An Account of
Upper Louisiana
by Nicolas de Finiels

An Account of
Upper Louisiana

by Nicolas de Finiels

Edited by Carl J. Ekberg and William E. Foley
Translated by Carl J. Ekberg

University of Missouri Press

Library of Congress Cataloging-in-Publication Data

Finiels, Nicolas de.
     [Notice sur la Louisiane supérieure. English]
     An account of upper Louisiana / by Nicolas de Finiels ;
edited by Carl J. Ekberg and William E. Foley ;
translated by Carl J. Ekberg.
          p.   cm.
     Translation of: Notice sur la Louisiane supérieure.
     Includes index.
     ISBN 0-8262-0702-2 (alk. paper)
     1. Mississippi River Valley—History—To 1803.
2. Louisiana—History—To 1803. 3. Finiels, Nicolas de.
I. Ekberg, Carl J. II. Foley, William E., 1938- .
III. Title.
F352.F5613   1989
976.3—dc19   88-39867
                                                            CIP

Illustration on pp. ii–iii: *Fort San Carlos, St. Louis, 1780,* by Clarence Hoblitzelle.
The original is an ink drawing commissioned by Pierre Chouteau in 1897 as support
material for his proposal to recreate the village of old St. Louis on the levee.
Courtesy Missouri Historical Society.

FOR ABRAHAM P. NASATIR
AND IN MEMORY OF
JOHN FRANCIS McDERMOTT

ACKNOWLEDGMENTS

The editors of this volume have accumulated many debts for assistance on various problems pertaining to its translation and editing. We wish to acknowledge our indebtedness to the following persons and institutions:

John Abbott, Louisa Bowen, and Gary N. Denue of the Lovejoy Library at Southern Illinois University–Edwardsville, for providing access to the Finiels manuscript and enabling us to prepare it for publicaton.

In New Orleans, Wayne Everard of the New Orleans Public Library, for helping track down documents that were important for understanding Finiels' life in that city at the end of the colonial era. Alfred Lemmon of the Historic New Orleans Collection, for identifying many examples of Finiels' cartographic work pertaining to Spanish Louisiana. Samuel Wilson, Jr., for explaining Finiels' position as an engineer in late colonial New Orleans.

F. Terry Norris of the U.S. Corps of Engineers, St. Louis District, for help in analyzing and photocopying Finiels' map of the Illinois Country.

Melburn D. Thurman of Ste. Genevieve, Missouri, for giving generously of his broad knowledge of Upper Louisiana to assist us in compiling the annotations for Finiels' text.

W. Raymond Wood, professor of anthropology at the University of Missouri–Columbia, for painstakingly checking Finiels' comments about the upper Missouri and assisting us with our annotations for that portion of the text.

Garold Cole, Bill Easton, and Helga Whitcomb of Illinois State University's Milner Library, for helping us locate the books and maps that were necessary for interpreting and annotating Finiels' "Account."

Finally, to Mathé Allain of the University of Southwestern Louisiana, for checking, sentence by sentence and word for word, our translation of Finiels' text. Scrupulous in catching nuances of meaning in Finiels' prose that we had missed, she never attempted to impose her sensibilities upon Finiels' views or our translation.

CONTENTS

Acknowledgments, vii

Introduction, 1

Illustrations, 17

An Account of Upper Louisiana, 25

Works Cited, 137

Index, 147

INTRODUCTION

Nicolas de Finiels, an expatriate French engineer who served the Spanish monarchy in Louisiana during the late colonial era, remains little known. Yet he enjoys the distinction of having prepared two of the most valuable source documents pertaining to Upper Louisiana in colonial times: a lengthy memoir entitled "Notice sur la Louisiane Supérieure" ("Account of Upper Louisiana") and a meticulously drawn map of the central Mississippi River valley, "Carte d'une partie du cours du Mississippi, depuis la rivière des Illinois, jusqu'au dessous de La Nouvelle Madrid."[1] The forty-thousand-word "Account," which appears here in print for the first time, provides important information about Upper Louisiana in the late 1790s on subjects ranging from great issues of geopolitics to details of domestic life. The map, undeniably the best ever done of the eighteenth-century Illinois Country, complements Finiels' text with a careful rendering of both physical and cultural features of the Mississippi valley from the mouth of the Illinois River south to the outpost of New Madrid. The original manuscript map, done in six panels, measures 68 cm by 262 cm and is noteworthy for its great accuracy, astonishing detail, and superb craftsmanship. Small-scale reproductions of sections of this important cartographic work are included in this volume.

Historians and other scholars will discover in these two documents a wealth of information about French Creole culture, social relations, black slavery, demography, agriculture, frontier economic activity, and the influx of Anglo-Americans into Upper Louisiana from east of the Mississippi. Archaeologists, anthropologists, cultural geographers, and historic preservationists will welcome the new and detailed data on roadways, Indian migrations, settlement patterns, town development, location of farmsteads, place names, and waterways—especially the course of the Mississippi during the late eighteenth century. The map also provides new data on flora and perhaps climate, for Finiels carefully delineated features of the landscape and distinguished woodlands from prairies. Ethnohistorians will find much new information in Finiels' reports of migrant Indians who settled in Upper Louisiana during the late eighteenth century. His descriptions of the Shawnee and Delaware villages situated between Ste. Genevieve and Cape Girardeau are the best available for the late colonial period. Finiels' account of the fur trade economy, based upon his interviews with fur merchants in St. Louis, is an informed précis of Indian-white trading practices at the turn of the nineteenth century.

1. Finiels' original manuscript is located in the John Francis McDermott Collection in the archives of the Lovejoy Library at Southern Illinois University–Edwardsville. The map, formerly housed in the now-disbanded Bibliothèque du Service Hydrographique in Paris, is located in the map division of the Service Historique de la Marine in the château of Vincennes outside Paris.

Finiels remains a rather shadowy figure. Much of what is known about this obscure Frenchman comes from a scattering of papers and maps in various Spanish archives.[2] This is appropriate, for only his work for the Spanish crown between 1797 and 1818 rescued him from anonymity and gave him a place in North American history. There is no direct evidence concerning his exact place and date of birth, his education, or the circumstances that prompted him to leave France and come to the New World. Historian Jack D. L. Holmes, whose short but informative pieces constitute the only published work on Finiels and his career, surmised that he first crossed the Atlantic as a member of the French expeditionary force sent by King Louis XVI in 1780 to assist the Americans in their struggle for independence from Great Britain.[3] This may be true, but it seems more likely that Finiels, a sharp critic of the French Revolution, was one of the numerous political refugees who fled France and came to the United States during the early 1790s. If Finiels had arrived from France as early as the American Revolution, documentary evidence of his presence would probably have come to light.

The first recorded account of Finiels in the United States places him in Philadelphia in 1797. His presence in that city was hardly surprising, for the American republic's cosmopolitan capital was a thriving center for international commerce and politics, and also home to a diverse mix of French nationals representing widely disparate political viewpoints.[4] According to Finiels himself, he served in the American government's employ, presumably as an engineer in the embryonic U.S. Army, but a search of official archival records turned up no mention of his American service.[5]

While in Philadelphia, Finiels made the acquaintance of Carlos Martínez de Irujo, the Spanish minister to the United States. Irujo was, at the time, actively seeking to strengthen Spain's position in its North American borderlands. The situation in Spanish Louisiana appeared to be especially precarious. Statesmen and military men throughout the western world sensed that the province was a plum waiting to be seized from atrophying Spanish hands. Spanish colonial officials were preoccupied with this problem, worrying whether Great Britain, France, or the United States would be the aggressor.[6]

2. Most of Finiels' extant papers are to be found in the Papeles de Cuba collection (hereafter cited as PC) of the Archivo General de Indias (hereafter cited as AG) in Seville and in the Archivo Histórico Nacional, Estado Unidos 1808, in Madrid. A number of the maps he drafted of New Orleans, Pensacola, and Spanish Louisiana are located in the map division of the Servicio Histórico Militar in Madrid.

3. See Holmes, "Some French Engineers in Spanish Louisiana," 136–39; Holmes, "The Marqués de Casa-Calvo, Nicolas de Finiels, and the 1805 Spanish Expedition through East Texas and Oklahoma," 325–29; Holmes, ed., *Documentos Inéditos para la Historia de la Luisiana, 1792–1810*, 359–68. The latter is an introduction to Holmes's edition of Finiels' description of Louisiana in 1810.

4. See the letter from Martínez de Irujo to Baron Hector de Carondelet cited in Holmes, ed., *Documentos*, 362. Concerning the interesting mix of French refugees residing in Philadelphia during the 1790s, see Frances Sergeant Childs, *French Refugee Life in the United States, 1790–1800;* Moreau de Saint-Méry, *Voyage aux Etats-Unis de l'Amérique, 1793–1798*, ed. Stewart L. Mims.

5. Finiels to Carondelet, 6 June 1797, AG, PC, legajo 188–3. Holmes, "The Casa-Calvo–Finiels Expedition," 327, n. 12.

6. A good introduction to the "Louisiana problem" is Alexander DeConde, *This Affair of Louisiana.*

St. Louis, Upper Louisiana's largest settlement and its provincial capital, was particularly vulnerable. Since the Anglo-Indian attack upon that city in 1780, Spanish
authorities in New Orleans had been concerned with strengthening St. Louis's inadequate defenses. In the midst of the renewed tensions of the 1790s, Louisiana's governor general, Don Francisco Luis Héctor de Carondelet, launched a major campaign
to improve the city's dilapidated fortifications.[7] To oversee that project, he hired
Louis Vandenbemden, a Flemish engineer who in 1794 had taken up residence in New
Madrid, a Spanish settlement and outpost on the west bank of the Mississippi some
two hundred miles downstream from St. Louis. Vandenbemden had impressed the
Spaniards with his architectural skills by designing a flourmill, and serviceable mills
were in short supply in Upper Louisiana. So too were competent military engineers,
and in the remote frontier setting a qualified engineer could easily move from designing flourmills to planning fortifications.[8]

The Spaniards were not alone in their efforts to assess Louisiana's military pre-
paredness. In 1796 the French agent General Georges-Victor Collot visited the western province on a reconnaissance mission. Despite an elaborate ploy by Collot to
keep his true intentions secret, the Spanish authorities arrested him as a spy. He
feigned innocence and secured release from prison, but officials in New Orleans
quietly ushered him out of their territory. Collot moved on to Philadelphia, a center of
intrigue as well as diplomacy, where he met Finiels and Irujo and shared with them his
impressions about Louisiana. The French agent continued to pass himself off as a
friend of the Spanish regime. He warned Irujo that the British were preparing to
launch an invasion of Louisiana from Canada, and he offered the Spanish minister
some recommendations for improving St. Louis's faulty defenses.[9]

Collot suggested that Finiels be appointed to oversee such a project. Without
authorization from his superiors, Irujo retained the French expatriate as an engineer
for the Spanish service at a monthly salary of one hundred pesos and dispatched him
to St. Louis with a hefty one thousand peso advance. Finiels' hostility to the French

Irujo's mission in Philadelphia is discussed in Arthur P. Whitaker, *The Mississippi Question, 1795–1803*.
Concerning Irujo's hiring of Finiels, see the publications of Holmes cited above in note 3, and also Liljegren, "The Commission of Carlos Howard," 77–78. The original of Finiels' appointment, dated 20
March 1797, is in the Bancroft Library at Berkeley. See Abraham P. Nasatir, "Anglo-Spanish Rivalry in
the Iowa Country, 1797–1798," 366.
  7. On the efforts to fortify Upper Louisiana against foreign aggression, see Abraham P. Nasatir, ed.,
Spanish War Vessels on the Mississippi, and James B. Musick, *St. Louis as a Fortified Town*. Some interesting documents pertaining to St. Louis's fortifications in the 1790s are printed in Louis Houck, ed., *The
Spanish Regime in Missouri*, 1:342–49, 2:123–39.
  8. Concerning Vandenbemden and his career in Upper Louisiana, see Louis Houck, *A History of
Missouri*, 2:143, 155; Nasatir, ed., *Spanish War Vessels*, 225, n. 79; Ernest R. Liljegren, "The Commission
of Carlos Howard," 78–85. The form of the stone towers used as defensive fortifications in Upper Louisiana was derived from the round stone windmills of France. See Musick, *St. Louis as a Fortified Town*,
59.
  9. Concerning Collot's activities in North America, see Victor Collot, *A Journey in North America*;
Durand Echeverria, "General Collot's Plan for a Reconnaissance of the Ohio and Mississippi Valleys,
1796"; George W. Kyte, "A Spy on the Western Waters: The Military Intelligence Mission of General
Collot in 1796."

Revolution and his open sympathy for the royal house of Bourbon evidently persuaded Irujo that he could be trusted with the assignment. Irujo issued Finiels a commission in Philadelphia on 20 March 1797, and shortly thereafter Finiels, with wife and mother-in-law in tow, headed westward.[10]

In the late eighteenth century, there were two principal routes between Philadelphia and St. Louis: the first by sailing ship to New Orleans and then up the Mississippi by *bateau* to Spanish Illinois; and the other overland from Philadelphia to Pittsburgh, down the Ohio River by riverboat to its mouth, and then up the Mississippi to St. Louis. Finiels and his family traveled to Upper Louisiana by way of the Ohio valley, the route usually preferred for westward travel because of the difficulty and slowness of ascending the Mississippi all the way from New Orleans.[11]

Finiels arrived in New Madrid, located just below the confluence of the Ohio and Mississippi rivers, in late May 1797 with just ten pesos in his pocket. His trip from Philadelphia had cost him the better part of a year's salary. Governor Carondelet wrote from his headquarters in New Orleans on 6 June to the commandant at New Madrid, Carlos Delassus: "I've learned by your letter that Don Nicolas Finiels with his [pregnant] wife and mother-in-law arrived at your post and that he continued his trip to the Illinois settlements [i.e., Ste. Genevieve and St. Louis] two days later. I approve of your supplying him with the guide that he requested."[12] Finiels probably met and married Marianne Rivière, who was a Creole from St. Domingue, in Philadelphia. By 3 June 1797 Finiels and his family were in St. Louis preparing to face the oppressive summer heat of Spanish Illinois's capital city.[13]

In St. Louis local officials received Finiels cautiously. Lieutenant Colonel Carlos Howard, the newly appointed Spanish military commander for Upper Louisiana, was understandably hesitant to involve a stranger in the sensitive task of constructing military fortifications. He preferred leaving that responsibility in Vandenbemden's hands. Vandenbemden was not a military man, however, and Finiels considered his plans for defending St. Louis flawed. Finiels communicated his concerns to the authorities in St. Louis and New Orleans, but he was powerless to effect any changes without more explicit authorization from the Spanish government. His several extant letters from St. Louis make it clear that he was not pleased with his situation in

10. On Finiels' relationship with Collot and Irujo, see Holmes, "The Casa-Calvo–Finiels Expedition," 327-29; Liljigren, "The Commission of Carlos Howard," 77-78.

11. On river travel in the West, see McDermott, "Travelers on the Western Waters."

12. Carondelet to Carlos Delassus, 6 June 1797, AG, PC, legajo 131A; copy in Pierre Chouteau Collection, Missouri Historical Society, St. Louis.

13. Finiels' wife's name is to be found on the baptismal record of their son, Pedro Juan Luis Nicolas Arturo de Finiels, 15 October 1805, which is located in the archives of the archdiocese of New Orleans. We are grateful to Dr. Charles Nolan, archdiocesan archivist, who helped us locate this baptismal record. We have found no evidence to support Jack D. L. Holmes's remark ("Some French Engineers in Spanish Louisiana," 138) that Finiels was married twice. The baptismal record also makes it clear that his wife, Marianne, was a native of St. Domingue. For a description of Finiels' arrival in St. Louis, see Carlos Howard to Carondelet, 7 June 1797, in Nasatir, "Anglo-Spanish Rivalry in the Iowa Country," 366-70.

Spanish Illinois—his salary was inadequate, his official position ambiguous, and his professional life frustrating.[14]

While he awaited a decision on his official status from Spanish administrators, Finiels reconnoitered Upper Louisiana's settlements, gathered information about the region and its people, and put his talents as a draftsman to work. James Mackay, a prominent trader recently returned from the upper Missouri country, employed him to prepare a final draft of the famed Evans-Mackay map that Lewis and Clark later found so helpful.[15] Moreover, Finiels established a friendship with the highly respected lieutenant governor of Upper Louisiana, Zenon Trudeau, a French Creole who had become an administrator in the Spanish colonial regime. Obviously Finiels and Trudeau had much in common, both Frenchmen serving the Spaniards, and Finiels became tutor in mathematics to Trudeau's son.[16]

During this time Finiels also drafted his map of the central Mississippi valley. Within the map's cartouche, Finiels explained that the map had been "Laid out and drafted during the course of 1797–98, by Don Nicholas de Finiels, special engineer serving His Most Catholic Majesty in Louisiana." Finiels appears to have drawn the map on his own initiative, for there are no extant orders concerning the cartographic project, and the map seems never to have been delivered to Spanish officials in Louisiana. Perhaps because the Spaniards subsequently suspended his salary, he considered the map a personal possession, which he apparently retained until 1803, when he turned it over to Napoleon's colonial prefect to Louisiana, Pierre-Clément de Laussat.[17]

Despite his frustrations, Finiels seemed ready to remain in St. Louis, for in April 1798 he purchased two town lots.[18] But his plans were dashed the following month when word reached Spanish Illinois that authorities in Madrid had rejected his appointment and ordered his removal from the King's payroll. In early summer, he took his wife and mother-in-law to New Orleans, where, in spite of the Spanish government's pronouncement, Louisiana's new governor, Manuel Gayoso de Lemos, decided to reemploy him. General Collot continued to tout Finiels' engineering talents and had written to Spanish authorities in New Orleans recommending him for

14. For Howard's attitude toward Finiels, see Howard's letter cited in the previous note. Letters from Finiels to Carondelet (6 June 1797 and 23 June 1797) are found in AG, PC, legajo 188–3.

15. W. Raymond Wood, "Nicholas de Finiels: Mapping the Mississippi and Missouri Rivers, 1797–1798."

16. Zenon Trudeau to Pedro Favrot, 31 August 1797, in *Transcriptions of the Manuscript Collections of Louisiana: The Favrot Papers, 1796–1799,* edited by the Louisiana Historical Records Survey, Tulane University, 5:94.

17. Marc Villiers du Terrage noted in his *Les dernières années de la Louisiane française* (p. 445, n. 1) that "Laussat brought back a very fine map drafted by Faniels [i.e., Finiels] for the Spanish government."

18. There is an abstract of a warranty deed between Finiels and Julien Roi dated 30 April 1798 in the St. Louis Recorded Archives Index, in the Missouri Historical Society, St. Louis. The original document (no. 759) is, however, missing from the files.

further service. In the cosmopolitan world of the eighteenth century, a former political prisoner had no trouble writing such a letter and getting results.[19]

Finiels remained in New Orleans for the duration of the Spanish regime, working under Governor Gayoso and his successors, Manuel de Salcedo and the Marquis de Casa Calvo. His residence was located near Fort San Carlos, the downriver bastion of fortified New Orleans, and at least one of his children was born there. He worked on a vast array of projects for the Spanish colonial government—drawing maps, repairing levees, planning fortifications for Baton Rouge and New Orleans, and even designing fire engines for the city government. After Gilbert Guillemard, another French engineer in Spanish service, designed the Cabildo building that stands next to the cathedral facing present-day Jackson Square, Finiels was one of the appraisers assigned to determine an accurate billing for the construction project.[20]

Following the transfer of Louisiana from Spain to France (1800) and its subsequent sale to the United States (1803), Finiels cast his lot with his Most Catholic Majesty, Carlos IV of Spain, rather than with the expanding young republic and its popular president, Thomas Jefferson. By choosing to serve the Spanish monarchy, Nicolas de Finiels rejected an America of the future in favor of a crumbling European colonial regime. Finiels participated in the Spanish expedition into east Texas in 1805–1806 and drew an excellent map of the region. He remained in the Spanish service and was stationed successively at Havana and Pensacola. He bought property at the latter place and was wounded there during Andrew Jackson's controversial 1818 raid into Spanish Florida. His four sons followed their father into the Spanish army, and the youngest, Pedro Arturo de Finiels, earned special honors for valor during the American siege of Pensacola in 1818.[21]

19. Concerning Finiels' work for the Spanish colonial regime in America, in addition to the publications of Holmes cited above in note 3, see the bundle of documents in the Archivo Histórico Nacional, Estados-Unidos 1808, legajo 5549, expediente 20 (microfilm in Library of Congress).

20. Finiels appears a number of times in the civil records from New Orleans during the end of the colonial era. In the notarial records (Civil Courts Building, Acts of Narcisse Broutin, vol. 6, 1803) are a series of powers of attorney that Finiels conveyed to friends in Havana, St. Domingue, and Philadelphia. These notarial documents reveal that Finiels and/or his wife still owned property of one kind or another in those locations; they also reveal that Finiels lived in New Orleans near the fort of San Carlos. In the New Orleans Public Library, the "Acts and Deliberations of the Cabildo, 1769–1803," book 4, vol. 3, reveal the various engineering tasks in which Finiels was employed for the Spanish government in and around New Orleans. We are grateful to Wayne Everard of the Louisiana Collection in the New Orleans Public Library, who helped us track this information on Finiels. See also Samuel Wilson, Jr., and Leonard V. Huber, *The Cabildo on Jackson Square,* 37. The Archivo Servicio Histórico Militar in Madrid has a collection of maps and plans done by Finiels of various locations in Louisiana and West Florida, including New Orleans, Pensacola, Baton Rouge, and San Carlos de Barrancas. The Historic New Orleans Collection in New Orleans has photocopies of these, and we are indebted to Dr. Alfred Lemmon for making them available to us. Several of these Finiels maps are reproduced in Holmes, ed., *Documentos Inéditos.*

21. See Holmes, "The Casa-Calvo–Finiels Expedition." Finiels' map of western Louisiana and east Texas is reproduced in Holmes, ed., *Documentos Inéditos.* Finiels' property in Pensacola is mentioned in *American State Papers, Public Lands,* 4:188. His land grant was conveyed by the Spanish intendant, Juan Morales. The service sheets of Finiels' two sons, Juan Bautista Emilio de Finiels and Pedro Arturo de Finiels, have been published in Holmes, ed., *Honor and Fidelity: The Louisiana Infantry Regiment and the Louisiana Militia Companies, 1766–1821,* 118–19.

* * *

Spain ceded Louisiana to France by the second Treaty of San Ildefonso, signed on 1 October 1800. The opening paragraphs of Finiels' "Account of Upper Louisiana" provide an elliptical history of France's pursuit of the province during the late eighteenth century. Finiels claims that it was during the European wars provoked by the French Revolution that Louisiana again became an object of French foreign policy. In fact, the success of the American Revolution in trimming the scope of British power in North America whetted the appetite of French statesmen for the retrocession of their former province. France, the first European power to recognize the fledgling United States government, had sent an army to America to help the revolutionaries wrench their independence from Great Britain. When peace was negotiated in Paris during 1782–1783, Louisiana did not appear on the table as a bargaining chip. Spain wished to keep the colony that it had acquired in 1762 at the end of the French and Indian War, and neither France nor the United States was prepared to reach for it in the early 1780s. Within several years, however, there had arrived in North America a Frenchman who possessed the energy, vision, and ambition to cast envious eyes on Louisiana.[22]

Eléonore François Moustier, French minister to the United States from 1787 to 1789, was the first French official to urge Louisiana's retrocession to France. Moustier, who never visited Louisiana, prepared a lengthy memoir more noteworthy for its liberal commercial and political ideas—Louisiana was to become part of metropolitan France with no restrictions upon international commerce—than for its information about Louisiana. Although the memoir had no immediate impact on French foreign policy, in government circles it superseded all previous documents concerning Louisiana, and during the French Revolution, when reacquisition of the colony became a lively topic, officials frequently turned to Moustier's work for arguments in support of retrocession.[23]

The expansion-minded revolutionaries enthusiastically considered the prospect of spreading their doctrines in the New World province and of tapping the region's vaunted riches. To a limited extent, the fervor for "Louisiane française" caught on in the province itself with the formation of fledgling Jacobin clubs in New Orleans and even in St. Louis.[24] It was not the French Revolution that brought these plans for French aggrandizement to fruition, but rather a creature of that revolution—Napoleon Bonaparte. Napoleon, junior officer in the revolutionary armies and youngest general in the French army under the Directory, possessed visions of grandeur as

22. Concerning the issue of Louisiana in European and American diplomacy, see the following works: DeConde, *This Affair of Louisiana*; E. Wilson Lyon, *Louisiana in French Diplomacy, 1659–1804*; Frederick Jackson Turner, "The Policy of France toward the Mississippi Valley in the Period of Washington and Adams"; Whitaker, *The Mississippi Question.*

23. A discussion of Moustier's unpublished 330-page "Mémoire sur une question intéressante souvent agitée en Amérique et quelque fois en Europe. S'il convient à la France de désirer la rétrocession de la Louisiane?" can be found in Lyon, *Louisiana in French Diplomacy*, 60–66.

24. See Ernest R. Liljegren, "Jacobinism in Spanish Louisiana, 1792–1797."

vast as the territory of Louisiana itself. By 1800 Napoleon as first consul and military dictator had brought order to France; Charles-Maurice de Talleyrand, well-known advocate of overseas colonization, had been reappointed minister of foreign affairs, and hostilities in the European theater of action were winding down.[25]

The revolutionary wars of the 1790s had devastated France's overseas empire. A bloody revolution, which Finiels blamed in part on "philanthropic fanaticism" in France, had wracked St. Domingue, the French pearl of the Antilles. Napoleon's plans for revivifying France's New World empire called for the creation of a commercial axis between Louisiana and the French Caribbean islands—St. Domingue, Guadeloupe, and Martinique. It was obvious that French Canada would never again be reunited with Louisiana to recreate the great continental arch of empire that had been shattered by the French and Indian War, but Louisiana's wealth of basic provisions—lumber, grain, and salted meat—constituted a perfect commercial complement to the rum, sugar, and molasses of the Antilles.[26]

Napoleon's colonial enterprise took form quickly between the autumn of 1800 and the autumn of 1801. France regained de jure sovereignty of Louisiana by the Treaty of San Ildefonso (October 1800); one year later the French agreed to end hostilities with Great Britain by the Treaty of Amiens (October 1801); and in November 1801 French troops were dispatched to St. Domingue for the purpose of retaking that island from the rebellious black leader Toussaint L'Ouverture. The timing, strategic vision, and deployment of resources were vintage Napoleon, and the grand plan seemed destined to succeed with all of the éclat characteristic of the great Bonaparte at that stage of his career. In January 1803, Pierre-Clément de Laussat, prefect-appointee of all Louisiana, sailed from La Rochelle for New Orleans to take charge of the province. Yet within a matter of months, Napoleon unexpectedly abandoned his plans in the western hemisphere and in hurried negotiations with the Americans agreed to sell all of Louisiana to the young republic.[27]

Complex reasons lay behind this sudden change of plans. General Charles-Victor Leclerc's initial brilliant success on St. Domingue was unraveling as logistical problems, tropical diseases, and difficult terrain dashed French hopes for recreating a lucrative colonial regime on the sugar island. Troops and supplies destined for Louisiana had to be diverted to St. Domingue. Great Britain's opposition to a French military expedition to Louisiana was also increasingly evident, as British warships cruised menacingly close to the Dutch ports where Napoleon's Louisiana task force was gathering. Moreover, as news of the supposedly secret retrocession clause in the Treaty of San Ildefonso leaked out, the United States government let it be known that it was not especially keen about Louisiana's return to France. The Americans consid-

25. See Lyon, *Louisiana in French Diplomacy*, 101–43. Napoleon was still first consul in 1803, not taking the title of emperor until 1804.
26. For references to the history of the French Antilles during the 1790s, see below, note 3 of the "Account."
27. See Lyon, *Louisiana in French Diplomacy*, 129–44.

ered a French empire in the Mississippi valley far more inimical to their interests than the continued presence of a faltering Spanish monarchy. What the United States lacked in regiments and warships, it made up for in masses of land-hungry farmers, the real foot soldiers of a trans-Mississippi empire. Napoleon could not ignore the fact that America's burgeoning western population had already begun to cross the Mississippi in droves.[28]

By mid-March 1803, the very moment that Laussat arrived in New Orleans to oversee the retrocession, Napoleon had decided to scratch his military expedition to Louisiana and redirect his resources to the European theater of action. Laussat, however, had no inkling of his ruler's dramatic change of plans. As the new French prefect busied himself preparing for the arrival of the French expeditionary force, he also set about gathering up-to-date information about the sprawling province he expected to oversee for France. Laussat particularly wanted to learn more about Upper Louisiana, whose vast reaches he did not have time to explore personally.[29] He prepared a lengthy questionnaire designed to elicit a clearer picture of conditions in that region. Pierre Chouteau, member of the prominent St. Louis trading family, received a copy while he was in New Orleans on business. Chouteau completed the questionnaire, which he subsequently discussed with Laussat, but the St. Louisan was a active merchant whose busy schedule did not afford him the luxury of providing the detailed responses the French prefect desired.[30]

Laussat needed someone who was intelligent and literate, who was knowledgeable about Upper Louisiana and willing to serve France. Nicolas de Finiels qualified on all counts. The circumstances of their initial encounter are unknown, but polite society in New Orleans was still intimate enough to give an incoming official numerous opportunities for meeting a French compatriot. Finiels was a royalist and a Roman Catholic, but his chronic financial problems and a lingering loyalty to France may have persuaded him to work for Laussat, even though the latter represented a revolutionary despot, Napoleon Bonaparte, whom Finiels probably found repugnant. It is unclear whether Laussat in fact hired Finiels to write his "Account" or whether the observant French engineer merely hoped to position himself for possible employment with the French regime by obliging Laussat.[31]

28. Ibid., 199–207.
29. See Pierre-Clément de Laussat, *Memoirs of My Life,* trans. Agnes-Josephine Pastwa, ed. Robert D. Bush, 21.
30. Ibid., 22; Pierre Chouteau to Laussat, 1803, in Laussat Papers, Historic New Orleans Collection, and Laussat to Chouteau, 30 April and 24 August 1803, Delassus Collection, Missouri Historical Society.
31. It is clear that Finiels was often in difficult financial straits. In 1804, two American merchants in New Orleans obtained a judgment against Finiels for a debt, and the new American governor of Louisiana, William C. C. Claiborne, wrote Casa-Calvo asking that one-half of Finiels' back pay be appropriated for satisfying his creditors. See *Official Letter Books of W. C. C. Claiborne,* ed. Dunbar Rowland, 2:296. Holmes also commented upon Finiels' chronic indebtedness ("Some French Engineers in Spanish Louisiana," 139). The fact that neither Laussat's published *Memoirs* nor his papers (now housed in the Historic New Orleans Collection) mention Finiels or his "Account of Upper Louisiana" suggests that Finiels drafted the document on the sly for Napoleon's prefect while he was still employed by the Spaniards.

According to the notation on the manuscript, Finiels wrote his "Account of Upper Louisiana" in June 1803. A short time later the astounding news that France had agreed to sell Louisiana to the United States reached New Orleans, and the disappointed Laussat was forced to turn his attention from planning for a revitalized French empire to arranging for the province's transfer to the American republic. When he packed his bags and returned to France, Laussat took his copy of Finiels' "Account" and kept it among his personal papers. He also carried with him Finiels' original manuscript map of the middle Mississippi valley. Although Laussat retained possession of Finiels' "Account," he treated the map as an official document and turned it over to French authorities. A notation under the map's cartouche states, "Brought back from Louisiana in 1804 by M. Laussat, Prefet-Colonial."[32]

* * *

In preparing the map and the "Account," Finiels drew heavily upon the extensive body of knowledge he had accumulated during his year's residence in Upper Louisiana. His acute powers of observation are readily apparent. But internal evidence suggests that he also drew on other sources, written and oral. Finiels specifically refers to the work of Thomas Hutchins in the "Account." Hutchins, a British military officer stationed in the Illinois Country during the late 1760s, had compiled an abundance of accurate information about the region in the form of maps and reports. During the American Revolution, he abandoned the British to join the American cause, and the U.S. government eventually rewarded him with an appointment as its official geographer. Hutchins's *A Topographical Description of Virginia, Pennsylvania, Maryland, and North Carolina,* published in 1778, contained the most accurate and detailed map of the Illinois Country then in existence; his *A Historical and Topographical Description of Louisiana and West Florida* came into print in 1784.[33]

Finiels likewise utilized information he acquired from General Collot, who had befriended him in Philadelphia. While traveling in Louisiana, Collot had taken copious notes, which he later used in the preparation of the descriptive narrative and map that he published in 1826 under the title *A Journey in North America.*[34] During his stay in St. Louis, Finiels also interviewed scores of informants—traders and *voyageurs*—with firsthand information about the upper Missouri country, and as he freely acknowledged in his "Account," those portions of the memoir dealing with that region were based solely on their data. So too was that part of the map that extends up

32. On the tribulations of Laussat as Napoleon's prefect in Louisiana during 1803 and 1804, see Laussat, *Memoirs of My Life;* Charles Gayarré, *History of Louisiana,* 3:576–628; Marc de Villiers du Terrage, *Les dernières années de Louisiane française,* chaps. 17–19; Lyon, *Louisiana in French Diplomacy,* 242–49; Laussat Papers, Historic New Orleans Collection, New Orleans. For the map's present location, see above, note 1.

33. Concerning the life and career of Thomas Hutchins, see the following works: Anna M. Quattrocchi, "Thomas Hutchins, 1730–1789"; the introduction in Frederick Charles Hicks's edition of Hutchins, *A Topographical Description of Virginia, Pennsylvania, Maryland, and North Carolina;* and the introduction in Joseph G. Tregle's facsimile edition of Hutchins's *A Historical and Topographical Description of Louisiana and West Florida.*

34. On Finiels' relationship with Collot, see Holmes, "The Casa-Calvo–Finiels Expedition," 327–29.

the Missouri as far as the mouth of the Femme Osage River. Although the largely derivative sections of the "Account" dealing with the upper Missouri provide little in the way of new factual information, they do give us a valuable summary of what was generally known in St. Louis during the 1790s about the upper Missouri and its people, based upon Finiels' prudent sifting of the locally available source materials.[35]

For many locations, Finiels' map is startlingly detailed and accurate. Of the various communities depicted on the map that remain in existence today, Ste. Genevieve most closely approximates its late-eighteenth-century configuration. The street plan and in some instances even the locations of buildings within the nucleus of modern Ste. Genevieve remain much the same today as they were in the 1790s. The town square, Main Street (then la Grande Rue), Merchant Street (then Rue à l'Eglise), the Jean-Baptiste Vallé house, the Louis Bolduc house, the Nicolas Janis House, and St. Mary's Road all appear on Finiels' map precisely as they are today. Archaeologists from Illinois State University, the University of Missouri–Columbia, and the U.S. Corps of Engineers have field-tested Finiels' map for certain specific sites outside developed areas and likewise found it to be extremely accurate.[36]

Finiels' depiction of east-bank sites appears to be less reliable. As an employee of the Spanish monarchy, he was obviously most concerned with providing a precise rendering of the geographical features on the west side of the Mississippi. He seems not to have drawn the settlement configurations of Cahokia, Prairie du Rocher, and Kaskaskia with the same care that he lavished on Ste. Genevieve or St. Louis. Kaskaskia, for example, is shown with what seems to be a generic waffle-iron grid, when in fact the extant records suggest that the town developed in a helter-skelter, unplanned fashion. Finiels' grid is too simple and geometrical. No surveyor in colonial Kaskaskia laid out the straight streets and right-angle corners he depicted.[37] This

35. F. Terry Norris, who is employed as a staff archaeologist for the U.S. Corps of Engineers in St. Louis and who is an expert on the mapping and geomorphology of the middle Mississippi valley, has observed that some unrelated minor errors appear in precisely the same areas on the Hutchins, Collot, and Finiels maps of the Illinois Country. His conclusion is that they were all working with the same basic original plan. Finiels may also have had access to the extensive "Mémoire sur la Louisiane et le pays des Illinois," written by Bonnevie de Pogniat in 1795. Bonnevie was a former officer in the French royal navy who became a refugee in North America during the French Revolution. In an effort to ingratiate himself with French authorities there, he made a bungled attempt to serve as a French agent in the Mississippi valley. His memoir, which is an interesting and unpublished description and commentary on the American scene during the mid-1790s, was written with the intention of persuading the Revolutionary government to pursue the reacquisition of Louisiana. Spanish authorities arrested Bonnevie at New Madrid in the autumn of 1795, confiscated his papers including the manuscript of his memoir, and sent him to New Orleans in chains. He was released when news of the Treaty of Basle reached New Orleans, and Finiels may have had access to a copy of his memoir at the time he was drafting his "Account of Upper Louisiana" during the spring of 1803. Bonnevie's "Mémoire" is in the Archives Nationales, section d'Outre Mer, in Aix-en-Provence. Carl J. Ekberg is currently preparing a translation of this document for publication.

36. Concerning the layout of colonial Ste. Genevieve, see Carl J. Ekberg, Colonial Ste. Genevieve: An Adventure on the Mississippi Frontier. These archaeologists are: from Illinois State University, Joseph Phillippe; from the University of Missouri, Michael K. Trimble; from the U.S. Corps of Engineers, St. Louis Branch, F. Terry Norris.

37. The best eighteenth-century plan of Kaskaskia was done by the British officer Philip Pittman in the 1760s and published in his The Present State of the European Settlements on the Mississippi (1770). It seems difficult to square Pittman's plan of Kaskaskia with that done by Finiels. Finiels' is clearly a much-

caveat aside, as previously noted, the Finiels map stands as the best piece of eighteenth-century cartography for the Illinois Country as a whole.

Finiels was a member of the generation positioned between the seminal eighteenth-century French proto-romantic, Jean-Jacques Rousseau, and the great nineteenth-century French romantic stylist and North American traveler, René de Chateaubriand, and careful readers of the "Account of Upper Louisiana" may detect romantic elements in his writing. Finiels' romantic sensibilities are especially evident in his portrayals of wildlife, primordial nature, French Creole society, and the Indians. He reveals, for example, a marked sympathy for the pathos of wild fauna threatened by encroaching white civilization in his description of Creve Coeur Marsh, located west of St. Louis: "It is . . . a refuge for many ducks, swans, and other aquatic birds. The proximity of the farmsteads that have gone up . . . during the past six years will surely frighten them off, but the fish, not having the birds' ability to escape man's voracity, will remain." By juxtaposing the terror of civilization and human rapacity with the innocence and vulnerability of the birds and fishes, he extols in a romantic fashion the virtues of nature over the ills of humanity.

In a later passage, Finiels returns to that theme when he observes that a tributary of the upper Missouri "serves as a habitat for untold numbers of beaver and otter, which have thus far lived in peace. The Indians, however, will soon discover the value of their pelts, and the timid animals will soon come to experience terror." Once again the underlying metaphor is warfare between timid nature and human greed. In this instance, the Indians represent humanity, and even though Finiels did not generally subscribe to the eighteenth-century myth of the noble savage, he clearly implies that the Indians' imminent assault upon the innocent animals was driven by the white traders' market economy.

Finiels was one of the first visitors to Upper Louisiana to portray the region's fauna within a framework of pathetic sensibility. The almost contemporaneous journals of Lewis and Clark express no similar sympathy for the pathos of western wildlife.[38] No doubt Finiels hunted game animals while he was a resident of Upper Louisiana, but at the same time his vision of the universe—natural as well as human—appears to have been refined enough, and romantic enough, to see the trans-Mississippi West as a haven for both wildlife and human beings.

The notion of external nature as Sublime—vast, picturesque, untamed, and frightening yet pleasing—was a literary and aesthetic concept pioneered in late-seventeenth-century England. By the late eighteenth century, it had spread across the Channel to the Continent and become part of a pan-European romantic movement.[39] Passages in Finiels' "Account" suggest that he was familiar with that literary tradi-

---

abstracted plan of the town.

38. The shooting of wild animals by the Lewis and Clark expedition was of course partly to procure food for a large party of men and partly for scientific reasons—the easiest way to describe or sketch an animal was to kill it and examine it up close.

39. For a good analysis of the Sublime in literature, see Marjorie Hope Nicolson, *Mountain Gloom and Mountain Glory*.

tion. In describing the Mississippi bluffs below the mouth of the Illinois River, Finiels was transported by the sublimity of the scene:

The bluffs . . . offer a most picturesque view of the plain, and from their heights there are delectable vistas and perspectives. In different places, perpendicular masses of rock protrude from these bluffs, which seem from a distance like vast walls covered with terraces. . . . But . . . up close to the bank of the Mississippi, [what] a striking spectacle meets your eyes. An immense panorama of rocks is deployed along the bank for more than four leagues, after which it disappears at the mouth of the Illinois River. These rocks . . . attain in several places heights of 130 to 140 feet above the river. . . . You can from there admire the confluences of the Mississippi, Missouri, and Illinois rivers, get drunk on an indescribable spectacle, and lose yourself in the profound meditations that it inspires.

Finiels evokes a more somber mood in describing his reaction to the bluffs over-looking the confluence of rivers with a passage that might well have come from a nineteenth-century Gothic novel: "The profound solitude that engulfs you on these heights; the majestic and imposing silence that reins as the murmuring waters of the Mississippi swirling around the rocks present the only intrusion; the wild and rustic appearance of those summits, which the luminous forest renders even more savage and desolate, darkens thoughts provoked by the spectacle of the rocks." It is unlikely that any seventeenth-century French author would have been induced by the sub-limity of a natural setting to write such a gloomy, introspective piece, but by the end of the eighteenth century, the Sublime had permeated the sensibilities of Nicolas de Finiels and an entire romantic generation throughout Europe.

He also displayed his interest in the Sublime in other parts of the narrative. His account of the Missouri River cascading down from its sources in the Rocky Moun-tains—a scene he had not witnessed in person—was equally romantic: "Its dizzy height stuns your gaze; its swiftness is a kind of impetuous fury, with the waters leaping out onto the plain as if they are indignant with the constraints just overcome." With this reference to "indignant" waters, Finiels employed another favorite romantic literary device, the anthropomorphizing of nature. In this instance the French engineer-turned-prose-stylist indulged his taste for romantic writing by utilizing the recollections of other persons.[40]

Finiels' "Account" suggests that he had been exposed to a hearty dose of romantic literature, perhaps both French and English, but in the absence of more direct cor-roborative evidence, all such conclusions remain largely speculative. Nonetheless, in some specific passages concerning French Creole morals, customs, and mores, Finiels' commentary bears a striking resemblance to certain of Rousseau's proto-romantic

40. According to W. Raymond Wood of the University of Missouri–Columbia, no white person had seen the sources of the Missouri River prior to 1803. Therefore, Finiels' account must have been based upon descriptions that originated with Indians.

notions. Examine, for example, the distinctions Finiels drew between society in St. Louis and Ste. Genevieve:

Although there is a noticeable difference in the moral character of the residents of St. Louis and those of Ste. Genevieve, you nevertheless still discover in the former traces of their native simplicity. . . . More affluent outsiders, more wealth, pretension to fine manners, and social distinctions are already tainting native customs, which are not yet entirely lost but which will certainly disappear. The women have cultivated more elegance than the men. Their finer sensibilities prompt them to adorn themselves, and they are beginning to laugh at the naive beauties of Ste. Genevieve; they do not perceive what they are really losing in the price they pay for acquiring affected appearances. Their dress is already more studied, and soon you will see an artificiality that until now has only just appeared.

Or consider the following rambling discourse on why the arts and sciences failed to make the French virtuous:

We have lost out in educating ourselves, in enlightening our minds too much beyond that which is necessary in order to control our passions. And if we dare to be sincere and appreciate the results of this vast and sublime knowledge, the acquisition of which makes us so proud, we should acknowledge that all we have really gained in Europe from this growth of knowledge boils down, as far as morals are concerned, to the art of mitigating our vices, of putting an attractive veneer on the numerous treacheries that have become, due to the poverty of spirits, the current coin of good society.

Finiels' conclusions in these passages—natural is good, artificial bad; modesty is good, pretension bad; equality is good, social distinction bad; simplicity is good, luxury bad; naïveté is good, sophistication bad; education is good, but too much of it bad—appear to have been taken directly from Rousseau's *Discours sur les sciences et les arts*.[41]

Yet Finiels defies easy categorization. He was not a thoroughgoing primitivist. He deplored the loss of vivacity by the Illinois Creoles in their isolated wilderness, and he likewise lamented that their imaginations had stagnated without the stimulation of city life. Finiels did not subscribe to the popular romantic canon of the noble savage, and unlike Chateaubriand who followed him, he chose not to make invidious comparisons between Indians and whites in order to cast aspersions on the quality of European society. Nor did he view the Indians through the rose-colored glasses of Chateaubriand's later romanticism.[42] To Finiels, the Shawnee were superior to the Delaware because they had advanced farther in the direction of European agricultural society; the Maha or Omahas were cruel, not noble, in their savagery; the

41. See *Discours sur les sciences et les arts,* esp. pp. 6–10, in Jean-Jacques Rousseau, *Oeuvres complètes,* vol. 3.
42. For some interesting remarks concerning the nobility of North American Indians, see François-Auguste-René de Chateaubriand, *Voyage en Amérique,* ed. Richard Switzer, 1:117, 2:396.

Ojibway or Chippewa were wretched nomads, made more miserable by their lack of permanent settlements and agriculture. These seeming contradictions merely confirm Finiels as a transitional figure whose ideas embodied a blending of clear-sighted realism with brooding romanticism.

* * *

The original manuscript of Nicolas de Finiels' "Account of Upper Louisiana" is deposited in the archives of the Lovejoy Library at Southern Illinois University–Edwardsville. Unlike his map of Upper Louisiana, which became a government document, the "Account" remained filed away among Laussat's papers, where it lay unnoticed until John Francis McDermott came upon it a century and a half later. McDermott, an authority on the cultural history of the upper Mississippi valley and an indefatigable pursuer of sources pertaining to the region's early history, was contemplating preparation of a special edition of Laussat's *Memoirs* when he traveled to Pau, France, in 1966 to examine the family archives in the possession of the Louisiana official's great-great-grandson, the Comte du Pré de Saint-Maur. The American scholar immediately recognized the importance of Finiels' long-forgotten memoir and launched a campaign to acquire it for an American archival depository. At McDermott's urging, the Comte du Pré agreed in 1970 to sell the manuscript to Southern Illinois University at Edwardsville, where McDermott held an appointment as Research Professor of Humanities until his death in 1981. McDermott had kept the document in his collection of manuscripts with the intent of preparing it for publication. Thus it remained unused by researchers until John Abbot and John Neal Hoover, Special Collections archivists at the Lovejoy Library, called it to the attention of William E. Foley, who initiated plans for bringing it into print in collaboration with Carl J. Ekberg. Ekberg prepared this translation.

Finiels' "Account of Upper Louisiana" runs two hundred manuscript pages, although the actual document is unpaginated. The original copy is in three distinct handwritings, indicating that it was transcribed by three different secretaries. None of the hands is recognizable as Finiels' own. These facts, along with the manuscript's rather haphazard organization, suggest that it was probably dictated in haste. Any revising or editing appears to have been superficial at best, and it is entirely possible that it was the only draft ever prepared. No other copy, outline, or notes have surfaced in Spanish, French, or American archives. Events and people were moving quickly in Louisiana during the summer of 1803, requiring Finiels to turn out his text for Laussat in very short order. Scholars can be grateful that he accomplished the task.

Although the text contains some repetitiveness and a few minor contradictions, Finiels' "Account" is neither chaotic nor slovenly. The spelling is modern and consistent; the paragraphing is usually logical and helpful; and, despite some convoluted constructions, the syntax and grammar are generally correct and comprehensible. Overall, the manuscript suggests that its engineer-author was both well-educated and well-organized.

In translating Finiels' "Account," we have attempted to remain as close as possible to the text's original meaning. Occasionally, Finiels' tortured romantic prose made it necessary to depart from a literal translation in order to convey the author's thoughts or feelings in coherent, modern English. In specific cases where meanings were ambiguous or doubtful, we have provided explanations either enclosed within brackets in the text or appended in the footnotes. The original paragraphing has been retained throughout. Although the manuscript is not paginated, we have placed appropriate page numbers within brackets in the translated text.

Place names and proper names always present a special problem for translators. We have retained Finiels' names and his spellings, except for those instances where a modern version has become so widely known that it would seem awkward to use any other. Thus we have rendered Finiels' "Nouvelle Orléans" as New Orleans, and his "Schawanones" as Shawnees. On other occasions, where modern names exist but are not well-known, we have used Finiels' version with the modern rendition following in brackets: Grand Détour [Dogtooth Bend].43 Conversely, in those instances where a well-known modern name exists but Finiels' appellation is interesting or significant, we have used the modern version in the text and placed Finiels' terminology in brackets: Rocky Mountains [Montagnes de Pierres].

43. Finiels' reference is to the Grand Détour of the Mississippi River, although there was also such a place on the Missouri River in what is present-day South Dakota.

The first page of the manuscript of Finiels' "Notice sur la Louisiane Supérieure." Courtesy the John Francis McDermott Collection, Lovejoy Library, Southern Illinois University–Edwardsville.

Finiels' signature, from a document dated 24 November 1803 in the Notarial Archives, Municipal Court Building, New Orleans.

Manuel Gayoso de Lemos, governor general of Spanish Louisiana from 1797 to 1799, by an unknown artist. Gayoso, who employed Finiels in 1798, died in New Orleans of yellow fever in 1799. Courtesy Louisiana Historical Association.

Tower Rock, View on the Mississippi, by Karl Bodmer. Color engraving from *Travels in the Interior of North America,* by Maximilian, Prince of Wied (London, 1843–1844). Courtesy State Historical Society of Missouri.

A Shawnee brave. Engraving from *A Journey in North America,* by Georges-Victor Collot (Paris, 1826). Finiels was favorably impressed with the Shawnees who entertained him in villages located between Cape Girardeau and Ste. Genevieve.

Bequette-Ribault House, Ste. Genevieve. According to tree-ring analysis completed recently by University of Missouri researchers, this *poteaux-en-terre* structure, which is a typical French house type that Finiels would have seen in the Illinois Country in 1797–1798, dates from about 1808. Photograph by Jack E. Boucher for the Historic American Buildings Survey, Washington, D.C.

Don Francisco Héctor de Carondelet, governor general of Spanish Louisiana from 1792 to 1797. This portrait appeared in *A History of Louisiana* by Alcée Fortier (1904). Photograph courtesy Historic New Orleans Collection.

The Chouteau House, St. Louis. Lithograph by J. C. Wild, 1841. Courtesy Missouri Historical Society.

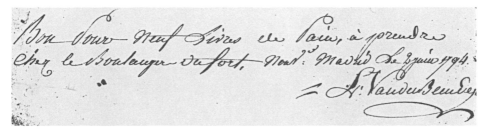

"Good for nine pounds of bread at the bakery of the fort. New Madrid, 2 June 1794." This IOU signed by Louis Vandenbemden provides an example of the paper financial transactions that Finiels remarks upon in his "Account." Courtesy Chicago Historical Society.

Pierre-Clément de Laussat, Napoleon's prefect in Louisiana during 1803. This rendering, which appeared in *A History of Louisiana* by Alcée Fortier (1904), was after a painting executed by François Gille Colson in 1786. Photograph courtesy Historic New Orleans Collection.

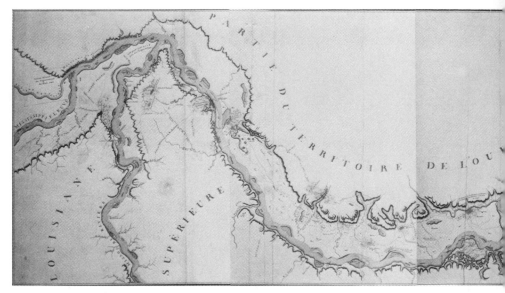

The Finiels map of 1797–1798. Courtesy Service Historique de la Marine, Vincennes. The details at bottom show the settlements of Cape Girardeau, Ste. Genevieve, New Bourbon, St. Louis, Carondelet, Florissant, Marais des Liards (now Bridgeton), and St. Charles.

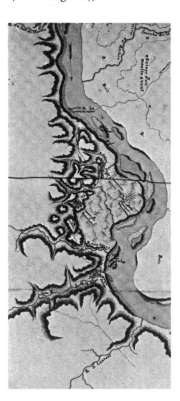

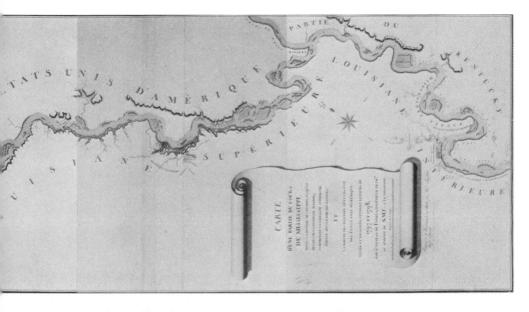

PARTIE DU

ÉTATS UNIS D'AMÉRIQUE

LOUISIANE

KENTUCKY

LOUISIANE SUPÉRIEURE

INFÉRIEURE

CARTE
D'UNE PARTIE DU COURS
DU MISSISSIPPI

1797 ET 1798.
PAR NICOLAS DE FINIELS, INGÉNIEUR ETC.
AU SERVICE DE S.M.C. A LA LOUISIANE

In some sense the text and the translator are locked in struggle—"I attacked that sentence, it resisted me, I attacked another, it eluded me"—a struggle in which curiously, when the translator wins, the text wins too, and when the translator loses, what wins is the demon inhabiting the space between the languages, champion of the inviolability of each language.

Lydia Davis

AN ACCOUNT OF UPPER LOUISIANA
Written by Monsieur de Finiels
at New Orleans in June 1803

During France's last war against Spain [1793–1795], the French government revived its interest in Louisiana, an interest that had been moribund for more than twenty years. Its minister to the United States [Edmond C. Genêt] planned an invasion in 1793, using refugees from St. Domingue, and he sent emissaries to explore the colony. All of their reports were crafted to cast a favorable light on the invasion favored by the minister and to justify it in the eyes of his constituents.[1]

This project soon evaporated, as do all of those spawned by overheated imaginations. But the reports endured.[2] They came into the hands of this minister's [Genêt's] successors; the path was cleared, and they willingly pursued it. Emissaries and reports multiplied. Perhaps these agents, who had to avoid detection by the Spanish government, got only a superficial view of the colony. Or perhaps they were seduced by the enthusiasm of those *habitants* who fervently desired the reunion of this colony with France and viewed things only through clouds of exaggeration and love for their native land. In any case, the result was that those who headed the French government developed a strong disposition in favor of the province and focused all of their energies on the task of reacquiring it. These officials were quite convinced that this reacquisition was the only thing that could heal the cruel wounds that philanthropic fanaticism had inflicted upon France by destroying the richest and most beautiful of its colonies in the Antilles [St. Domingue].[3]

As long as the French government wanted to keep a secret of the acquisition [2][4] it

1. Concerning French interest in Louisiana between 1762 and 1804, see Alexander DeConde, *This Affair of Louisiana;* E. Wilson Lyon, *Louisiana in French Diplomacy, 1759–1804;* and Frederick Jackson Turner, "The Policy of France toward the Mississippi Valley in the Period of Washington and Adams." The most comprehensive account of the mission is Harry Ammon, *The Genêt Mission.* Also see F. R. Hall, "Genêt's Western Intrigue, 1793–1794."

2. Finiels was in all likelihood referring to the accounts of the French spy, General Georges-Victor Collot. Collot reported that the French inhabitants of St. Louis exhibited "that sentiment of attachment to their country which characterizes the French nation; they appeared to be excellent patriots, whose lives and fortunes are devoted to France. . . . The people in general would be happy, were it not for the viciousness of the [Spanish] administration . . . ." Collot, *A Journey in North America,* 1:247–48. See also George W. Kyte, "A Spy on the Western Waters: The Military Intelligence Mission of General Collot in 1796." Finiels' relationship with Collot is dealt with in our Introduction above.

3. Finiels here alludes to French Revolutionary policies that led to a series of slave revolts on St. Domingue beginning in 1791. The National Convention abolished slavery on the island in 1794, and the famous Toussaint L'Ouverture eventually created the free black republic of Haiti. See T. Lothrop Stoddard, *The French Revolution in San Domingo;* Thomas O. Ott, *The Haitian Revolution, 1789–1804;* and David P. Geggus, *Slavery, War, and Revolution: The British Occupation of Saint Domingue, 1793–1798.*

4. Although Finiels' "Account" is not paginated, we have placed appropriate page numbers for the manuscript in brackets in our text.

had just made, documents concerning Louisiana remained exclusively in the hands of those who needed to be convinced.[5] But hardly was it revealed that France was going to take possession of Louisiana than printed descriptions of the province flowed from the presses; men who had never even glimpsed the Mississippi boldly declared that its marshy banks would transcend the most radiant images of heavenly and enchanted places depicted for us by [Konrad von] Gesner;[6] its climate—sometimes fiery, sometimes icy, sometimes damp, and sometimes capable of being all three in the same day—became the finest and loveliest climate in the universe; its quivering alluviums were presented as soils superior to the best in France; all of nature's wonders appeared in the chaos of its marshes, cypress swamps, and forests; novels celebrated its inhabitants, who were depicted as more wild and rugged than the place itself; they peopled it with persons more beautiful than those of Circassia, Georgia, and Mingrelia; they placed in the ignorant, rustic, and barbaric mouths of savage children from the wilderness the harmonious and heroic language of Greece's Golden Age. After such intense and persuasive argumentation, the superiority of Louisiana over all other countries of the universe was taken for granted in France; it appeared to be manifestly demonstrated, as rigorously proved as the geometrical axiom that the largest angle of a right triangle is a right angle.

It would be easy to explain the objective of all these agreeable—or treacherous—fictions, but for what purpose? Deceived by such seductive stories, a crowd of greedy persons will descend upon the boggy shores of the Mississippi; they [3] will abandon the true felicity that they enjoy in the bosom of their fatherland, which their fevered imaginations will ignore, in favor of illusory advantages of which not even a shadow will remain when they obtain the object of their desire—swamps, quicksand, and unhealthy sloughs. They will wage continual war against Mother Nature, who will be indignant over the audacity that has interrupted her work. That mother, so prodigal of the industry required to produce wealth, will deny them the expected fruits of their labors; poverty, which they could perhaps have eradicated in their fatherland, will again be the result of their error.

This error will be just as damaging to the [French] government, which, confident of the advantages that have been promised, will expect the happiest results from an acquisition that is only a burden. Soon seeing reality, but not wishing to retreat after having proceeded so arrogantly in view of the entire world, it [the government] will redouble its efforts to overcome all the snares, which have been cleverly concealed and will continually spring up underfoot. Political issues, the interests of Louisiana, will add new difficulties to those that its policies have already unraveled. Soon it will

5. France reacquired Louisiana in the Treaty of San Ildefonso of October 1800. Concerning the high hopes for Louisiana evinced in France following this treaty, see Lyon, *Louisiana in French Diplomacy*, 112–13.

6. Konrad von Gesner (1516–1565) was a Swiss botanist, naturalist, and Renaissance proto-Romantic who was well known in eighteenth-century France. See his *Descriptio Montis Fracti sive Montis Pilati*.

understand that enormous and onerous labors would be required to accomplish what nature has not yet had time to do for this province. Its highly touted resources—its fertility, productivity, climate, and even its salubrity—will appear in somber hues that are closer to reality than the smiling canvasses embellished by deft brush strokes. Finally, stripped of its exotic ornaments, should it not be feared that Louisiana will provide nothing more to the [4] French government than the regret of being burdened with one more load?

Are they not guilty, these treacherous men, who, honored with their government's trust, wish to profit from it, and present only roses when thorns would have been more appropriate? Whether false, or greedy, or ignorant, the damage they do to their country can in no way be excused. They should know that the greatest honor that can be rendered to the magistrates, and to the people themselves, of a great country is to tell them the truth or remain silent.

Until now I have adopted the latter course because of the persistent way in which this province has been accorded an importance that it does not have and *cannot* have to the extent that has been suggested. My voice could not have stanched a torrent fed by so many sources; and it has pained me to be considered a denigrator of a province that was to be united with France—but it seems to me that both Louisiana and France would be served best by telling the truth and nothing but the truth. France, when she had decided to request Louisiana from Spain, would then more likely have taken the measures necessary to succeed. And the colony itself should not have to experience the unpleasantness of failing to measure up to her reputation.

In this report I deal only with Upper Louisiana. Because of its distance from New Orleans it is less well known than Lower Louisiana; moreover, it is altogether different. Its agriculture [*culture*], its products, its needs, and its climate are not the same. Life there is healthier, [5] more varied, and more agreeable, and its topography is much more interesting. All of these characteristics, which are real advantages for Upper Louisiana when comparing it to Lower Louisiana, do not, however, justify all that has been said about Louisiana in general. One can only presume that with a large population, some energy, and an intelligent government the Illinois Country could begin to approximate the portrayals that have been made of it—and then only if the exaggerations could be eliminated.[7]

UPPER LOUISIANA
LOCATION, BOUNDARIES, COMMUNICATION

The Ohio, or the Belle Rivière, is created by the confluence of the Allegheny and Monongahela rivers at the site once occupied by Fort Duquesne and now occupied by

7. Throughout this translation the place name *Illinois Country* will be used rather than *Illinois* in reference to the region lying on both sides of the Mississippi from the mouth of the Illinois River to the mouth of the Ohio.

the city of Pittsburgh (40–31–44 latitude north). After flowing 1,188 miles along the southern boundary of that part of the United States that is called the Northwest Territory, with the states of Pennsylvania, Virginia, and Kentucky to the south, it empties into the Mississippi at 37–00–23 latitude north. This is eighteen leagues below [Finiels means *above*] New Madrid and fifteen leagues below Cape Girardeau.[8]

Proceeding up the Mississippi (long ago called Michacépé, that is, "The Distant Old Man") from the mouth of the Ohio, Upper Louisiana begins on the right bank of the Mississippi. This is more commonly called Spanish Illinois to distinguish it from the Northwest Territory, which—on the left bank of the river, facing Spanish Illinois—is occupied under the same name [Upper Louisiana] by the United States.[9]

The boundaries of Upper Louisiana to the west and to the north have never been established by any treaty and remain unknown; those of New Mexico, Upper Canada, and the United States, its neighbors, are as yet undetermined. This needs to be done in a definitive fashion, however, in order to establish [6] on a firm base the [fur] trade of Upper Louisiana. Future trade with the Indians of the Missouri River and its tributaries requires regulation because the English, who derive much advantage from it, continue to poach there despite the efforts and protests of the Spaniards.[10]

Upper Louisiana has contacts with Upper Canada to the north, the United States to the east, and Lower Louisiana to the south. In the west it is adjacent to the heights of New Mexico, with which it still has no contact, and it conducts trade with the Indian tribes of the Missouri River and its tributaries that flow from the south. All these issues could supply material for an interesting discourse, which would distract me too much from my principal subject at the present. I am going to speak now only of its communications with New Orleans, reserving the other issues until I deal with commerce.

Communications are ordinarily carried on between New Orleans and the Illinois Country via the Mississippi. The difference in latitude between the capital [i.e., New Orleans] and St. Louis is only 9 degrees, or 225 leagues at 25 to the degree, and their

8. In general, the mouth of the Ohio River was the line of demarcation between Lower and Upper Louisiana, although New Madrid, located below the Ohio's mouth, was usually included within the jurisdiction of Upper Louisiana. Captain Amos Stoddard, however, the first American commandant of Upper Louisiana, identified the Arkansas River as the boundary between Upper and Lower Louisiana (see Stoddard, *Sketches, Historical and Descriptive of Upper Louisiana*, 205).

9. Missouri was very rarely used as a place name (except for the river) during colonial times, and in the 1790s St. Louis was located in what was known as Spanish Illinois. It should be noted that Finiels' "right bank" and "left bank" always refer to the banks as seen when facing *downstream*.

10. Upper Louisiana, whose boundaries were never precisely defined in colonial times, was at first deemed to lie south of Upper Canada, but as the valleys of the upper Mississippi and Missouri rivers became known, those regions came to be considered a part of Upper Louisiana. And so it was when the United States purchased Louisiana in 1803. See DeConde, *This Affair of Louisiana*, 169–71. Following the close of the American Revolution, the British steadily increased their control over the Indian trade on both sides of the upper Mississippi valley. See Abraham P. Nasatir, *Borderland in Retreat*, 21–50.

longitude is about the same.[11] Nonetheless, because of the numerous twists and turns in the Mississippi, which continually doubles back on itself and seems to delight in snaking across the alluviums that it alternately creates and destroys along its banks, the route between the two cities is nearly 450 leagues by river.[12]

The man who decides to tackle this arduous route by boat will despair as he views this immense labyrinth, which almost triples his labor, his travail, and his time by its incredible sinuosity, and which seems to be a whim of nature. Yet he knows that it is this tortuous course that permits him to ascend the river. If the Mississippi flowed, as do some other rivers, in a more or less straight course, or proceeded with larger and more regular curves, with what impetuous speed its waters would rush to the sea and what efforts would be required to ascend it! A man would then be compelled to seek—across forests, across swamps and marshes, across choppy hills, across new rivers, across obstacles without end—an apparently shorter route [7] to Illinois, but it would be more taxing and painful. And by such a route he would not be able to take to the settlers along the Mississippi the merchandise from which he derives the profits that give him the courage to make the trip.

Thus the current of the Mississippi, even in time of the greatest floods, is not so rapid as one would naturally suppose it to be. It is slower than several rivers in Europe and even slower than some other rivers in America that have a shorter course, but its bed is deeper than any known river. It can be ascended by the largest boats for two hundred leagues even during the lowest water. Its channels leading to the sea [i.e., the Gulf] easily accommodate ships of all widths, but those which draw more than twelve feet of water have great difficulty when fully loaded. This difficulty, which prevents large ships from entering the river, together with the swamps that occupy the banks near the river's mouth, mean that Louisiana is safe and secure in time of war. An enemy can, it is true, anchor near the passes in order to intercept commerce, but he cannot penetrate into the province's heartland with those most terrible scourges of war—pillage and destruction.[13]

From New Orleans to Natchez the Mississippi runs for one hundred leagues. This

11. New Orleans and St. Louis are in fact 8½ degrees of latitude apart and are located at approximately the same longitude.

12. During the eighteenth century, estimates varied considerably concerning the river distance between New Orleans and St. Louis. Usually the estimates fell between 400 and 500 leagues. Finiels reckoned the league at 25 to the degree latitude and the river distance between St. Louis and New Orleans as 450 leagues. Reckoning a degree of latitude at 69 (English) miles (which means that Finiels' league would be 2.76 miles) and using his distance of 450 leagues between the two cities, St. Louis and New Orleans were 1,242 miles apart by river. Concerning the length of a league, see Roland Chardon, "The Linear League in North America."

13. Twelve French feet equaled almost thirteen English feet, reckoning a French foot at 12.79 English inches. This depth of water did prevent some ships from moving up the Mississippi to New Orleans, but to increase security, fortifications had been erected at various places—La Balise, Plaquemines Bend, and the English Turn—between the mouth of the river and New Orleans. See Carl J. Ekberg, "The English Bend: Forgotten Gateway to New Orleans."

entire section of the river is navigable even during low water. That is to say, navigation is not impeded by any of the islands, sandbars, and snags that occur for the
remainder of the river's course heading north, and which crop up at every step all
the way to St. Louis. Navigators consider this part of the voyage upriver a piece of
cake [*les fleurs de la route*], for the work is straightforward. Farther upstream,
however, the work is consistently dangerous. In the lower region they can sometimes make eight or ten leagues in a day, while higher up they are lucky to make
three leagues. In descending, boats glide along peacefully day and night after passing Natchez, and the navigators abandon the vigilance that kept them on edge ever
since leaving the Illinois Country.[14]

[8] I'm not going to interrupt myself here to describe further the river trip from
New Orleans to the Illinois Country. This would bog me down in details and really
requires an article unto itself. I will only remark that this is a very difficult trip,
despite what I said about the Mississippi's moderate current. The current is, however,
rather swift in the main channel, which would make the trip much longer if you did
not make use of the counter-current (called here the *remoux*). This is located alter-
natively on one bank and the other along points of land facing coves, and navigators
must seek it out by continually crossing the river, losing a bit of headway with each
crossing. A *bateau* manned by twenty to thirty oarsmen, husky and accustomed to
ascending the river, requires a minimum of sixty days to reach St. Louis from New
Orleans. And even then such a *bateau* must be guided by a good skipper [*patron*], a
man able to take advantage of all possibilities, a man with long experience and a
perfect knowledge of the river. In less favorable circumstances, a boat will require
seventy-five to eighty days to make the same trip.[15]

The best time to ascend the Mississippi to the Illinois Country is during February,
March, and April. Later than this, you are likely to be overtaken by hot weather that
will make the crew ill; earlier, cold weather may compel you to winter on the riverbanks. Few merchants in the Illinois Country have not experienced one or the other
of these inconveniences because of bad timing and as a consequence suffered losses in
their business. To these inconveniences you must add the persistent danger of found-
ering on a sandbar (several of which are famous for shipwrecks), the lurking misfortune of breaking up on one of the snags that fill the river, and the risks that you face
along the banks of being crushed by monstrous falling trees or buried by the
mudslides that accompany their fall. This done, you will have some idea [9] of naviga-

14. Natchez was a strategic site during late colonial times, and the Spanish government kept a governor
posted there. See Jack D. L. Holmes, *Gayoso: The Life of a Spanish Governor in the Mississippi Valley,
1789–1799*.
15. Finiels' data pertain to the 1790s. In earlier times, especially when the Chickasaw Indians harassed
river boats, the trip from New Orleans to the Illinois Country often required four or five months. See
Nancy M. Surrey, *The Commerce of Louisiana During the French Regime, 1699–1763*.

tion that would shock the bravest Europeans and compel them to admit that there is absolutely no work in Europe to compare with the travail of Mississippi boatmen.[16]

You can make the trip overland from New Orleans to the Illinois on either side of the Mississippi. On the left side you can get to Natchez in three days by going via Lake Pontchartrain; from Natchez you can proceed to Nashville in twelve to fifteen days,[17] and from Nashville to Louisville on the Ohio River in five days. At Louisville you cross the Ohio to Fort Clarksville, and from there you proceed to Vincennes on the Wabash in four days; from Vincennes you pass on to Kaskaskia in six days, and then on to St. Louis in two more. Thus thirty-five days, or less in the right circumstances, are required to make this journey entirely in United States territory, across land that has only recently been ceded by Spain—then through Georgia, Tennessee, Kentucky, and the Northwest Territory. This route is practical only in summer and autumn; in winter ice, and in spring flooded rivers, render it impassable.[18]

On the right side of the Mississippi, you can proceed from New Orleans to Attakapas, to Opelousas, to Avoyelles, to Natchitoches, to Ouachitas, and to the Arks [i.e., Arkansas Post]. All of these outposts are linked with each other rather easily by journeys of three to six days during the summer and autumn. From the Arks you can travel overland to New Madrid in twelve to fifteen days, and from New Madrid to St. Louis in three to four days, the entire journey thus requiring about thirty days.[19]

I've rapidly outlined these two routes without discussing the obstacles that might encumber them, and at first glance it may seem that there are no obstacles on the overland routes. But in Louisiana, you must completely forget the conveniences of European routes, in order to be [10] prepared for the difficulties that characterize each step of the way in countries inhabited by savages. On the Mississippi, the entire burden falls upon the boatmen; a passenger experiences only boredom and fear of the journey. Overland, all the hardship falls upon him, and if he wishes to undertake such a trip he must be seasoned and endowed with an even temperament in order to withstand the travail. He must expect to pass most of his nights upon the ground, and

16. Perrin du Lac, who traveled on the Mississippi about the same time as Finiels, said this about the existence of riverboatmen: "On long voyages they suffer indescribably. They wear no clothes except those necessary to provide decency, and their skins, burned by the sun, peel off several times. . . . It is not unusual for them to succumb to fatigue and die oar in hand" (*Voyage dans les deux Louisianes*, 166).

17. By the late 1790s, the Natchez Trace from Natchez to Nashville had become a standard route for boatmen who sold their craft in New Orleans and returned to the Ohio Valley via the overland route that Finiels here describes. See Jonathan Daniels, *The Devil's Backbone: The Story of the Natchez Trace*.

18. In the Treaty of San Lorenzo, or Pinckney's Treaty (1795), Spain had ceded to the United States all territory east of the Mississippi that lay north of the 31st parallel. See Samuel F. Bemis, *Pinckney's Treaty: America's Advantage from Europe's Distress, 1783–1800*. Georgia claimed land west as far as the Mississippi until 1802.

19. Both the Arkansas Indians and the Arkansas Post were often referred to simply as the *Arks*. From the French *aux Arks* eventually came *Ozarks*. The latter term was being used as early as 1780. See John Montgomery to George Rogers Clark, 18 February 1780, Clark Family Papers, Missouri Historical Society.

under the burning rays of a pitiless sun perpetually to be crossing rivers, hills, and plains that are sometimes swampy and sometimes sandy. Cloudy weather is sometimes the most stifling; torrential rains raise the water level in swamps, leaving no refuge; the forests are so wild that they are virtually impenetrable; ancient trees, which the hand of time and violent winds have struck down, lie scattered hither and thither at the feet of their numerous successors; many trees, thwarted in their ascent, grow crossways through the forest in thick bunches only three or four feet off the ground; native vines, snaking without leaves from tree to tree, block the path in all directions; often the ground in these forests is flooded, and their shadowy atmosphere retains moisture long after the heat has dried out the prairies. The traveler must carry tents, beds, food, and clothing, and all this equipment multiplies the difficulties of crossing forests and rivers.

SETTLEMENTS

I now return to describing the Illinois Country, whose communications with New Orleans diverted me, but which I must describe before guiding my reader there.

Upper Louisiana is as yet only settled in the lower part, from Cap à la Cruche to the Rivière d'Ardennes [Dardenne Creek], which empties into the Mississippi two leagues above the mouth of the Illinois River.[20] The settlements are Cap à la Cruche, Cape [11] Girardeau, the Saline, New Bourbon, Ste. Genevieve or Misery, Carondelet or Vide Poche [Empty Pocket], St. Louis or Pain Cour [Short of Bread], St. Ferdinand or Fleurissant,[21] Marais des Liards [Cottonwood Swamp] (named after a common tree in the Illinois), Bon Homme Creek on the right bank of the Missouri eight leagues from St. Louis, St. Charles or Petites Côtes [Little Hills] on the left bank of the Missouri, a settlement established four years ago on the Rivière d'Ardennes, and several farmsteads located on the bank of the Mississippi between St. Louis and the mouth of the Missouri River, on the Missouri above its mouth, on Rivière aux Pères [Des Peres Creek], between St. Louis and Ste. Genevieve, and between Ste. Genevieve and Cape Girardeau.

CAPE GIRARDEAU AND ENVIRONS

When you enter the Mississippi valley from the Ohio, the first region you encounter consists of low-lying alluvial lands, which are similar to those along the right bank of the Mississippi all the way to its mouth. During high water they are covered by about

20. Finiels' Cap à la Cruche is now called Cape la Croix, a clear case of garbled meaning as translations and pronunciations got jumbled and confused over time. When Louis Houck remarked (*History of Missouri*, 2:190) that *Cruz* was the correct spelling and *Cruche* incorrect, he was probably wrong, for *Cruche*, "jug" in French, describes the configuration of the Mississippi as it swirls around Cape la Croix. For more controversy and confusion about the name of this cape, see Milo M. Quaife, ed., *The Journals of Captain Meriwether Lewis and Sergeant John Ordway*, 58.

21. The town is now called Florissant, while the local township is St. Ferdinand.

four feet of water, and after having seen them covered like that, you are surprised to find them twenty feet above the river during the months of July, August, September, and October. These lands persist for eleven leagues above Cap à la Cruche. They are covered with thick woods, and although composed of a mixture of mud, soil, and sand, they are fertile enough to sustain myriad plants and vigorous trees. West of the river above the woods you find vast prairies dotted here and there with clusters of woods, which the Mississippi does not inundate even at highest flood stage. Although these lands appear good for agriculture, farmers hesitate to locate there because there is no water supply to sustain them. After leaving the prairies, you come upon small hills crowned with woods and surrounded by water and marshes; then after four or five leagues you come upon the highlands of Cap à la Cruche. This region [i.e., below Cap à la Cruche] is called the low country and extends all the way to the high ground of Cap à la Cruche. It is covered with swampy woods, which are rarely dry and sometimes have water three feet deep. As soon as you pass through them you head for Cape Girardeau. After leaving [12] New Madrid, the European traveler following his guide through this chaos of trees, water, and mire is surprised at not getting lost a thousand times and admires what ability and memory can accomplish when there is nothing else to serve as a guide.[22]

Immediately after these lowlands come those of Cap à la Cruche, which rise toward Cap Pointe de Rocher [Cape Rocky Point]. They are slightly elevated, are covered with black soil, and extend for thirteen leagues up the Mississippi from the mouth of the Ohio. Cap Pointe de Rocher is like an advance guard for Cape Girardeau, which is only two leagues away. At Cap Pointe de Rocher the current of the river is slowed by two features: a bank of rocks facing the cape a short distance from the east bank of the river, and a sandbar that begins at the cape and extends down the west bank of the river. The first high ground on the west bank of the Mississippi begins a little below Cap Pointe de Rocher. This high ground extends westward from the river for a considerable distance and connects with the high ground drained by the St. Francis, Arkansas, Ouachita, and other rivers of Lower Louisiana.[23]

Shortly after leaving the mouth of the Ohio to head upriver toward Cap à la Cruche, you find yourself in the midst of a multitude of various sized islands. These islands surround the Grand Détour [Dogtooth Bend], and the largest group of them has been christened Isles à la Course, probably because at low water boats must be

22. In the 1780s Canadian traders François and Joseph Le Sieur established a trading post on the bend of the Mississippi below the mouth of the Ohio at a site known as L'Anse à la Graisse (Greasy Cove) because the Indians often boiled down buffalo and bear grease there. Colonel George Morgan, an Anglo-American merchant, chose that west-bank location in 1789 for the settlement of New Madrid. For the early history of New Madrid, see Max Savelle, *George Morgan: Colony Builder,* and Lynn Morrow, "New Madrid and Its Hinterland, 1783–1826."

23. Cap à la Cruche (Cape la Croix) is below Cape Girardeau; Cap Pointe de Rocher (Cape Rock) is above. Finiels' geography is obviously a bit fuzzy in this passage, and he seems to have been ignorant of the many rivers flowing southeastward out of the Ozark highlands toward the Mississippi River.

pulled over their sandbars with a towline. These islands greatly increase the width of the Mississippi's channel at this spot, and the human eye can scarcely see across it. When, after struggling through its numerous detours, you emerge from this area, you find yourself between two parallel chains of rocks located in the channel of the river; these rocks are exposed during low water. This passage, immediately below Cap à la Cruche, is difficult and dangerous whether you are ascending or descending the river.

In 1798 there were only three [13] farmsteads at Cap à la Cruche; they are on the bank of the river and are dependencies of Cape Girardeau, which has similar lands and forests.

Cape Girardeau follows immediately after Cap à la Cruche and is located fifteen leagues above the mouth of the Ohio. It is composed of a vast block of granite covered with a thin layer of black soil. The Cape from its nearly perpendicular height dominates the entire course of the Mississippi, whose waters swirl at the foot of its rocks. Great efforts are required to overcome the current of the river and ascend it at this spot, and, when coming downriver, you must be very careful landing there.

Eleven or twelve years ago, Monsieur [Louis] Lorimier, whose outpost on the headwaters of the Big Miami was being harried by General [Anthony] Wayne, arrived to occupy old Cape Girardeau; he was accompanied by bands of Shawnees and Loups [Delawares] of which he was the leader.[24] Some years later, Monsieur the Baron de Carondelet appointed him commandant of the post, and he then abandoned the old post in order to occupy the new Cape, which is now his principal settlement.[25] He settled the Indians who had accompanied him in three villages a short distance away.[26] These villages were more systematically and solidly constructed than the usual Indian villages. Around their villages the Indians soon cleared the land, which was securely fenced around in the American style in order to protect their harvests from animals. The first of these villages is located five or six leagues from Cape

24. After supporting the British cause during the American Revolution, the Canadian-born trader Louis Lorimier fled to Spanish Illinois in 1786 and initially settled at the Saline Creek south of Ste. Genevieve. With the approval of Spanish authorities, he actively recruited members of the Shawnee and Delaware tribes to follow him west of the Mississippi. In 1792 he moved to Cape Girardeau to be near the Shawnee and Delaware bands that had established themselves between the Cinque Hommes and Apple creeks. Concerning Lorimier and his settlement at Cape Girardeau, see the excellent biographical note in Abraham P. Nasatir, ed., *Spanish War Vessels on the Mississippi*, 71–72, note 27; Louis Houck, *Memorial Sketches of Pioneers and Early Residents of Southeast Missouri*, 1–18; and Houck, *History of Missouri*, 2:167–84.

25. Don Francisco Hector de Carondelet, a Fleming, was governor general of Spanish Louisiana from 1792 to 1797. He was in office when Finiels arrived in Upper Louisiana in the spring of 1797.

26. Spanish officials had encouraged the relocation of eastern tribes west of the Mississippi in the belief that they could serve as a buffer between Upper Louisiana's exposed settlements and the hostile Osages to the west. According to a 1787 report, 1,200 Shawnee and 600 Delaware had relocated along the Saline, Apple, Cinque Hommes, and Flora creeks south of Ste. Genevieve. See Reuben Gold Thwaites, ed., *British Regime in Wisconsin, 1760–1800*, 435, n. 48. On the arrival of the Shawnee and Delaware in Spanish Upper Louisiana, also see William C. Sturtevant, gen. ed., *Handbook of North American Indians*, vol. 15, *Northeast*, ed. Bruce G. Trigger, 600–601, 623–35; and Melburn D. Thurman, "The Delaware Indians: A Study in Ethnohistory." We have consistently translated Finiels' *sauvages* as "Indians," which seems the best rendering into modern English.

Girardeau along the road to Ste. Genevieve, and the second is five or six leagues farther up the same route. Both of them are on high ground some distance from the river and are inhabited by the Shawnees. The third is farther inland, approximately halfway between the other two, and is inhabited by the Loups [Delawares].[27]

I passed through the two Shawnee villages in 1797 when I traveled overland between New Madrid and St. Louis. I arrived at the first between 9:00 and 10:00 a.m., and the Indians were loath to let me continue on my way. I was forced to spend the rest of the day and that night in the chief's house, where the most important of the Indians gathered. They kept me company around the hearth of hospitality, especially those who spoke English, [14] for they noticed that I myself spoke that language. During the evening they entertained me with several dances and games with which they pass the time not consumed in hunting and agriculture and which invigorate the youth of both sexes in their leisure time. The next day I encountered the same hospitality in the second village, and I was again compelled to oblige them.[28]

Everything suggested that the Shawnees are already less savage than other tribes in North America; they are good men and capable of more civilization than has generally been thought possible for Indians. Indeed, the Shawnees seem to have a marked superiority over all other peoples who are equally barbarous: they are generally large and well-built, lighter than other Indians, and possessing more regular features; they are cleaner and more particular about their dress. Their women share this predilection for cleanliness and good taste. These Indians no longer have a thirst to kill, a desire to take scalps that always heats Indian blood when spring arrives. I don't doubt that with some encouragement this tribe—while maintaining its taste for the hunt, which should not be completely extinguished—could become a stable agricultural people and would be useful residents of Upper Louisiana.

In reflecting upon the first steps toward civilization that the Shawnees seem to have made, I believe that I perceive the reasons for this progress precisely in the little interest that has been shown for civilizing them, and in the example set for them by several whites who while mingling with them seem to have adopted their customs. This is especially true of Monsieur Lorimier, son of a white man and a Shawnee woman, who alternately adopts European and Indian customs and who appears, along with his son, sometimes in European garb and sometimes in the dress of these children of nature.[29] If you recall our missionaries' futile efforts in Canada to civilize

27. In his *Sketches, Historical and Descriptive of Louisiana*, 215, Amos Stoddard stated that the "three villages of Indians, one of Delawares, and two of Shawnees" were located about twenty miles up Apple Creek. Stoddard claimed that in all three villages the Indians' houses were substantial log structures.

28. This paragraph suggests that the Shawnees spoke more English than French, although Lorimier, who had led them from the Ohio Valley into Spanish Illinois, was a French Canadian and did not speak English. He was, however, adept at Indian languages.

29. Finiels' remark in this passage that Lorimier was of mixed Indian blood makes sense. Cyprien Tanguay's monumental *Dictionnaire généalogique des familles canadiennes*, 7 vols., contains no record for the baptism of a Louis Lorimier, which suggests that his mother was an Indian woman. Claude Delorimier, born at Montreal in 1709, may have been his father.

the Iroquois and Hurons and [15] compare these to the progress that the Shawnees have made in so little time in Louisiana, you will perhaps be persuaded that it was the impatience and inflexibility of the missionaries that doomed their efforts to failure. In fact, the free man of nature reacts when something is forced upon him but yields unwittingly to everything that is not demanded of him, which he seems to adopt of his own accord when he has had the opportunity to appreciate how it may contribute to his happiness.

The Loups that occupy the third village differ much from the Shawnees. They are still savages in the full sense of the term, but one must hope that the example of the Shawnees will have an effect upon them.[30]

Besides the Indian tribes that occupy the area north of Cape Girardeau, about thirty American families, taking advantage of the Spanish government's generous land policy of 1796, have left Kentucky in order to settle at Cape Girardeau. Several of these families have settled near Monsieur Lorimier's concession, which occupies the entire cove of new Cape Girardeau, being ninety arpents across and about the same in depth. But most of them have settled a little further inland, creating the settlement of Levana. This is linked to Cape Girardeau by a road that passes over Monsieur Lorimier's land and over the lands of the families settled at the southern end of his concession.[31]

The population of Cape Girardeau, which could supply nearly one hundred fifty men able to bear arms, has existed very peacefully up to now and seems very loyal to Spain.[32] These people possess the industry that one cannot deny to the Kentuckians, as well as the energy that was missing in the old colonists of Upper Louisiana. But one should not conceive of this industry and energy in European terms, nor must one base upon them hope for the future growth of this colony. Kentuckian industry must necessarily precede the European variety in uninhabited and wild regions. But this industry is limited to supplying the first indispensable needs of life by rustic and imperfect means, which are not [16] yet enlightened or directed by the methodical processes of the mechanical arts [procédés réguliers des arts]. It breathes life into barren areas by substituting for the disorder with which nature commences her most sublime compositions a plan unknown to nature; it warns nature henceforth to yield

30. *Loups* (Wolves) was a name used somewhat loosely by the French to refer to a number of eastern Indian tribes (see Trigger, *Handbook of North American Indians*, 15:211). The Loups of Upper Louisiana were a part of the large Delaware tribe (see Thurman, "The Delaware Indians"). In part the oft-noted distinctions between Missouri's early Shawnee and Delaware emigrants may have been a result of the individuals from those tribes who chose to migrate. The Shawnee settlers appear to have been established bands with influential tribal leaders, whereas the first Delawares were often dissident and renegade factions led by persons of lesser standing.

31. Spain's "generous land policy of 1796" had been implemented by Governor Carondelet. When he was replaced by Gayoso de Lemos in 1797, American immigration into Spanish Louisiana was restricted on religious grounds. See Lawrence Kinnaird, "American Penetration into Spanish Territory, 1776–1802"; Jonas Viles, "Population and Extent of Settlement in Missouri before 1804."

32. The Spanish colonial definition of "men able to bear arms" was all males between the ages of fourteen and fifty, and these age categories were used in the census tabulations. For an example of a Spanish colonial census, see Carl J. Ekberg, *Colonial Ste. Genevieve*, 243.

in the face of man, who arrives to settle areas that previously had sustained only a multitude of nature's animals. Kentuckian industry can clear and seed a field, build a crude cabin, raise scattered herds, construct grist and saw mills, trace roadways, do primitive mining, and weave some coarse cloth. It accomplishes all of this without producing a single thing of quality, as the products of Kentucky demonstrate. It is at first useful and perhaps indispensable in a difficult country, which requires indefatigable men to blaze the trail. But it is soon insufficient for the capacity, the growth, the orderliness, and the splendor toward which a colony must be swiftly guided; it must give way in the face of better and more useful strategies, of more advanced techniques, of science and technology, just as the pencil strokes of a sketch must be eradicated by the brush strokes that complete and give life to a painting.

Cape Girardeau's population would have grown very rapidly and would be considerable at this time if the Spanish government had not decided to halt its growth. It did this by insisting that immigrants raise their children as Roman Catholics and by prohibiting the practice of any other religion. This is not the place to examine the question of whether Spanish policy was reasonable or not; whether it was good or bad for the colony; whether the population that, without this policy, would have been drawn to Cape Girardeau and to the other settlements in the Illinois Country would have been advantageous to France.[33] France can still make up for this [17] error (if it is one) by ceasing to believe that the colony should be reserved for Frenchmen. To shake off the stagnation of the colony, all France needs to do is say the word, and thousands of men will stream out of Kentucky to strip away its ancient forest, to lacerate its breast with plowshares, and to create the cornucopia that they are eager to produce.

One branch, and perhaps several, of the St. Francis River, after having passed behind New Madrid, drains the hinterlands of Cape Girardeau at a distance of twelve to fifteen leagues while descending toward the Missouri [i.e., the Mississippi]. The lands along its banks are just as good as those of Cape Girardeau, and they could sustain a large population. Although the farmers that will settle there could easily communicate with Cape Girardeau by overland routes, the St. Francis River would provide them with an easier and faster outlet to the Mississippi and to New Orleans. It is assumed that iron mines will be found on the back branches of the St. Francis River.[34]

All the lands of Cape Girardeau are not, however, uniformly good. They are often

33. During the 1780s and 1790s, Spanish colonial authorities in Louisiana hotly debated the issues of immigration and religion. They were caught in a dilemma of wanting immigrants but being wary of Americans, especially Protestant Americans. See Kinnaird, "American Penetration into Spanish Territory."

34. Iron deposits do in fact occur in the highlands west of the upper St. Francis River, and during the nineteenth century they supported a substantial iron-mining industry. Iron mining is, however, no longer an important part of Missouri's economy. Dating all the way back to the John Law schemes of the early 1720s, the French had been hoping to discover rich mines of various sorts in Upper Louisiana. Unfortunately, lead—rather than gold or silver—turned out to be the most plentiful mineral.

dissected by hillocks, creating gullies and ravines; in rainy seasons these become torrents that are very difficult to cross. The hillocks seem for the most part to be composed of sandy soil, mixed with pebbles and stones, that is not well suited to agriculture. This soil does sustain some isolated trees that attain a considerable size. But they in no way compare to forests growing on richer soil, whose mere presence suggests a soil eager to produce, a happy sign of fertility. On the one hand this speaks well for Cape Girardeau's trees, for they must possess a hardiness lacking in [18] humid, low-lying, and wet regions. They are also seasoned by the air that circulates throughout these thin forests, which thicker forests enjoy only along their fringes; this is demonstrated by the superior quality of trees that grow on the outer perimeter.

I won't repeat here other persons' claims about the importance of Cape Girardeau, which, according to them, exercises surveillance over everything that leaves the Ohio in order to ascend or descend the Mississippi.[35] Certainly, when you consider that the Cape is fifteen leagues above the mouth of the Ohio, you begin to think that this is an illusion. It, and Cap à la Cruche below it, are the two sites on the west side of the Mississippi where solid forts could be built above the mouth of the Ohio. That is all that can be said on the subject. The importance of Cape Girardeau, which consists of being in a position to stop convoys of munitions or provisions from ascending the Mississippi in case of an American invasion of the Illinois Country, would not have been exaggerated if it had been clear that some other route could be used. Sufficient attention has not been paid to the fact that if a fort guarded this route, convoys would not be compelled to use it; its problems are known, and there are two overland alternatives whose difficulties are not insurmountable. In fact, it is above the mouth of the Ohio that navigation of the Mississippi becomes the most difficult and dangerous. Without mentioning the double chain of rocks above Cap à la Cruche, there are even more dangers above Cape Girardeau before you arrive at the Kaskaskia River. There are numerous locations where the smallest detachment of men would have good sport destroying a convoy that attempted to come upriver to that point. It would therefore be only through the grossest ignorance that an enemy would send convoys via a route that is as difficult as it is dangerous. He would thus risk seeing all of his plans founder, while he could have assured himself of success by using the overland route to Kaskaskia, which [19] is the rendezvous point in the Illinois Country.

If the United States should ever threaten the settlements in Spanish Illinois, its first logistical base, whether for munitions or for provisions, would be Cincinnati. Also called Fort Washington, it is located on the right bank of the Ohio, a few leagues below the mouth of the Little Miami and facing the mouth of the Licking River. From there, troops and munitions could descend the Ohio River to rendezvous with those from Kentucky at Fort Clarksville, which is across the river from Louisville. These

35. In all likelihood Finiels was referring to the claims of General Georges-Victor Collot, who described Cape Girardeau as "the first military point on the river from the mouth of the Ohio" (*A Journey in North America*, 1:217–18).

allied forces could then proceed down the Ohio to Fort Massiac [Massac], located on the right bank of the Ohio forty-six miles above its mouth. Or better yet, part of the force could take this route while the rest proceeded overland from Fort Washington to the Vincennes post on the Wabash and from there, still by land, to the point where the Kaskaskia River becomes navigable, which would carry them safely to the town of that name. The troops that had gone on to Fort Massiac could also proceed overland to Kaskaskia and thereby avoid the difficulties presented by ascending the Mississippi. Recall the campaigns of Generals [Arthur] St. Clair and [Anthony] Wayne in 1791 and 1795 during the last American war against the Indians and the route the generals took from the Ohio River up to the mouth of the Miami. This should easily convince you of the route that Americans would likely take in attacking the Illinois Country, which would be both shorter and less difficult than via the Mississippi.[36]

Thus the Americans would never descend the Ohio and ascend the Mississippi for an attack upon the Illinois Country, for they have rendezvous points in Illinois that they can reach by land. They would take the rivers only if they wished to attack Lower Louisiana, and then Cape Girardeau would be utterly useless.

I do not conclude from this that it is unnecessary to establish a fort at Cape Girardeau and neglect control of the Mississippi above the mouth of the Ohio. [20] Construction of forts on provincial frontiers is absolutely necessary. They provide farmers with the confidence that creates loyalty to their lands and to the government and encourages them in their work. Cape Girardeau is one of the best sites for building a fort, but after having built it, one must not be deluded into thinking that the entire colony is thus protected from its neighbors.

Cap à la Cruche and Cape Girardeau are still covered with primeval forests. Like their environs, they are drained in all directions by several creeks and small rivers, of which the principal are the Cap à la Cruche, the Albion, and the Canes. Their headwaters are not far removed in the hinterland and seem to originate in the highlands behind the two capes. Cap à la Cruche River empties into the Mississippi immediately above this cape; the Albion River midway between Cap à la Cruche and Cape Girardeau; and the Canes River a little above Cape Girardeau. The Albion already has three mill sites. It flows across the entire concession of Monsieur Lorimier, and one of its branches crosses the American settlements south of this concession.

Numerous advantages guarantee that Cape Girardeau will one day have a large population and will command the attention of a government enlightened enough to profit from its virtues; all of this suggests that it will someday be one of the Illinois

36. In this paragraph, Finiels' geography is accurate and his strategic remarks succinct and penetrating. Although he does not specifically refer to it, George Rogers Clark's campaign of 1778 runs between the lines of this paragraph. In that well-remembered campaign, Clark proceeded overland from Fort Massac on the lower Ohio to Kaskaskia, thus avoiding the ascent of the Mississippi from the mouth of the Ohio northward. See James A. James, *The Life of George Rogers Clark*.

Country's leading settlements [21] and that it will become one of the firmest bases upon which will be founded the splendor of Upper Louisiana—water flowing from several nearby sources; many highlands beyond the river's reach and sufficiently productive; good wood for construction; stone that can be easily quarried from the flanks of the hills and turned into houses and lime; the relative beauty of a location that agreeably freshens eyes grown weary by the monotonous spectacle of the Mississippi and lower Ohio floodplains; healthfulness radiating from the site.[37]

THE TWO SALINES, NEW BOURBON, AND STE. GENEVIEVE

Leaving Cape Girardeau to ascend the Mississippi toward Ste. Genevieve, the only obstacle that you encounter for eleven leagues is the current of the river itself. Then you arrive at Grand Tower, which is infamous among skippers on the Mississippi for its danger, for the rocks that surround it, for the rocky mass of which it is composed, for its isolation in the middle of the river (which is unique in the known course of the river), and for the rocks lying just beneath the surface of the water that link it to an island just downriver. From Cape Girardeau the lands on the right bank of the Mississippi become lower for a distance of five leagues, but the bluffs are not far from the river. After five leagues they return to the riverbank and remain there until you come to Cap St. Antoine, a league and a half above Grand Tower. On the American side, the bluffs that were close to the bank all the way from the Isles à la Course begin to recede at Cap à la Cruche, leaving a vast floodplain facing Cape Girardeau. They return to the [left] bank only at Cap St. Croix, facing Grand Tower. It seems as if they relish the spectacle of the rocky peaks crowned with trees and the roaring of the Mississippi's waves as they, one after the other, smash upon the rocks, indignant that an indomitable obstacle should be placed in their path. If you wish to ascend this passage you must be careful to take the channel that is between the right bank and the first island. You then pass between two islands, opposite the larger of which the Rivière aux Vases [22] flows from the American side and empties into the Mississippi. Then you must head directly toward the point on the left bank opposite the channel and surge ahead with the oars until you have passed Cap St. Antoine. At that point you begin to feel safe from the danger of being swept away by the current and dashed against fearsome Grand Tower. You will have already passed Cap St. Antoine when

37. The Spanish census of Cape Girardeau in 1803 can be found in Louis Houck, *The Spanish Regime in Missouri* (cited hereafter as *SRM*), 2:403–7. The census shows a total population of 1,206 souls of all ages and colors, both sexes, free and slave. Cape Girardeau was in many ways unlike any of the other Spanish administrative districts. It was inhabited predominantly by Anglo-Americans, who in typical American fashion dispersed themselves in small settlement clusters and on scattered farmsteads in what they considered to be the healthier uplands away from the rivers. There was not a single town or village of any size in the entire district. Louis Lorimier's trading post served as the administrative headquarters. The town of Cape Girardeau was not formally platted until 1806. See Floyd Shoemaker, "Cape Girardeau, Most American of Missouri's Original Five Counties."

you perceive once again the roaring of the waves, which perpetuate in your mind the sense of the peril you have just escaped.[38]

In the region between Cape Girardeau and Tower Rock, you encounter several neighboring bayous on the right bank, then three rivers empty into the Mississippi. The first is the Rivière à la Glaise, which flows in a bit below Isle à la Glaise; the second, called Rivière à la Table, flows in a little above the same island; and the third, called Rivière à la Pomme, which is the largest of the three, flows in a league above the Rivière à la Table. All three of these rivers arrive from the west, but their courses are known only by Indian hunters. The entire region between Cape Girardeau and St. Laurent Creek is in fact frequented only by them and a few white boatmen who pass between Cape Girardeau and Ste. Genevieve.[39]

From Cap St. Antoine you ascend the Mississippi rather easily as far as the Roches Brutales, which are located four leagues above Cap à l'Ail and half a league below Cap St. Cosme. These rocks emerge only during low water and can be easily avoided; they were named by some careless navigator who smashed into them before they were exposed enough to be visible. His resentment is salutary for those navigating the river, for the name inspires a healthy fear; and the danger that you sense long before you pass these rocks keeps you in a state of enhanced alertness.[40]

Six leagues further up you encounter Anse du Bois Brulé [Bois Brule Bend], which is sweeping and difficult to ascend. But during high water you can avoid it by passing amidst the Isles aux Perches, opposite the largest of which is the Rivière à Marie. Two leagues higher on the same side is [23] the Kaskaskia River, where the Mississippi turns toward the west and forms Anse à Coco [Coco Bend] on the east side of the river. This bend is almost as large and difficult to ascend as Bois Brule, and toward the

38. The bluff just below the town of Wittenberg, Missouri, is probably Finiels' Cap St. Antoine, and his Cap St. Croix is now called the Devil's Bake Oven. Finiels' Rivière aux Vases entering the Mississippi from the American side (i.e., east) is now named the Big Muddy. Meriwether Lewis called it the "River Avaise" (*Journals of Lewis and Ordway,* 65). There were many *aux Vases* streams in French Louisiana. *Vase* means silt or mud in French, and thus many of the *aux Vases* streams were later renamed "Muddy."

39. Of the three streams mentioned in this paragraph, the Rivière à la Pomme (Apple Creek) has the same name and is clearly identifiable. Rivière à la Table is present-day Indian Creek, and Rivière à la Glaise may be Bainbridge Creek.

40. Finiels' Roches Brutales is perhaps the area now known as the Devil's Backbone. The Nicolas Bellin map of 1755 places "La Roche brutale" near where Cape Girardeau was later founded (see Melburn D. Thurman, "Cartography of the Illinois Country: An Analysis of Middle Mississippi Maps Drawn during the British Regime," 283). Finiels' Cap à l'Ail would seem to be present-day Cape Cinque Hommes, and his Cap St. Cosme, the bluff called Backbone. The nomenclature for these various capes is very confused, in part because the name *Cinque Hommes* originated as a mispronounciation of *St. Cosme* and in part because somehow over time names have gotten switched around. What is now Backbone seems originally to have been St. Cosme, then became Cinque Hommes (Cinque Hommes Creek still enters the Mississippi just upstream from Backbone), and then Cinque Hommes got attached to the cape some ten miles down the Mississippi. The name *St. Cosme* originated with the missionary priest Jean-François de St. Cosme, who traveled on this section of the Mississippi during the winter of 1698–1699. For more on the problems of this nomenclature, see *Journals of Lewis and Ordway,* 66; Houck, *History of Missouri,* 1:241–42. The names on the Lewis and Clark map of 1804 (Gary E. Moulton, ed., *Atlas of the Lewis and Clark Expedition,* map no. 6) correspond very precisely to those on Finiels' map.

top of it you meet St. Laurent Creek arriving from the west. At the mouth of this creek several American families have established farmsteads.[41]

Both of these bends are very difficult. The current of the Mississippi is restricted here by banks of beautiful reddish sand, much coarser grained than those of Lower Louisiana; it occurs from Bois Brule Bend to the largest Isle aux Perches, and along the American side from the Kaskaskia River to St. Laurent Creek in Coco Bend. The [Mississippi] river, squeezed against the right bank by these sand banks, runs as fast as lightning and continuously erodes the bank. These two bends daily cut into the alluvial lands that the river has deposited at the foot of the bluffs. The bluffs, which leave the riverbank at Cap St. Cosme, proceed in a northwesterly direction to the mouth of St. Laurent Creek. Between the bluffs and the river is a lowland that Coco and Bois Brule bends continuously gnaw away at as they enlarge themselves. Some pitiful trees, whose appearance is as sad as it is dismal and across which fire scars run in all directions, cover this lowland. Someday this lowland will disappear, only to reappear on the American side of the river, which today is lined with shady heights, forests whose edge casts into relief the gloomy scene of Bois Brule Bend.[42]

Two leagues above St. Laurent Creek is Saline Creek, which has been occupied since the beginning of the Illinois settlements. The first residents of Ste. Genevieve exploited the saline springs, which are scattered along the banks. [24] At this time, they supply salt not only to the Illinois settlements but also to the lower part of the colony, where the residents of Ste. Genevieve and Kaskaskia ship it every year.[43]

A league above Saline Creek is the Rivière aux Vases, the second of that name. Normally this stream runs shallow, but when [Mississippi] river floodwaters back up into the Rivière aux Vases they do much damage along its banks. There are some Americans and farmers from Ste. Genevieve settled along this river. Above its mouth begins the famous Pointe Basse, so fertile and rich, to which the farmers of New Bourbon and Ste. Genevieve commit their seed grain every year. Ordinarily, the yield is richly profuse, but sometimes the farmers' hopes are dashed when the waters of the Mississippi rise up out of their bed. More than thirty years of experience has demonstrated that the farmers lose two out of five plantings. But the fertility of this soil so captivates their minds that one year after a lost harvest they are back at the plow

41. Finiels' Anse de Bois Brulé is now the Missouri Chute of the Mississippi River near the town of Belgique. His Isles aux Perches are Marys (or Crains) Island and Pucketts Island, and his Rivière à Marie is now Marys River. Anse à Coco is now Ste. Genevieve Bend, although it is markedly different than in Finiels' time because of the dramatic leap of the Mississippi's channel during the 1880s, when old Kaskaskia was destroyed. *Anse* may translate either as bend or cove. St. Laurent Creek now enters the former channel of the Mississippi at the village of St. Marys south of Ste. Genevieve. In this passage, Finiels establishes the origins of St. Marys in the late 1790s.

42. Although the name *Bois Brulé* had long been used to describe the alluvial lowland below Ste. Genevieve, Finiels here suggests a possible origin for the name, which may have come from the fire-scarred woods that covered the area.

43. Henri Joutel, a survivor of La Salle's ill-fated expedition of 1687, was the first European to describe the salt springs along the Saline River. See Henry Reed Stiles, ed., *Joutel's Journal of La Salle's Last Voyage, 1684–1687*, 186; David Denman, "History of 'La Saline': Salt Manufacturing Site, 1675–1825."

cutting furrows in this unwilling, ungrateful bosom. They do this without knowing whether the Mississippi will return and seize the produce of the seed grain that their foolhardy hands devoted to the land.[44]

After having passed the cove that the river is cutting into this low land [Pointe Basse] and into the point upon which was established the first town of Ste. Genevieve, you enter the channel between Gabouri Island and the right bank of the Mississippi. Soon you are at the mouth of Gabouri Creek. This creek empties into the channel a little above the island and serves as a limit to Pointe Basse, of which I spoke. Boats are moored at the mouth, and you ascend a channel for about a league to [25] find yourself in Ste. Genevieve. The hills that receded from the Mississippi's bank at the Rivière aux Vases, creating the Pointe Basse of Ste. Genevieve, return to the river at the mouth of Gabouri Creek; they remain more or less along the river bank all the way to the mouth of the Missouri River.[45]

Let me return to Cape Girardeau in order to guide you to Ste. Genevieve by an overland route. This route does not provide the same sights but it is shorter and less dangerous. The trip can easily be accomplished in thirty-six hours, and some *voyageurs* in a hurry have done it in twenty-four.[46]

I've already mentioned the two Shawnee villages on the route outside of Cape Girardeau. All that part of the trail runs through woods and is passable only on foot or horseback. It is a succession of ups and downs across ravines that lead to the Mississippi. The torrents that arise in these ravines during a rain disappear as soon as the rain stops; several of the streambeds, however, contain rivulets that flow tranquilly over gravel and seem impatiently to await the next downpour in order to resume their furious and rapid course. At some distance from the last Shawnee village the land begins to open up. Then you pass over empty plains, copses of woods, and numerous ravines and rivers that I have already noted in my discussion of the route up the Mississippi. This entire region has not yet attracted the attention of the residents of Upper Louisiana. It will not be surveyed until the population of Cape Girardeau, after having consumed all of the arable land to the west, is obliged to flow northward. What I have seen of these lands makes me think that they will be adequate to fulfill the needs and desires of the population.

44. The Pointe Basse or the Grand Champ of Ste. Genevieve later came to be known as the Big Field Commons, which did not mean that arable land was held in common but merely that open field agriculture was practiced and that there was a common fence around the plowlands (see Ekberg, *Colonial Ste. Genevieve*, 129–32). The ratio of two lost crops for every five planted that Finiels cites in this passage is the same ratio given by the lieutenant governor of Upper Louisiana, Zenon Trudeau, in his report of 1798 (see *SRM*, 2:248).

45. As Finiels' map indicates, there were two branches, a north and a south, to Gabouri Creek, which joined together before flowing eastward into the Mississippi. In this passage Finiels uses *league* very loosely, for the channel of Gabouri Creek from the Mississippi to Ste. Genevieve was not nearly that long. The future governor general of Louisiana, Gayoso de Lemos, who visited Ste. Genevieve in 1795, wrote in his journal (see Nasatir, ed., *Spanish War Vessels*, 303) that the distance was one mile.

46. Finiels' map indicates that there was not really an established overland route laid out between Cape Girardeau and Ste. Genevieve. Probably it was little more than an Indian trail.

In this region when you are compelled to cross a river you must rely solely on your own resources. Some are fordable at low water. But the others must be swum leading your horse behind you, or, if you cannot swim, by constructing a raft. I fell into this category, and luckily I had a good guide. He was very zealous in helping me overcome obstacles, but I was not always successful in preventing my belongings from getting soaked.

You approach Saline Creek over the bluffs that come to an end near its banks. A league before this the road [26] forks; one road goes to the old Saline and the other goes to the left, passing on to the little Saline, which is located on the right bank of the same stream a league above the other one.[47]

Saline Creek is easy to cross in one of the pirogues that come and go between its banks. All you need do is call out and summon one of the boatmen who will appear on the bank. If you do not wish to stop over at the Saline, you immediately reascend the bluffs and continue your route toward the Rivière aux Vases. This is about a league distant and is just as easy to cross as the Saline during low water. Some American houses are located on the north bank a little above the road, and they [i.e., the Americans] will get you across. If the water is up you'll experience some difficulties that will slow you down, and if you're traveling in the spring you can expect this to happen.[48]

From the Rivière aux Vases you can follow a road atop the bluffs and arrive at New Bourbon in less than an hour; this road passes by the house of Monsieur de Luzières, who is commandant of New Bourbon.[49] From New Bourbon a half hour suffices to get to Ste. Genevieve, which you approach by descending from the hills. Ste. Genevieve is located at the foot of the hills upon a patch of ground that is a little higher in elevation than the Pointe Basse, which I've described. Gabouri Creek passes through the village at the bottom of a steep ravine; it gathers the waters from the bluffs and carries them down to the Mississippi. In hot, dry seasons this creek is tranquil and calm; in rainy seasons it sometimes comes out of its banks and can be unpleasantly swift.[50]

As I have already mentioned, there are some American families settled on the banks of St. Laurent Creek two leagues below the Saline. I know little about this settlement,

47. As was customary in early times, roads tended to follow the high ground, which meant that routes were often longer but were passable for larger portions of the year. Finiels' geography for the Saline area is remarkably accurate.

48. Recently, archaeologists led by Michael K. Trimble of the University of Missouri–Columbia have begun excavations at a number of the Saline sites. Their findings should cast new light upon the history of this fascinating area.

49. Concerning Pierre-Charles Delassus de Luzières and New Bourbon, the community he developed, see Ekberg, *Colonial Ste. Genevieve,* 445–55; Houck, *History of Missouri,* 1:362–66. At about the time that Finiels arrived in the Illinois Country, Governor General Carondelet created a new administrative district for New Bourbon and made Delassus de Luzières commandant.

50. This paragraph makes it clear that the main road from the Rivière aux Vases to Ste. Genevieve went across the high bluffs and did not follow the present route of U.S. Highway 61.

which consists of five or six families at most. They cultivate wheat, maize, mountain rice [barley?], some vegetables, and raise cattle; some of them work at extracting salt from the little Saline.

The big Saline has been exploited ever since the days of the first settlements in the Illinois Country. Since then it has passed between several [27] proprietors. It now belongs to Monsieur Peyroux, present commandant at New Madrid.[51] He—or, in his absence, his wife—used to oversee its exploitation. Now, however, given the fact that they live in New Madrid, they have leased it out, and it is being exploited by the lessee. The big Saline is located a little above the mouth of Saline Creek, on the left [i.e., north] bank, and at the foot of the neighboring hills. The springs that supply the saline water seem to be inexhaustible and have not diminished at all during the time they've been exploited. A sort of small village, of little consequence, has sprung up near the Saline. On the right bank about a league upstream, new springs have attracted the attention of some American families who settled there six or seven years ago and asked for a concession. I saw that settlement when it was only an embryo. They were making a great deal of salt there at that time, and they must have perfected their operations since then. Saline springs are numerous and rich in the Illinois Country, and in the hinterland there is even rock salt. At St. Louis, Monsieur Auguste Chouteau gave me a sample taken from a larger piece that he had brought back from the Osage Post.[52] He assured me that he had taken it from a very large vein that he had discovered near the Osage River. I do not know the exact production figures of the two salines just discussed. However, at the present time they supply not only the needs of the Illinois Country, but a major part of their production is shipped each year to New Orleans, and sometimes even to Kentucky via the Ohio River.[53]

New Bourbon is a small village that was founded eight years ago by a combination of farmers from Ste. Genevieve and several American families that wished to settle in the area. It is located halfway down the hills facing the Pointe Basse, which consists of river-deposited land lying between the village and the Mississippi. The farmers from New Bourbon and Ste. Genevieve work primarily this alluvial soil. New Bourbon's location is fresh and healthy, and it is a bit more cheerful than most [28] of the settlements that are situated immediately upon the bank of the Mississippi, for its

51. Henri Peyroux de la Coudrenière was former commandant in Ste. Genevieve and a notorious character in Louisiana politics during the 1790s. On his fascinating career, see Ekberg, Colonial Ste. Genevieve, and Oscar W. Winzerling, Acadian Odyssey.

52. Auguste Chouteau, who helped found St. Louis in 1764, was widely acclaimed as Upper Louisiana's first citizen. See William E. Foley and C. David Rice, The First Chouteaus: River Barons of Early St. Louis. In 1804 Chouteau sent President Thomas Jefferson "a specimen of salt formed by concretion, procured at the great Saline of the Osage nation, situated on a Southern branch of the Arkansas River, about six hundred miles West of St. Louis." See Meriwether Lewis to Thomas Jefferson, 18 May 1804, in Donald Jackson, ed., Letters of the Lewis and Clark Expedition with Related Documents, 1783-1854, 2d ed., 1:193.

53. Salt from local deposits, enormously important to the settlements in the Illinois Country during the colonial times, became insignificant with the coming of the steamboats about 1820, for salt from the huge deposits in Louisiana could be supplied much more cheaply than the local mineral.

view is not restricted by the tedious and unchanging perspective of a forest-covered river bank. At its feet unfolds a vast plain, which during different seasons offers diverse tableaux that are rare in this region. A brook flows out of the hills, after having meandered for some while, and enters the plain at the foot of the New Bourbon hills, dissecting it with various curves before emptying into the Mississippi. During different seasons this plain is covered with men and beasts and plows, which furrow it in all directions. Once this work is completed, the eye can follow the progress of the growing crops. The furrowed earth at first takes on a deeper hue than the rest of the surface; then, a light shading of green appears and sweeps over the entire surface of the field; the earth disappears and is replaced by a spread of brilliant green that billows with each breeze that crosses it. Then the anxiety begins; eyes that had complacently admired the progress of the plain glance nervously at the Mississippi in order to judge the uncertain and threatening advance of its flood waters; satisfaction is thwarted by fear until it is finally apparent that the river will recede and thus assure a harvest that is all the more satisfying because fear had at first been aroused. The plants mature and under the farmers' gaze become covered with clusters of grain. Soon the plain takes on a color that is less pleasing to the eye but which raises sweet hopes for the coming of a guaranteed harvest. Then perhaps arrive new scenes, even more animated and gay, that finally complete our series of observations. Business and pleasure intermingle to brighten the experience—or, if the river has gone over its banks, perhaps to darken it. If that occurs, the undulating carpet of greenery is reduced to a gray sheet of water with an occasional isolated tree protruding above it. The trees add to the desolation of the scene, [29] which does not regain its allure for the farmers until it is once again sown with the seeds of new hopes—and new fears.

The tableau of this fine plain is not the only one that New Bourbon's residents have to enjoy. The eye, sweeping across the plain and passing rapidly beyond the Mississippi, can range all the way to the lands facing the Kaskaskia River and discern some of their richness. The city of Kaskaskia—its fields, its prairies, its copses of woods, its river, the hills on the south bank; the village of Prairie du Rocher; the ruins of Fort de Chartres; the plains curiously dissected by woods that snake between the hills rising to the north, alternately covered with trees and pinnacles; the irregularities and recesses that shape the contours; the spectacle of wild flowers sprinkled liberally across the plains; all of these sights make the view from New Bourbon one of the most picturesque in the entire Illinois Country.[54]

Monsieur de Luzières' house, which is located between New Bourbon and the Saline at a higher spot on the hills [*montagnes*], enjoys the full scope of this seductive

---

54. Although there is nothing left of the former village of New Bourbon, there is still a fine view of the Mississippi valley from the hills where it once stood. Fort de Chartres, however, is not visible from these hills.

view; indeed this view is even more sweeping, for it extends off to the north. This elevation goes far toward making a visit there as healthy as it is agreeable.[55]

New Bourbon has 460 to 480 inhabitants of all ages, male and female, black and white, slave and free. The community possesses 400 to 500 head of cattle and 60 to 80 horses. It annually harvests 400 to 500 bushels of wheat and nearly 3,000 of maize. Furthermore, the residents produce 12,000 to 15,000 [pounds] of lead each year.[56]

The colonists who founded Ste. Genevieve were drawn there by the expectation of abundant harvests that the fertility of [30] the Point Basse, located at the foot of the hills, promised them. They erected their houses on the same land that they planned to cultivate and placed them near the bank of the Mississippi, as is shown on the map; they paid no attention to the fact that they would be disturbed every year by the flooding river. They soon learned of this trouble and should then have abandoned this precarious site; but the idea of clearing a new area on higher ground and erecting new buildings discouraged them. They hoped that destructive floods would occur only rarely, and they remained on the original site. Despite this slothful calculation, the river's rampages increased, and a struggle between the residents and the river ensued. The river won, and in 1792 the residents finally decided to leave its banks and retire to the location where the village is located today; they left only ruins to witness the fury of the rampaging river, which comes all too often to cover these vain witnesses of its triumph.[57]

At its new location Ste. Genevieve bravely endures the floods of the Mississippi, but Gabouri Creek, which cuts through it, sometimes gives cause for alarm. The village is located on the face of a long hill that veers toward the river. Atop the hill is a wooden fort that dominates the village but does not really secure it from an enemy invasion.[58] The population has increased since 1795, when several American families, finding no

55. This passage makes it clear that De Luzières' *habitation* stood some distance off from New Bourbon proper and could not have been the structure located just off of U.S. Highway 61 that has recently been identified as the De Luzières' residence. The residence is identified on the Finiels map as being on a bluff south of New Bourbon.

56. The New Bourbon District included the settlements at the Saline and the Bois Brule, and in his census of 1797 De Luzières recorded a total population for the district of 459 souls (see Archivo General des Indias, Papeles de Cuba [hereafter cited as AGI, PC], legajo 2365). Therefore the population figures that Finiels presents here (probably from late 1797) are in accord with those that De Luzières compiled and obviously pertain to the entire district rather than merely to the village of New Bourbon. On the other hand, Finiels' figures for grain production are dramatically lower than those contained in the official census records for 1795 (*SRM*, 1:326) and for 1796 (ibid., 2:143). This suggests three things: Finiels based his figures upon the harvests of 1797; the flood of 1797 had devastating effects on the harvests in the Ste. Genevieve area; Finiels' ideas on the fertility and productivity of the Illinois Country were skewed because he relied upon statistics from an atypical year. Throughout this translation, we will render *minot* as "bushel," although a minot was in fact approximately 1.1 bushels (see John Francis McDermott, *A Glossary of Mississippi Valley French, 1673–1850*, 104). Similarly, we will render *livre* as "pound," although the French livre equaled approximately 1.08 English pounds (ibid., 94).

57. Concerning the founding of the Old Town of Ste. Genevieve (c. 1750) and the move to the New Town, see Ekberg, *Colonial Ste. Genevieve,* chaps. 1 and 13.

58. The wooden stockaded fort, located on the hill overlooking South Gabouri Creek, was built early

more land available on the Pointe Basse, acquired some higher land to the northwest of the village. These lands, which had been poorly thought of, [31] responded to hope and effort; they produce handsome, wholesome grain and in quantities as bountiful as the lowlands.

Ste. Genevieve has added another source of revenue to agriculture, which has been so generous to her, one which is further encouragement to industry. This is the exploitation of lead mines that were discovered long ago about eighteen or twenty leagues to the northwest. They are located in an area around the branches of the Meramec River, which flows through the hinterlands of this village. These mines are plentiful and rich, since they commonly produce eighty livres to the hundredweight. They are shallow and easy to reach. Those who exploit them excavate pits, for subsurface layers of rock prevent penetrating deeper than eight feet. From one of these pits they usually acquire enough of the mineral to do several smeltings; when one pit is exhausted they move on and dig another pit somewhere else. Smelting is even easier than the mining. They pile the ore on the ground, cover it with wood, and set it afire. When the metal melts out, they gather it up and pour it into rectangular pig molds. This crude, primitive method must be a wasteful way of smelting. But they don't give up; they repeat the process and finally succeed.[59]

It is time for these irregular and wasteful methods to be replaced by operations based upon science and technical skill. But it is up to the government to do something about it, and until now nothing has been done. The old methods have persisted for many reasons: because [32] they are compatible with the indolence and laziness of the residents; because they have always brought results adequate for the very limited ambitions of the people; because the people, being content with what they get, have no interest in knowing about what they are missing; because they don't worry about wasting nature's bountiful treasures, which might make them think of ways to multiply and increase productivity.

Traces of tin and iron have also been discovered near the lead mines of Ste. Genevieve, and we shall see further along that the shores of the Meramec should contain such mines. The [French] government will surely be interested in this type of production in Upper Louisiana and will encourage artisans who will be able to develop the mineralogical resources of the colony. Five or six years ago, they could have taken some steps in this direction if the residents had not rejected and thwarted the efforts of an American named Osten [i.e., Moses Austin]. He came here, attracted by the reputation of these mines, from Kentucky [Virginia], where

in 1794 in reaction to rumors of an imminent Franco-American invasion from east of the Mississippi. Antoine Soulard, future surveyor general of Upper Louisiana, helped design the fort (ibid., 73, 436).

59. There is a large literature on early lead mining in the hinterlands of the Ste. Genevieve District. For a recent survey, see ibid., 144–58. The livre was worth 20 percent of the American dollar, the Spanish peso, or the Spanish piastre. A quintal was a French hundredweight, which was equivalent to 108 English pounds.

he had been engaged in mining. But his example did not sink in, and the old habits prevailed.[60]

Some remains of the Kaskaskia, Peoria, and Michegamea Indian tribes, who inhabited the plains of Illinois when Europeans arrived here, have taken refuge at Ste. Genevieve.[61] They are not very numerous and are settled along the banks of Gabouri Creek; their cabins are virtually in the center of the village. These Indians in the middle of a white population provide a contrast as striking as it is sad for humankind. It is painful to observe that nothing has been able to draw these savage men out of the miserable condition into which their lack of civilization has thrust them. In sharp contrast to the Shawnees, they have taken from Europeans [33] the vices that appealed to their depraved proclivities, while at the same time they have retained their primitive laziness and indolence in the face of European industry and activity. Twenty-five years ago [Thomas] Hutchins already called them a debauched people, given over to drunkenness, which had dramatically undermined the traditional bravery of their forefathers. Today they have fallen farther still and are interested only in wallowing in their vices.[62]

The land around Ste. Genevieve is suitable for many things: agriculture; grist and saw mills, of which there are already several; forges, which this remote area sorely needs, for the scarcity and expense of iron are among the greatest impediments to the growth of agriculture. Near Ste. Genevieve is located one of the finest flour mills ever built in the Illinois Country. It is located on a brook [Valle Spring Branch] that separates the parishes of New Bourbon and Ste. Genevieve; this brook flows down out of the hills, crosses the Plaine Basse, and then empties into the Mississippi. The mill is built of neatly dressed rubble stone that has been smoothly mortared to give it the appearance of cut stone. It belongs to Monsieur François Vallé.[63]

The population of Ste. Genevieve is nearly 950 persons of all ages, male and female, black and white, free and slave; this does not count the Indians who live there. The village has nearly 1,200 head of cattle and 250 horses; it produces annually 3,000 bushels of wheat, 3,500 to 4,000 bushels of maize, 5,000 to 6,000 of tobacco,

60. Concerning Moses Austin's career in lead mining, see David B. Gracy II, *Moses Austin: His Life*.

61. The Kaskaskia, Peoria, and Michegamea were all tribes of the Iliniwek "confederacy" and belonged to the Algonquian linguistic group. Concerning their history in colonial times, see Trigger, *Handbook of North American Indians*, 15:594–97, and Wayne C. Temple, *Indian Villages of the Illinois Country*, 11–56.

62. In his *A Topographical Description of Virginia, Pennsylvania, Maryland, and North Carolina*, Hutchins observed, "They [the Kaskaskia Indians] were formerly brave and warlike, but are degenerated into a drunken, and debauched tribe, and so indolent as scarcely to provide a sufficiency of Skins and Furs to barter for cloathing" (p. 37).

63. Concerning the Vallé family, which was the most important family in colonial Ste. Genevieve, see Ekberg, *Colonial Ste. Genevieve*. The Valle Spring Branch now flows northward into Gabouri Creek instead of southward across the "Plaine Basse," the Big Field Commons, to the Mississippi.

900 to 1,000 of salt, and 80,000 to 100,000 pounds of lead. Oats and hay are also grown for winter fodder.[64]

I cannot leave Ste. Genevieve without rendering homage to its residents, a tribute, I should hope, that every visitor will pay them for a long time to come. They maintain the mark of friendliness and simplicity that characterized their forefathers, who in turn had received it during the prosperous days of Kaskaskia, a small town that was the first French settlement in the Illinois Country. The few strangers [34] that have settled among them have in no way altered these traits, which isolation deepens and strengthens, although their affluence and influence will soon begin to have some effect. Seduced by the charms of that primitive and natural simplicity, sufficiently tempered by moral and religious principles, they found it easier to follow its guidance than to seek other direction. The people of Ste. Genevieve and New Bourbon offer to the attentive traveler's eye simply an extended family, bound together more by camaraderie than by blood. All these families grow and are linked by innumerable branches, and everyone in these villages is cousin so-and-so. Strangers themselves are soon part of this patriarchal family, which quickly adopts them and whose hospitality is limited only by how widely it must be shared. Their pains are endured together; they are shared, and in being experienced by the entire family they are easier to endure. Likewise their pleasures belong to everyone; only vice or bad character can make one an outcast, and these exclusions are rare. Perhaps the ultrasophisticated man would not find these pleasures all that attractive because they are not exquisite and lack the refinement that Europeans believe necessary. But everything that produces fun and gaiety, everything that brings forth ringing laughter and joy, all these unaffected frivolities, which might be called foolery somewhere else, are sweet pleasure for these children of nature. As yet they are unaffected by the exquisite taste that makes us Europeans so difficult once we have acquired it and deprives us of all enjoyment since we can no longer enjoy pleasures that are not clearly labeled as such.[65]

Monsieur François Vallé, commandant of Ste. Genevieve, is head of the principal family of these two villages [i.e., Ste. Genevieve and New Bourbon]. His contribution to the sweet harmony, which is so hard to find elsewhere, is not insignificant. He is loved and esteemed like a father; his wife is modest, unaffected, and always as caring

64. The official Spanish census of 1795 (SRM, 1:326) gave the population of Ste. Genevieve as 849 souls. Rather inexplicably, the census of 1796 (SRM, 2:141) showed a decrease to 773. On the other hand, the Abbé de St. Pierre, parish priest of Ste. Genevieve, took a census of his entire parish (rather than simply the village) in 1796 (University of Notre Dame Archives, New Orleans Diocesan Collection, IV-5-1), and he tabulated 1,214 total souls. These census numbers suggest that Finiels' figures on Ste. Genevieve's population are about right for 1797. Finiels' statistics on grain production in Ste. Genevieve are just as atypical as those for New Bourbon, probably for the same reasons (see above, note 56).

65. Many visitors remarked on the close-knit quality of society in colonial Ste. Genevieve. Lieutenant Governor Zenon Trudeau noted (SRM, 2:248), for example, that the people of the town "are united by the most narrow bonds. For nearly all of them being related, blood binds them to maintain the fast friendship and harmony which has always existed among them."

as a mother. How could they not be loved?—they both conduct themselves as if all the good people here were their own children.[66]

[35] Now we're going on to St. Louis, and if I were to say more about this village [i.e., Ste. Genevieve] we would too much regret having to leave the peaceful place with its rustic hospitality, unity, and happiness. Our memories of it will sustain us during our journey, and we will not forget it when we arrive in St. Louis and begin to inhale the air of this capital of Spanish Illinois.

CARONDELET, ST. LOUIS, ST. FERDINAND, AND MARAIS DES LIARDS

Traveling from Ste. Genevieve to St. Louis via the Mississippi, there are few dangers: they consist only of passing two shoals [platins], some small rocks, and those snags that fill the river all the way between Natchez and the Illinois Country. The pain and the labor are the same as before, as is the continual crossing and recrossing of the river in order to avoid the current through the bends. But the skipper's courage is rekindled with the thought of soon reaching the end of the voyage. A well-manned boat can make the trip in two days; two and a half or three days is usual; four days rare.

The first thing you encounter on this trip is a series of rocky heights along the right bank, half a league above Gabouri Creek; these run for a distance of more than two leagues. Four leagues above Gabouri Creek you find the Rivière de Chartres, which flows into the Mississippi from the Spanish side and whose mouth is marked by two small islands. Immediately after comes the Isle à Duclos, which is large and creates a deep channel along the left bank. Opposite the middle of this [island] Fort de Chartres, now in ruins, was located. This was the work of the first Frenchmen to occupy the left bank of the river in the Illinois Country; it was very solidly constructed of stone, had four bastions, and contained all the necessary buildings. The powder magazine, which was very carefully built, is still to be seen. The fort used to be at some distance [36] from the river, but the portion that still stands is now immediately on the river bank, and other parts have fallen into the water. The residents of the village of Prairie du Rocher, which is behind the fort, have made use of the remains— brick, stone, lumber, and ironwork—in order to build their houses; when they needed stone, it was the quarry from which they obtained it. There was once a village with the same name [Chartres] below the fort. It was probably abandoned because of the river's floods, and now, in the midst of the weeds, brush, and woods that cover the area, its ruins are very hard to locate.[67]

66. Perrin du Lac (*Voyage dans les deux Louisianes,* 169-70) described Madame François Vallé as a woman who "never refuses her aid when an aggrieved mother comes to her. Day and night she serves the sick, from whom she does not even ask for thanks."

67. There was in fact a succession of Forts de Chartres, beginning with the wooden palisaded fort of 1719 (see Anna Price, "The Three Lives of Fort de Chartres: French Outpost on the Mississippi"). The stone fort, built in the 1750s in preparation for the French and Indian War, is now being rebuilt by the Illinois Historic Preservation Agency. The village of Chartres is now entirely obliterated.

It is difficult to guess why the stone fort was built behind an island that entirely blocked the view of the river and prevented its guns from controlling the ascending and descending river traffic. A much more advantageous location would have been on the point of land just upriver from the island; the river narrows at this point, and everything passing on it would have been directly under the guns. It was abandoned thirty-one years ago.[68]

As you proceed upstream, several bayous appear on both the left and right banks until you reach the Isle au Bois. After passing the point above this island, you encounter another bayou and the Roche Déboullée, which seems to be a large fragment of rock that broke off the bluffs, fell, and landed on the bank. During high water it is invisible, but during low water it is wholly out of the water. Above the Roche Déboullée is the Isle du Platin, into the channel of which empties still another bayou. Almost a league above that island are the Grand and Petit Platin; [the Grand Platin] is a bank of rocks that extends along the right bank of the river. During high water the river boils swiftly over it, and during low water it is exposed. It requires extra effort to get past this spot, after which you are at the mouth of St. Joachim Creek. This creek, which is not well known, is shallow during low water, but you can [37] ascend it for some distance when the Mississippi floods. Four leagues further up, you encounter the Petit Platin, which is difficult to get past because of the swiftness of the current. You can ascend only with a tow rope, and you must be careful to have a good rope, for it is not unusual to see one broken by the current, and then the boat will be swept far downstream before coming to a halt. This small rock is composed of two semicircular blocks of stone, one atop the other. The *engagés* use the lower one when pulling on the tow rope, and usually passengers are invited to do the same thing in order to prevent accidents from happening. *Bateaux* that make it from Ste. Genevieve to Petit Rocher in one day surely arrive in St. Louis before nightfall the next day. Some Americans have built a few cabins on Petit Rocher. Count on *them* to pick an advantageous spot; they select it with a very fine touch and calculate at a glance all of its advantages. Hardly had they set foot in the Mississippi Valley than they sighted them [the advantageous spots] all and seized them, while Frenchmen, who had occupied these shores for sixty years, never thought of building there.[69]

The mouth of the Meramec River is a league above Petit Rocher. This is a fine river and one of the largest that flows into the Mississippi from the west anywhere between

68. Fort de Chartres became part of British territory with the Treaty of Paris (1763), which ended the French and Indian War. A British detachment arrived from Pittsburgh in October 1765 to replace the French marines at the fort, and the British remained until 1772. Therefore, Finiels' observation that the fort had been "abandoned thirty-one years ago" is correct, given the fact that he was writing in 1803.

69. Isle au Bois is no longer identifiable, but Isle de Bois Creek, flowing into the Mississippi from the west, is on the boundary between Jefferson and Ste. Genevieve counties. Roche Déboullée seems to have disappeared, but Platin and Joachim creeks enter the Mississippi near Festus and Herculaneum, Missouri. Sulphur Springs, Missouri, is at, or near, Finiels' Petit Rocher, which may mean that Sulphur Springs is one of the oldest American communities in Missouri.

the St. Francis and Missouri rivers.⁷⁰ It is navigable far inland and has salt springs on both banks near its mouth. Five leagues farther up you come to Des Peres Creek, and a little above that the village of Carondelet, whose appearance reflects the poverty of its inhabitants. From there it is only two leagues to St. Louis, and for most of that distance the right bank is covered with rocks. Upon one of these, a half league below St. Louis, there was a ferry boatman's house six years ago, but since then it has been replaced by a ferry based on the other side of the river, [38] across from the upper part of St. Louis. From Ste. Genevieve to St. Louis the right bank of the Mississippi is lined by bluffs and rocks; for most of the distance this bank is immune from river floods. The entire facing American bank is low-lying; for more than twenty-five leagues, from the mouth of the Kaskaskia River up to the Missouri River, there is one vast plain. This plain, upon which are located all of the American settlements in the Illinois Country, is bordered on the east by a chain of bluffs running north and south, which is a league, and often a league and a quarter, from the bank of the Mississippi.

You can proceed overland from Ste. Genevieve to St. Louis by two different routes. One is on the Spanish side of the Mississippi, and the other passes through all the American settlements in the Illinois Country except Kaskaskia. The route on the Spanish side is rarely used except occasionally in summer and autumn. This is because there are too many bayous and rivers to cross, of which the Joachim and the Meramec are the most difficult and dangerous. This route is similar to that between Cape Girardeau and Ste. Genevieve. For nearly eighteen leagues it crosses lands that are little known but which are suitable for the same agriculture as those between Cape Girardeau and Ste. Genevieve. If the population of the Illinois Country increases, it will soon penetrate into this region because of the different kinds of mines that are almost certain to be found there.⁷¹

If you wish to travel overland from Ste. Genevieve to St. Louis during the high-water season, the route that passes through American territory is preferable, and, unless you have some particular reason to take the other, it is preferable during any season. You proceed on foot to Little Rock [Petit Rocher], which is a league and a half above the mouth of Gabouri Creek; at this spot begins the line of rocks that, as I have already mentioned, borders the right bank of the river. [39] There you find the cabin of an Indian named Maringouin who will take you in his pirogue up along the rocky bank.⁷² He proceeds upstream until you are abreast two islands on the other side of

70. French explorers and missionaries in the Illinois Country had known about the Meramec River since the very early eighteenth century. See Reuben G. Thwaites, ed., *The Jesuit Relations and Allied Documents,* 65:101.

71. After Spain declared war on Great Britain in 1779, a road was built between St. Louis and Ste. Genevieve for strategic reasons (see Lawrence Kinnaird, ed., *Spain in the Mississippi Valley, 1765–1794,* pt. 1, 348). It is apparent, however, that this route remained largely impassable and that the preferred overland route between the two towns remained on the east side of the Mississippi during the entire colonial period.

72. *Maringouin* was Mississippi Valley French for "mosquito." *Rigoley,* more often spelled *rigolet,* usu-

the river. Just above that point he crosses the river and lands about a league below the ruins of the old town of Chartres. There you find a road that leads to Prairie du Rocher through the woods bordering the river. Leaving the woods, you cross the plain cultivated by this little town's farmers. Then you have your choice of two roads: One crosses the plain all the way to Cahokia; the other climbs the bluffs immediately after leaving Prairie du Rocher, follows the bluff line and passes by Ogle, Corne à Cerf, and Belle Fontaine.[73] After leaving Belle Source, the road heads left, descends from the bluffs, and reenters the plain at Tucker's plantation. There the road proceeds to Cahokia, after passing by the ancient Indian tombs and Prairie du Pont, another small village half a league from Cahokia. This route can be traveled between sunrise and sunset, either along the bluffs or across the plain. The latter route, however, can be difficult during periods of high water and may then require two days to pass. At Cahokia you can embark in a pirogue [*rigoley*] or you can proceed a league upstream to the new ferry, which will take you across to St. Louis.

Of the entire course of the river that we have traveled from the mouth of the Ohio to St. Louis, the most difficult and arduous section is between the Ohio and Ste. Genevieve—many lengthy detours, endless islands, bends where the current moves as swiftly as lightning, innumerable sand bars, snags, fallen trees here and there, rocks, sometimes in the channel, sometimes along the banks. In recapitulating all of these obstacles, [40] you can easily see that I did not exaggerate when I mentioned the difficulties of moving convoys of provisions or munitions up this route and of the ease with which they could be destroyed. It is true that when the Ohio is very high and "gives" [*donne*], as they say, it rushes into the Mississippi with such force that it functions like a dam and creates virtually a backflow as far up as Cape Girardeau. Then you can ascend the Mississippi as far as the Isles à la Course without too much trouble. But there the main difficulties begin, and it doesn't make any difference what time of year it is because the Ohio's waters never have any effect that far up. From Ste. Genevieve to St. Louis the Mississippi's course is less difficult; there are fewer islands; the bends are less sweeping; the river describes circle segments, without the constant switchbacks that considerably protract the route downstream. And in observing it carefully, you will notice that it is more rapid in this section than in any other. It ordinarily takes eight or ten days to ascend the river by boat from the mouth of the Ohio River to St. Louis; three days suffice by land if you begin the journey at the Ohio, which is not impossible if you have a horse and it's the dry season. If not, you absolutely must leave from New Madrid, and the best way is to drift down to this town [i.e., New Madrid], which is the way I did it.

---

ally meant "creek" in colonial Louisiana, but in this context it would seem to mean "pirogue" or "canoe."

73. Along the road atop the bluffs between Prairie du Rocher and Cahokia was located New Design, which was the largest English-speaking community in Illinois during the mid-1790s (see Clarence W. Alvord, *The Illinois Country, 1673–1818*, 409–10). Although Finiels does not mention New Design in this paragraph, he showed it prominently on his map of the area.

The little village of Carondelet, or Vide Poche [Empty Pocket], is located on the right bank of the Mississippi.[74] It is two leagues below St. Louis, a little above the mouth of Des Peres Creek, and at the foot of the hills that recede a bit at this point, leaving a small, low plain along the river. The village consists of a single street running north and south, and it looks more substantial than it in fact is. It was founded by some farmers from St. Louis who were attracted by the fertility of the soil near the mouth of Des Peres Creek. They built dwellings there about twenty years ago in order to be [41] closer to their work. Soon the number of farmers increased, and they were compelled to seek more land to cultivate beyond the hills, where they easily found enough for their needs. As soon as Carondelet took on the appearance of a village, residents from St. Louis began to visit. The sense of solitude that its location conveyed from the beginning, romantic and isolated at the foot of the hills, made it appear like a country retreat; it seemed an appropriate refuge for pleasures that are no longer available in towns and to which one is always attracted by nature. Carondelet thus became the site of their festivities; its humble cabins echoed the clamor of their gaiety, and no holiday was complete unless Carondelet was included on the itinerary. But soon more refined tastes replaced the rustic ones, and Carondelet was no longer an attraction. For eight or nine years now it has not been frequented by the citizens of St. Louis except when business affairs call them there.

The population of Carondelet is composed of [French] Canadians and Creoles from Illinois.[75] Paltry wooden cabins serve as their dwellings. In general they are poor; they sow grain only in proportion to their needs and to pay any debts they have. They supply some to St. Louis, however, as well as fruits, vegetables, and milk. They are naturally lazy, and necessity alone forces them into the fields. Older folks take care of the agriculture; the younger men are busy making trips to New Orleans, up the Missouri, to Michilimackinac, and sometimes up the Ohio to Pittsburgh. They prefer to endure three consecutive months of hard work in order to pass eight or nine months in sloth, rather than as youths take up a vocation that would lead more surely to success, but whose permanence [42] would leave little time to idle away, to doze in indolence and sloth.

Carondelet is composed of scarcely 160 or 180 inhabitants of both sexes and all ages; I won't say of all colors because there are only two or three slaves there. It has 190 to 200 cattle and 30 or so horses. It annually harvests close to 3,000 bushels of

74. Carondelet was established in 1767 when Clement Delor de Treget, a former French naval officer, settled near the mouth of Des Peres Creek three miles south of the original townsite of St. Louis. Initially it was called Delor's Village, and then Louisbourg. In the 1790s, it was renamed Carondelet in honor of the governor general, Luis Hector, the Baron de Carondelet. As Finiels notes, the village's nickname was Vide Poche or Empty Pocket. See James Neal Primm, *Lion of the Valley: St. Louis, Missouri*, 65–66, and Houck, *History of Missouri*, 2:64.

75. In his report of 1798 (*SRM*, 2:249), Lieutenant Governor Zenon Trudeau remarked about Carondelet that "its *habitants* are poor and the greater part Canadians and Creoles. The married men cultivate their fields, and the young men are employed in the voyages of the Misispy and Misury."

wheat, 2,000 bushels of maize, and 2,600 to 3,000 pounds of tobacco. Its industry is limited to one horse mill for grinding flour.[76]

St. Louis is the capitol of all the settlements in Spanish Illinois. It is the residence of the lieutenant governor, who subsumes in his person all power—military, civil, fiscal, and judicial. It is the only town in Illinois with a garrison, which at some times has had as many as two hundred men, although usually has only forty to sixty at most. St. Louis is twenty leagues from Ste. Genevieve, two leagues above Carondelet, and five leagues below the mouth of the Missouri River.[77]

Frenchmen occupied the part of Illinois that is now American for a long time before any thought was given to founding a town at the present site of St. Louis. Hunters attracted to that side of the river by game; *voyageurs* on their way to Michilimackinac; traders who ascended the Missouri River—all of these frequented the future site of St. Louis, with its high banks and stony defenses against the river. The area was only lightly forested; there were vast natural prairies that seemed to call out for cultivation; the air was pure and healthy, the enjoyment of which was sometimes disturbed by springtime fevers (often fatal) on the plains of Kaskaskia and Cahokia. Traders wanted access to the Missouri, and a few cabins were already located on the site when Monsieur Laclède, a French officer, received orders to lay out and found a town there.[78]

The choice of its location was determined by the existence of a small bayou, which began among the hills a short distance from the Mississippi and snaked its way to the river through a deep, wide ravine. This ravine was formed on the right by rather high hills and on the left by an irregular and fissured curtain [of rocks] that approached the plain. It [43] seemed easy to retain the bayou's waters some distance from their source by building a small dam from one high point to another, thereby creating a rather large reservoir. This pond [Chouteau's mill pond] could supply water the year around to operate a flour mill, which in fact the commandant had built at that spot. Thus the

76. Much of Carondelet's surplus produce was transported to St. Louis for sale in wooden carts called *charettes*. The official Spanish census of 1796 (*SRM*, 2:142–43) listed 181 inhabitants in Carondelet, of which 3 were black slaves. Finiels' grain production figures for Carondelet are much closer to those in the official censuses than was the case in Ste. Genevieve and New Bourbon (see notes 56 and 64 above). This suggests that the great flood of 1797 damaged the crops less at Carondelet than at Ste. Genevieve. At the end of the colonial period, horse mills remained the usual way of grinding grain in the Illinois Country.

77. Although Ste. Genevieve, established c. 1750, was older than St. Louis, founded in 1764, the Spaniards formally designated the latter as the seat of their government in Upper Louisiana in 1770.

78. St. Louis's founder, Pierre de Laclède Liguest, contrary to Finiels' statement, was not a French officer and was not acting under government orders when he founded St. Louis. Laclède selected the site as a trading headquarters for his New Orleans–based firm Maxent, Laclède, and Company in December 1763. Again contrary to Finiels' account, there were no cabins at that location when Laclède's stepson and clerk, Auguste Chouteau, supervised construction of the first buildings there in February 1764. Unlike many cities, St. Louis has an eyewitness description of its founding. Although it was written long after the actual event, Auguste Chouteau's "Narrative of the Settlement of St. Louis" gives many details of the city's early history. The original manuscript is in the collections of the St. Louis Mercantile Library, and an exact translation can be found in John Francis McDermott, ed., *The Early Histories of St. Louis*, 47–49. See also McDermott, "Myths and Realities Concerning the Founding of St. Louis," and his "The Exclusive Trade Privileges of Maxent, Laclède, and Company."

selection of St. Louis's site was based upon private interests. Enlightened and objective military opinion would have placed the town higher up, where the Bayou de Pierre would have been almost as close.[79]

In fact, St. Louis's site is very much dissected by irregularities in the terrain. The area is riddled with hills, bluffs, cliffs, and ravines, which make it very difficult to fortify the position in an effective, economical, and practical manner. The hills that border the creek to the south overlook the fort from a distance of 400 toise [almost .5 miles, for 1 toise equals 6.38 English feet]; moreover, there is a plateau close to the pond southwest of town that is at most 200 toises from the fort; deep ravines commence near the foot of the fort, some heading for the large ravine of the bayou and some for the town itself. The latter would provide an enemy with a veritable covered way to approach the town. The fort, which is located on a small plateau behind the town, commands only a portion of the area. Its guns cannot reach the river at all, and the town is too dispersed to be completely covered. In addition to these general defects of location, St. Louis's plan poses another problem. As with all the other towns in Louisiana, its streets are too narrow, which creates problems in any climate.[80]

For a long time St. Louis existed in a state of torpor, which did not bode well for its future. Indians, disturbed by a settlement on the [west] bank of the river, impeded progress with their continual depredations—stray cattle were stolen; farmers dared not extend [44] their fields and were obliged to plow with guns in hand.[81] Those who were not engaged in agriculture were on alert in town; the first shot they heard from the fields brought them out on horseback to pursue the Indians. Sometimes they were attacked right in St. Louis by these barbarians, who repeatedly aroused fear and terror. The residents still remember these disastrous episodes when Indians struck right in their midst. Some even carry scars from wounds they received, and they still shudder at the remembrance of what they endured, even though there is no chance that anything like it can happen again. They now show visitors who ascend the

79. St. Louis was well situated for a commercial center. Its elevation afforded natural protection against the dangers of flooding, and its strategic location offered easy access to the Mississippi, Missouri, and Illinois rivers. It was, as Finiels notes, less well suited for defense. The town site was open and easily accessible from the north and the west. The bayou or small stream on the south known as La Petite Rivière and later called Mill Creek afforded only minimal protection. Finiels' map shows a Ruisseau de Pierre flowing into the Mississippi just north of St. Louis. On issues relating to St. Louis's defenses, see James B. Musick, *St. Louis as a Fortified Town*, and for details concerning the mill and mill pond, see note 87 below.

80. The terrain in the vicinity of La Petite Rivière was dissected by numerous ravines. The fort Finiels refers to here was a two-story block house constructed in 1797 near the southwest corner of the village between Chouteau Avenue and Lombard Avenue not far from Fourth Street. See ibid., 103-4.

81. Since St. Louis was poorly fortified and exposed to attack, its inhabitants often lived in fear that an Indian assault was imminent. In fact, attacks in or near the city were a rarity. The major exception occurred during the American Revolution when a combined British-Indian party attempted to take the city in 1780. That invasion was repulsed by hastily arranged defensive measures instituted by Lieutenant Governor Fernando de Leyba. For a recent version of that encounter, see McDermott, "The Battle of St. Louis, 26 May 1780."

Missouri River the famous Portage des Sioux, where the warriors of these ferocious people crossed from the Mississippi to the Missouri in order to attack St. Louis.[82]

It was during the days of desolation and anxiety, when harvests were often snatched from the farmers, that St. Louis received the name Pain Cour [Short of Bread], which was only too true in those miserable and distressed times. Ste. Genevieve had already received the nickname Misère [Misery], and in this area the habit still persists of using these names, coined in a calamitous time, instead of their official names. But soon such traces will be only distant memories; they have begun to disappear in the face of faint rays of prosperity that a decade of peace has brought to both of these villages. The Indians have retreated since those times; settlements have developed on the lands around St. Louis, providing the town with security that thenceforth cannot be threatened.[83]

St. Louis is located on a narrow ledge [45] composed of a bank of rocks. This bank is high enough to be above the floods of the Mississippi, which in this area of Illinois can sometimes rise twenty-five feet above low-water stage. The ledge serves as the base for a small bluff, twenty-five or thirty feet high, that covers the town in the west and upon whose slope the rear portion [of the town] rises for most of its length. This bluff runs north and south 20 degrees west; main street in the town runs north and south 9 degrees west. The town extends 900 toises [north and south] and is 120 to 150 toises deep.[84]

The bluff upon which the town is located does not consist entirely of rocks. They begin roughly one-third of the way up from the south end and extend for about a league northward. Thus the last town lots to the south are located on a bank of alluvial ground that erodes some every year. This is true even though there is a large sandbar at the foot of the bluff that keeps the river away during low water. The public square, located across from Monsieur Auguste Chouteau's, is the same way. Town

82. Portage des Sioux is the alluvial tongue of land between the Mississippi and Missouri rivers in St. Charles County. There are many stories about the origin of this ambiguous place name. Lewis C. Beck attributed the name to an occasion when a group of Sioux Indians outsmarted a party of Missouri Indians by portaging across the alluvial lowland instead of going by water to the mouth of the Missouri and then proceeding upriver (*A Gazetteer of the States of Illinois and Missouri*, 310). For an alternative story, see note 121 below.

83. Following its founding in 1764, St. Louis quickly emerged as the focal point of fur-trading operations in Upper Louisiana. Because the people of early St. Louis often ignored agriculture in favor of the lucrative fur trade, they sometimes found it necessary to import foodstuffs from nearby Ste. Genevieve. As a consequence, the settlement earned its nickname. However, as historian John Francis McDermott has pointed out (see his article "Paincourt and Poverty"), that term was a misnomer, inasmuch as the settlement, which served as Upper Louisiana's commercial and political capital, prospered from its earliest days.

84. St. Louis was built on a limestone bluff that jutted up from the Mississippi and extended about two miles along the shore. Laclède laid out the original townsite on the long, narrow strip of level land that sloped gently from the riverbank westward to the area between what are now Third and Fourth streets, where the ground rose more abruptly to form a hill. Beyond that stretched the gradually sloping prairie to the west. Laclède's plan followed a gridiron pattern similar to the layout used in New Orleans. The three original streets paralleling the river were the Grande Rue (Main or First Street), the rue a l'Eglise (Church or Second Street), and the rue des Granges (Barn or Third Street). See Primm, *Lion of the Valley*, 15–16.

parcels are almost always 240 feet across and 300 feet deep and are supposed to be subdivided into four lots. Many, however, are only divided into two lots, and sometimes an entire parcel belongs to one owner.[85]

The small bluff [referred to above] arises in the south approximately opposite the point where the rocks begin along the river bank, and 200 toises from them. There it forms a small plateau, a few feet higher than the top of the bluff, where the stone fort is located. This is the oldest stronghold in St. Louis. In 1797 this fort was very dilapidated, and by now it must be out of service. It houses the garrison, which occupies a stone building that could hold a hundred men. Inside the walls of the fort was a stone tower [Fort St. Charles] intended as a place from which to monitor the movements of the Indians out on the plain, and there was also a small powder magazine. A well was also dug for the use of the garrison, but it fell into disrepair, and attempts at repairing it have been in vain. From there [i.e., the fort], the bluff [46] proceeds north-northeast and heads toward the river, from which it is no more than 110 to 120 toises at the upper end of town. Then it runs more or less parallel to the river off toward the mouth of the Missouri River. Above this small bluff there is a plain, which is about the same general elevation as the interior lands; these are, however, dotted here and there by hills.[86]

In the south the bluff turns westward and finally peters out near the mill pond. There it creates a plateau that for some distance commands the fort and also the pond, which is at most three hundred toises southwest of town. This pond is surrounded by steep wooded hills to the south and the west and was created by building a dam across the streambed from one bank to the other. The mill, which was built long ago close to the dam by the commandant, now belongs to Monsieur Auguste Chouteau. It is one of the area's busiest and most important for milling wheat and maize. Both grains are milled at the same time by using millstones and pestles that run off the same drive shaft. It is driven by a horizontal wheel that is fitted with scoops requiring a good deal of water. The flour produced is often burned by the excessive speed of its action. This defect is caused by having too much water in the millrun and

85. The public or market square, known as the *Place d'Armes,* was located facing the riverfront at the center of the village and was bordered on the west by Main Street, on the north by La Rue de La Place (Market Street), and on the south by La Rue de La Tour (Market Street). Immediately to the west of the public square and facing Main Street was Laclède's original trading headquarters, which Auguste Chouteau converted into the city's most elegant residence after he purchased it in 1789.

86. The Fort on the Hill, constructed in 1792–1793 at the crest of the hill in the vicinity of present-day Walnut and Fourth streets, was a rectangular palisaded enclosure with earthen parapets, built around the large round stone tower known as Fort San Carlos. The stone tower, which was approximately thirty feet in diameter and between thirty and forty feet in height, had been erected hurriedly in 1780 and had served as the centerpiece of the city's defenses during the Battle of St. Louis. In addition to the stone tower, the fort, as Finiels notes, also enclosed a barracks, a powder magazine, and a kitchen with an adjoining prison. The stockaded fort was itself surrounded by a ditch or moat approximately two feet deep and six feet wide. Despite its poor condition, the fort served as the Spanish and later the American military headquarters in St. Louis until the U.S. government constructed Fort Bellefontaine in 1806. St. Louis officials continued to use the old Spanish fortification as the local jail for several more years. For a more detailed description of the fort, see Musick, *St. Louis as a Fortified Town,* 28, 79–81.

could be easily corrected. A spillway at the top of the dam would permit excess water to be detoured around the mill, and this water could then flow back into the streambed below the mill, and so on to the Mississippi through the old streambed.[87]

When Indians were sorely threatening St. Louis, an attempt was made to protect it from their incursions. Earthworks were laid out that were supposed to encircle the entire town, from the Mississippi on the north down to the bank of the millstream in the south, and from there over to the river. A stone half-tower was built upon a rock along the bank of the river above the town. This tower had a gun platform with cannon embrasures and was capped off with a roof. Facing the tower, on the edge of the bluff 133 toises distant, a stone bastion was likewise built with cannon embrasures. The half-tower, the bastion, and the fort were interconnected by a strong palisade that served as a curtain wall. From the fort to the millstream, and then on to the river, earthworks were thrown up flanked by several bastions. These overlooked the ravine of the stream and were fortified with wooden blockhouses that had cannon platforms. One of these blockhouses can still be seen on the bank of the large ravine facing the hills. This fortified periphery made up the [47] defenses of St. Louis. But the town was too dispersed, and the available forces could not maintain the periphery. Nonetheless, it was adequate to fend off Indians. The presence of cannons, mounted at several high points, served to keep them at a distance.[88]

In 1797 I was dispatched from Philadelphia to St. Louis in order to prepare its defenses. Monsieur de Carondelet had already sent some troops from New Orleans and had dispatched Monsieur [Louis] Vandenbemden from New Madrid to fortify the place. The fortifications that Vandenbemden had planned were at most half-completed.[89] There was nothing that could be done to alter his plans because the

87. In 1765 Joseph Taillon (Tayon) constructed a dam on the La Petite Rivière, subsequently known as Mill Creek, and built a grist mill. Laclède acquired the mill from Taillon in 1767 and over the next several years raised the dam and improved the mill. Finiels seems mistakenly to have assumed that Laclède built the mill and that he was "commandant" in St. Louis; neither assumption was correct in fact. In 1779 Auguste Chouteau purchased the mill from Laclède's estate, and the Mill Creek Pond was thereafter referred to as Chouteau's Pond. In 1820 Auguste Chouteau had considerable difficulty locating suitable new millstones to replace the old ones worn out by many years of use. François Ménard to Auguste Chouteau, 22 March and 6 June 1820, Missouri Historical Society, Chouteau Collections.

88. The various fortifications Finiels describes were constructed at different times. Following the Battle of St. Louis, Lieutenant Governor Francisco Cruzat ordered the construction of a wooden stockade around the city as protection against a rumored spring offensive. In 1781, the Spaniards built the stone half-tower situated on a cliff overlooking the Mississippi near the foot of what is now Franklin Avenue at the northern end of Cruzat's line. Early reports generally referred to it as a demilune, but Finiels' account confirms that it was a fully enclosed structure with a roof. The picket stockade quickly deteriorated, and at the urging of Lieutenant Governor Manuel Pérez, a stone bastion was constructed sometime between 1789 and 1792 as a replacement for the rotting wooden bastion on the village's northwest corner near the corner of what are now Franklin Avenue and Third Street. In 1797, Colonel Carlos Howard supervised construction of the wooden blockhouse mentioned by Finiels. The cedar log structure was located at the southwest corner of the village between Chouteau and Lombard avenues near Fourth Street. More information concerning these fortifications can be found in Musick, *St. Louis as a Fortified Town*.

89. Louis Vandenbemden, a native of Flanders and an engineer, arrived in Upper Louisiana in 1794 and was employed in 1797 to work on the St. Louis fortifications. See Houck, *History of Missouri*, 2:155. Vandenbemden took strong exception to certain other plans for fortifying St. Louis, presumably those drawn up by George-Victor Collot, that had been prepared before his arrival. See Vandenbemden to

funds appropriated for the project were almost exhausted, and it was preferable to complete those plans rather than to start something new that could not be completed. Therefore I confined myself to providing some advice in order to derive the most benefit from the project already begun. For lack of money this project had not been completed, and I never liked its conception or arrangement. It is in these terms that I explained everything [i.e., by letter] to Monsieur the Baron de Carondelet as soon as I arrived in St. Louis, wishing to make it clear that I had had no part in planning the fortifications; this had been done by Monsieur Vandenbemden.

I have no desire to undermine the reputation of this craftsman [*artiste*], who had many talents and who possessed a profound knowledge of architecture. I wish to render him the justice that he deserves, and his premature death is a genuine loss for the colony. But he was not a military man. He relied exclusively upon the writings of [Guillaume] Leblond and [Marc-René de] Montalambert, and everything he did was done with the best of intentions.[90]

Thus the defenses of St. Louis were buttressed with the addition of four stone towers. One of these is opposite the bridge that crosses the creek on the way out of town toward Carondelet. It is thirty feet in diameter and almost sixteen feet high; it overlooks the Mississippi and commands nearly the entire course of the creek in the ravine. The second tower is southwest of town, bordering the ravine and facing the mill, from where it overlooks the depression that the ravine creates toward town. Its walls are four feet thick at the base, forty feet in diameter, and twenty-four feet high; inside there is a small [48] stone powder magazine. Between these two stone towers is the old blockhouse that I mentioned earlier. These three structures are all commanded by the hills facing them a good musket shot away; the tower to the southwest is also commanded by the plateau that borders the pond. These structures are too isolated and too far from town, with which they could not communicate if the hills were occupied by enemy forces; and this is the first thing an enemy would do if it had any intention of attacking St. Louis. The two other stone towers are better placed, between the fort and the stone bastion. However, if they had been built a bit further forward they would better serve to defend the fort and the bastion. As it is, the fort and the bastion effectively protect the towers by which they themselves were supposed to be protected. These two towers are twenty-four feet in diameter, and each has a stone powder magazine inside. Each of the four towers has a gun platform, above which is a stone parapet pierced with embrasures. The parapets have eight-foot crenelations all around for the use of musketeers.[91]

Carlos Howard, 23 May 1797, PC 214. Concerning Collot, see above, note 2.

90. Vandenbemden died on 9 September 1799 (see Nasatir, *Spanish War Vessels,* 225n). Guillaume Leblond (1704–1781) was a mathemetician and tutor to the French royal family who wrote several treatises on military affairs, including *Eléments de fortification* (1786). Marc-René de Montalambert (1714–1800) was a French general, member of the Academie des Sciences, and author of the eleven-volume *La fortification perpendiculaire* (1776–1786).

91. The four stone towers constructed in 1797 were probably located as follows: (1) on the west side of Third Street between Vine Street and Washington Avenue, (2) near the southwest corner of Third and

As I have described it, this configuration gives St. Louis the appearance of an amphitheater. This will be even more true when the edge of the small bluff becomes built-up with houses, which will soon occur with the growth of the population. The residents have thus far avoided doing this, and they prefer to locate their houses on the ledge in order to be close to the Mississippi, whose waters they prefer to well water. This is despite the fact that the wells in St. Louis are very good, the few that exist having been pierced down through the rock.

Houses in St. Louis are generally built of stone or timbers, and the interstices between the posts are filled either with masonry or mud and straw; the roofs are always shingled. Nearly all of the houses have galleries front and back, which is the usual manner of building in the whole colony. At first glance St. Louis appears to be of considerable size, and you are surprised to see the figures, which show that its population is quite small. This is explained by the fact that most of the residential parcels are occupied by only two owners, or sometimes three; others are owned by only one person, and the most densely settled are occupied by four families. [49] This apportioning seems generous compared to New Orleans, where the parcels are usually divided into twelve lots. But in a region where each family must provide everything for itself, instead of relying upon markets and butcher shops, the lots are scarcely sufficient. St. Louis has never had a central market, and each resident must have a substantial garden in order to be able to lay in a supply of vegetables for the winter. He must have a poultry yard, a stable, a barn, and sheds in order to house his animals and to store his fodder and farm equipment. His residence in town is a microcosm of a farm, which either provides him with everything he needs or places him in a position to obtain it.

St. Louis's streets are miserable. The least bit of rain renders them absolutely impassable, and there are no sidewalks. The sandy soil of the plateau is always mixed with rocks and rich clay, making it slippery in many places. Almost all of the cross streets are deeply rutted by the water that flows off the bluff behind town and rushes toward the river. When it rains you must remain at home for days on end or put on Creole clothing in order to face the mud, which covers you from head to toe by the time you return home. A horse is the only option in these circumstances, for carriages are very rare in the Illinois Country. Despite its pretentious title, "Capital," St. Louis is in fact only a medium-sized village, and it never seems more like one than when the heavens unleash their cataracts, which happens only too often.[92]

There are not enough cattle in this part of Louisiana to supply the needs of the

Pine streets, (3) on the block bounded by Broadway, Sixth, Cedar, and Gratiot streets, and (4) near the intersection of Second and LaSalle streets. See Musick, *St. Louis as a Fortified Town*, 103.

92. As early as 1778, concerns about poor drainage had prompted the residents of St. Louis to create a gutter or canal to "draw the water to the Mississippi, and to allow a constant drainage to the water from the gullies and sink-holes." Frederic L. Billon, *Annals of St. Louis in Its Early Days under the French and Spanish Dominations, 1764–1804,* 140–41.

area, and it is often difficult to obtain subsistence here.[93] Slaughtering is done only sporadically in the summer and never in the winter. Animals graze far from the villages—on the lowlands that border the Missouri, or on Grande Isle and the Isle à Cabaret, which are located between St. Louis and the mouth of the Missouri. On these low, damp lands the cattle graze on horsetail [*presle*] that grows in the shady [50] woods, and which is their sole source of food during winter. Its hollow stems contain water that slakes their thirst. The cattle are so accustomed to this annual migration that when November arrives they take it upon themselves to leave the St. Louis area and roam as far as ten leagues in search of food. Farmers who do not wish to risk losing precious cattle (some always get lost during that season) preempt this migration. Early on, they round up all of their cattle and lead them toward the Isle à Cabaret or Grande Isle. Then they compel them with great difficulty to cross over to one or the other of these islands. In this way they are more likely to find them all when time comes to lead them back.[94]

Once again, it is sloth that creates this destructive custom, which stifles the growth of the herds and which should be abandoned as soon as possible. With a bit more work and effort, shelters could be built to protect the cattle during the winter; and abundant fodder for this bitter season could be obtained from hay, which is common around St. Louis and often of excellent quality. It grows for the most part on public land, and everyone would have the right to harvest it.

The necessity to ensure future subsistence for St. Louis will surely call for wiser and more rational measures, which would in fact serve the interests of the land owners. This is all the more necessary because other sources of subsistence are very precarious. Fishing is confined to the summer because of ice. Some ponds and marshes, however, could furnish an abundance of fish if someone would devote some attention to it. But it is the hunt that is the real mother of subsistence during winter in the Illinois Country— deer, wild turkeys, ducks, coots, geese, swans, rabbits, raccoons,[95] opossums, squirrels are the prey. [51] Some years, however, the hunt is lean. Indians do most of the hunting, and sometimes they are slow getting started; other times there is virtually no game at all, which was true during the winter that I spent in St. Louis during 1797–1798. In such instances, fasting necessarily becomes the order of the day unless you have a well-stocked chicken yard and a good supply of vegetables.[96]

93. Finiels' remarks stand in sharp contrast with Amos Stoddard's observation that "it is common for a farmer to own from a hundred to a hundred and fifty head of cattle, and as many swine; nor ought this to be deemed extraordinary, when it is considered, that the rearing of them is productive of very little expense and trouble" (*Sketches*, 229).

94. It was the general practice in the Illinois Country to fence cattle out rather than in. Residential property and arable land were enclosed by fences, leaving livestock free to graze wherever else they chose.

95. One might think that *chat sauvage* should translate as "wild cat," but in the Illinois Country it had come to mean "raccoon." See McDermott, *Glossary*, 49.

96. It is curious that Finiels failed to mention the great flood of 1797 and the severe hardships that it created during the winter of 1797–1798. See Ekberg, *Colonial Ste. Genevieve*, 140, 142, 247. Juan Ventura

Six years ago [i.e., 1797] sheep were introduced to the Illinois Country; previously they had been very rare. The first to arrive in St. Louis were shipped from Ecores à Margot [later Memphis] by Monsieur de Bellechasse, who was then an officer in the Louisiana regiment. Later, some came by way of Kentucky. They have multiplied rapidly in the abundant Illinois pastures despite fearsome enemies—wolves—that abound in Illinois. The bitter winter cold abets their pursuit of these timid animals, which makes them easier prey than horses, oxen, or cows, who are better able to defend themselves. Attentiveness, precautions, and hard work—which will surely be found too irksome in Illinois—will be required in order to raise them there. That is, if these inconveniences have not already dashed the hope of raising them there.97

Another resource, which demands neither as much care nor as much effort and whose importance is now beginning to be recognized, is swine. They proliferate prodigiously, and the Americans raise a much larger quantity than has thus far been done [in Spanish Illinois]; they find rich fodder in forests composed of several varieties of oak; they put on weight easily and acquire a delicacy surpassing those that the old-time *habitants* fattened in feedlots.98

All the arable lands near St. Louis are high enough to escape flooding. They are generally good, although not so good as the low plains [52] found at intervals along the river. They [the lands] have not promoted the development of individual farm-steads, except two or three leagues apart. They are concentrated north and west of town and are divided only by some boundary markers. Each *habitant* maintains several toises of a common fence, which protects the fields from the cattle that graze on a common pasture that is located between the fence and the town. While there is grass they graze contentedly, but if a dry spell stifles its growth, they soon cast a greedy glance over the fence at the green expanse of the plowlands. They browse along the fence testing its strength; finding a weak spot, they gather together, redouble their efforts, and soon break down the barrier. One can imagine how quickly they range over the fields and with what voracity they consume the sprouting wheat. The alarm is immediately sounded in town, and people come running from all quarters in pursuit of the avid and illegal foragers. Against their will they are led back, and the fence is speedily repaired. A gate in this fence on the road to St. Charles permits passage at any time. It is left open after the harvest, but from the moment that green sprouts appear until the mowing scythes cut the grain for sheaving, the gate is closed.

Morales, the Spanish intendant in New Orleans, referred to the "notorious" 1797 flooding in St. Louis and Ste. Genevieve and observed that provisions were scarce and the residents had suffered a great deal as a result of their lost crops. Morales to Charles Dehault Delassus, 18 January 1799, Chouteau Collections.

97. Sheep were never plentiful enough in the Illinois Country to be listed in the official Spanish censuses with other livestock.

98. Pork had long been a specialty of the Illinois Country. As early as the 1720s, Illinois hams were being shipped downriver to New Orleans, and they continued to be an important trade commodity for the remainder of the colonial period.

A black man is housed in a cabin near the gate, and he opens and closes it for each passing traveler.[99]

The only water near St. Louis flows out of the [mill] pond and empties into the river. This is used by the laundresses, who set up their washboards on the pond's banks and the shores of the creek. They prefer this to using the Mississippi, whose waters must always be left to settle before being used. The Mississippi carries much more sediment in the St. Louis area than in the lower colony. Water taken close to the right bank and allowed to settle in a glass always leaves from one-fifth [53] to one-fourth of the glass full of sediment; taken from the left bank opposite St. Louis it is much clearer, leaving only a small deposit compared to the first.

This muddy water—whose mere appearance would quench the thirst of a man accustomed to the limpid, pure water of fountains—is nevertheless preferred to clearer waters. These could be taken from the Mississippi above the mouth of the Missouri, or from springs, which in several places flow out of the bluffs or can be tapped from the bowels of the earth with wells. It [the muddy water] is eagerly drunk, often even before it has settled. Panting boatmen, dripping with sweat, take it along the bank and eagerly gulp it down, and there is no evidence that it has ever caused any problems. Nature knows how to handle quantities of earth that enter the stomach and intestines, but she has not yet revealed her secret.[100]

St. Louis was given a boost when some Americans settled in the area six years ago. They grasped the advantages that they might derive from the natural indolence of the native *habitants,* and their industry has already opened avenues of business that that indolence had precluded. Sawmills now supply abundant planks at twenty-five sous apiece, whereas they used to be scarce and cost four escalins or even one piastre.[101] Iron is available at a better price; masonry, cabinetry, carpentry, and furniture are less expensive, and the residents can enjoy the fruits of labor that they once hesitated to undertake and only rarely brought to completion. Negligent workers left houses unfinished; you had to wait four to six years for windows, doors, and furniture, which grew old in the workshops before they were completed. Vegetables, eggs, [54] poultry, milk, butter, and grain are more readily available, and thanks to the Americans' industry subsistence is generally more secure than before.

99. This open-field style of agriculture was common to all French communities in the Illinois Country on both sides of the Mississippi. Instead of separating individually owned arable strips with fences, all owners of plowland within the common field were responsible for maintaining a fence enclosing the entire block of arable land. This system was similar to village agriculture in France. See Ekberg, *Colonial Ste. Genevieve,* 129–32.

100. Mark Twain (*Life on the Mississippi,* 24) wrote, "The man they called Ed said the muddy Mississippi water was wholesomer to drink than the clear water of the Ohio; he said if you let a pint of this yaller Mississippi water settle, you would have about a half to three-quarters of an inch of mud in the bottom, according to the stage of the river, and then it warn't no better than Ohio water."

101. Twenty-five sous were equivalent to twenty-five cents; four escalins were equivalent to fifty cents; one piastre was equivalent to one dollar.

The population of St. Louis is composed of Canadians, Creoles, Americans, and some French who have settled there during the last eight to ten years.[102] Earlier, the only way in which the population of the Illinois Country grew was owing to the journeys that some merchants made to Canada. These merchants always returned with ten or twelve *engagés,* all workmen and artisans who obligated themselves to serve in the Illinois Country for several years at modest wages. This was advantageous for Canadians who could not find such wages at home. These useful men, finding Louisiana's climate agreeable, especially in comparison with theirs, immigrated. They were also attracted by the ease with which they could settle there, which was difficult in Canada even with much labor, and by the higher wages. Some of them became farmers, who were all the more precious for Upper Louisiana. In addition to their labor, they brought gentle and steady dispositions, characteristics that earned them the esteem and friendship of a people who have always valued such qualities. There are many Canadians in the Illinois Country, and many of them arrived there thanks to the indefatigable spirit of Monsieur [Gabriel] Cerré in traveling to Canada, his native land. Age has never prevented him from making these difficult trips. The winter that I spent in St. Louis, I saw him arrive on foot from Detroit with two or three Indians, who would not have been able to endure the fatigue and bitter cold of such a trip without him. I must remark that this indefatigable old man was at Fort Duquesne in 1755 when the garrison so courageously defeated the English, under General [Edward] Braddock's command, who were marching to attack them. He was one of the Frenchmen who covered himself in glory in that action and who thus provided the Indians with an exalted opinion of his valor.[103]

[55] St. Louis's temperature is generally healthy and agreeable, although there may be frequent fluctuations during the same day—as is true in all regions of America. In summer, the heat is often as intense as at New Orleans. In winter, there is bitter cold, which is healthy, and also good for agriculture because it provides the soil with an opportunity to rejuvenate itself. However, the cold makes a considerable dent in your wallet because of the firewood that is required to defend against it.[104] The land is

102. Concerning the colonizing of the Illinois Country, a research group at Laval University has been doing seminal work. See Renald Lessard, Jacques Mathieu, and Lina Gouger, "Peuplement colonisateur au pays des Illinois."

103. Jean-Gabriel Cerré first established himself as a merchant in Kaskaskia but moved to St. Louis at the time of the American Revolution. Concerning Cerré's life, see Walter B. Douglas, "Jean-Gabriel Cerré—A Sketch"; Julius T. Muench, "Jean-Gabriel Cerré"; and Clarence W. Alvord, ed., *Cahokia Records, 1778–1790,* xx, note 2, and passim. Finiels' interesting comment that Cerré was present at Braddock's defeat in southwestern Pennsylvania in 1755 substantiates the fact that men from the Illinois Country, whites as well as Indians, participated in the French and Indian War.

104. Cast-iron stoves, as opposed to fireplaces, did not become commonplace in Upper Louisiana until after the turn of the nineteenth century and the coming of steamboat transportation. Deforestation around the settlements was extensive because of the very low efficiency of fireplaces.

often covered with snow a foot or two deep, which pleases the residents, especially the youngsters. For them it is one of the virtues of winter and provides them with a sport which they love passionately. Scarcely do they notice the delicate flakes gathering on the prairies and fields than they prepare their sleighs; the horses are shod for ice and their harnesses ornamented with bells. Vying with one another, they leap forward, and in the midst of joyous cries of pleasure they cross the milky plain, carving the surface into a myriad of figures. Sometimes the frail vehicles overturn and bury the youngsters in the snow. These repeated accidents only double the fun, and also prolong it by providing subject matter for storytelling upon the return. The river's waters suspend their swift race; they stop, and on their surface forms a layer of ice, thick and solid enough for wagonloads of wood to cross it without danger. Springtime is always rainy. April, May, and June bring torrents of water that scar the earth and carry to the river the soil for alluvial lands. Following violent claps of thunder, hail often mixes with the rain and damages the crops. Tornadoes sweep across the sky more swiftly than streaks of lightning can dissect the scene; with a frightful din they uproot old trees that have survived many a windstorm; they carve swaths across the thickest forests, stripping them of their finest [56] foliage; the earth, covered with debris, is witness to their trail and to the enormous force with which they blazed it. I was in Prairie du Rocher when one of these impetuous tornadoes, preceded by a hailstorm, compelled me to spend the night there. The following day the road along the bluff tops was littered with trees, which forced me to make frequent detours through the woods. Autumn is the finest season in the Illinois Country. It brings serene and temperate days that bridge the gap between crushing heat and bitter cold; it offers to the residents fruits that assuage tempers aroused by the heat. The prairies lose the tall grasses that make them difficult to cross. It's the season for travel. The sun's burning rays descend only obliquely; marshy lands dry out; rivers flow within their channels; all lines of communication are open and easily used.

Although there is a noticeable difference in the moral character of the residents of St. Louis and those of Ste. Genevieve, you nevertheless still discover in the former the imprint of their native simplicity, and you can still easily detect traces of the good nature that they inherited from their forefathers. More affluent outsiders, more wealth, pretension to fine manners, and social distinctions are already tainting native customs, which are not yet entirely lost but which will certainly disappear. The women have cultivated more elegance than the men. Their finer sensibilities prompt them to adorn themselves, and they are beginning to laugh at the naive beauties of Ste. Genevieve; they do not perceive that they are [57] really losing by the price they pay for acquiring affected appearances. Their dress is already more studied, and soon you will clearly see an artificiality that until now has only just appeared. The young men remain far behind in these developments. Although the Indian breechclout hardly ever appears anymore under their tunics, the woolen capot (a hooded cloak) has not yet vanished; it still appears at the most glittering fetes, where it makes a marked contrast to the finery of the young beauties.[105]

During its more than fifty years [sic] of existence, St. Louis has enjoyed a sort of privilege, which might be considered an exemption from one of the general laws of nature; this must be reckoned one of the finest gifts that indulgent Mother Nature has ever bestowed upon an area. During this entire period of time, and without the least suggestion of why, this town has been spared the scourge that is most destructive of beauty; from this cruel illness that can in a brief while utterly efface that beautiful flower, so fresh and delicate, and replace it with deformity; from this illness that ferociously ravages regions with warm climates. On several occasions, Indians covered with this disease's virulent pustules sought refuge in town and spent the entire term of the disease there without communicating it to anyone else. It was well established in public opinion that the residents of St. Louis were immune to smallpox, which on several occasions had visited other settlements in the Illinois Country. Last summer, this illusion (so comforting for vanity) was shattered, and mothers were given one more thing to worry about. The illness finally broke down the barriers that nature had seemingly raised against it, and almost all of the residents were afflicted. Some of them succumbed to this mortal disease, and other young beauties had dashed their hopes of numerous conquests, which had earlier been prophesied in their mirrors.[106]

[58] This visitation, as unexpected as it was unpleasant, followed close on the heels of a real loss that the city of St. Louis had just suffered—the recall of a commandant that she was lucky enough to have had for seven years, but who was supposed to have remained for ten. Don Zenon Trudeau,[107] named commandant of the Illinois by Monsieur de Carondelet, quickly came to be idolized for his kindliness, gentleness, and paternal friendship, which are so rarely found in commandants and which can still be seen in Natchitoches. As disinterested as he was just and generous, he never oppressed these good people with that urge to get rich that beckons officials to seek commands in Louisiana. He never meddled in the enterprises that individuals under-

105. This is the first passage in which Finiels gives evidence of the influence of Rousseau's romantic notion that rusticity is good and the artificiality of civilization bad.

106. According to Auguste Chouteau's recollection, smallpox first appeared in St. Louis on 15 May 1801. See Auguste Chouteau's interview in Testimony before Theodore Hunt, Recorder of Land Titles, St. Louis, 1825 (commonly known as Hunt's Minutes), in the Missouri State Archives, Jefferson City. A transcript of Chouteau's testimony can be found in McDermott, The Early Histories of St. Louis, 93.

107. Zenon Trudeau, lieutenant governor of Upper Louisiana, 1792–1799, was by all accounts a popular figure and effective leader in the region. In 1797, De Lassus de Luzières commented, "It will be infinitely advantageous for the general welfare of the residents of [Spanish] Illinois to maintain Monsieur Zenon Trudeau for a long time as commander in chief" ("Observations sur le caractère, qualités et professions des habitants blancs du District de la Nouvelle Bourbon," attached to the New Bourbon census of 1797, AGI, PC, legajo 2365). For a biographical sketch of Trudeau, see Nasatir, Spanish War Vessels, 59–60. A sampling of Trudeau's correspondence can be found in Nasatir, ed., Before Louis and Clark (hereafter cited as BLC).

took in order to further their own interests. Family disputes, quarrels, and bickering over money were all calmed by his conciliatory voice and very often ended by sacrifices that he was always glad to make. He provided solace, support, and charity for everyone who was down on his luck; he welcomed and encouraged strangers, persuading them to settle in a region where they found it easy to respect the man who governed it. In a twinkling all this happiness was destroyed. It has been three years since he was recalled, but the wound has not yet healed. In moments of distress, which misfortune so often brings to the lives of most of the residents of the Illinois Country, the people call out in vain for the father of the downtrodden—he can do nothing but wish them good luck.

St. Louis is composed of 1,100 to 1,200 persons of all ages, male and female, black and white, free and slave.[108] [59] They own 1,200 to 1,500 head of cattle and nearly 250 horses; harvest 5,000 to 6,000 bushels of wheat, 5,000 of maize, and 2,000 pounds of tobacco; and produce oats and hay for fodder.[109] They cultivate all varieties of vegetables and several European fruits—apples, pears, peaches, grapes, tart cherries, and currants. In the woods not far from town you can find hazelnuts, wild cherries, persimmons, pawpaws, pecans, wild grapes, blackberries, mulberries, and American walnuts, which are different from the European variety. Wild strawberries abound in the fields and woods. This region only requires a bit of domesticating in order to provide man with the better part of his needs.

Within its jurisdiction, St. Louis has several settlements that have developed on the right bank of the Mississippi up to the mouth of the Missouri, along Des Peres Creek, and on the Meramec River. These settlements are inhabited by people from St. Louis and by Americans, who about six years ago received some concessions upon which to settle. I have included produce from the first two [areas] with the totals for St. Louis and counted the landowners in the town's population. The settlements on the Meramec are more distant. They consist of 80 to 100 persons, have 120 head of cattle and a score or so of horses, harvest close to 3,000 bushels of maize and 1,000 to 1,200 pounds of tobacco, and produce about the same amount of salt. Wheat was not being grown there when I was in the Illinois Country, but the residents have probably begun to cultivate it since then.[110]

---

108. The official Spanish census of 1796 listed St. Louis's population at 975 souls of all statuses and colors (see *SRM*, 2:142–43).

109. As in the case of Carondelet (see above, note 76), Finiels' figures on grain production for St. Louis more or less agree with those from the official census reports, which suggests that the flood of 1797 did not devastate the crops at St. Louis. This was probably because the arable fields outside St. Louis were on higher ground than the Plaine Basse of Ste. Genevieve.

110. The Spanish census of 1796 (*SRM*, 2:142–43) lists 57 persons at the Meramec settlement and maize production at 900 bushels. The significant increases in both population and grain production that Finiels provides for 1797 suggest that the American settlements on the Meramec were growing very rapidly. In 1779 an American, John Hilderbrand (Albrane to the Spaniards), received a large land grant from De Leyba, Spanish lieutenant governor of Upper Louisiana, that was located "about four leagues" upstream from the mouth of the Meramec River (*American State Papers: Public Lands*, 6:836). Hilderbrand's property may have been the nucleus around which the early American settlement on the Meramec River developed.

From St. Louis you can travel overland to St. Ferdinand and Marais des Liards, which are two settlements located between the Mississippi and Missouri, at some distance from the rivers.

St. Ferdinand is a little village located on the bank of Cold Water Creek, which flows into the Missouri two leagues above its mouth; the creek flows over a rock bottom before emptying into the Missouri River. The village is situated four leagues north-northwest of St. Louis and was founded by a group of farmers who wished to till the lands bordering the cold-water stream. [60] During the fifteen or sixteen years of its existence it has done as well as can be expected given the sparse population and limited resources of the Illinois Country. It cannot really expand further because all the arable land in the region is occupied. This is the yardstick by which you must measure the potential of a settlement in the Illinois Country, given the present state of the colony: a tabulation of the arable lands indicates the number of families that can live there, and it was observed that when that number was reached there could be no farther growth; it remained stagnant and quickly sloughed off the excess population by sending it to other places, which will, in their turn, go through the same cycle.[111]

The residents of St. Ferdinand are utterly devoted to their work, which is confined, as in all the settlements of Upper Louisiana, to the cultivation of wheat, maize, and tobacco. They raise some oats and hay, which need only to be cut and stored in a barn. But in general they also want to make their lands as profitable as possible, and they should soon imitate enlightened farmers and provide an example of work guided by experience, along with the judgment required to bring it to perfection. This desire [to prosper] comes from the nickname Florissant, which has been given to this settlement and which indicates that progress has been made. This would have seemed surprising at the time of its founding, and must be appreciated within the context of the old-fashioned farming at St. Louis.[112]

St. Ferdinand has a total of 250 persons of both sexes, all ages, black and white, free and slave. It has 300 head of cattle and 50 horses. It harvests annually 6,000 bushels of wheat, 3,000 bushels of maize, and 6,000 pounds of tobacco.[113]

Marais des Liards, another small village situated three-quarters of a league from St. Ferdinand, is of even less consequence. It was settled seven years ago by several American families, who found enough arable land on the other side of St. Ferdinand to provide a basis for their settlement.[114] [61] Its total population of both sexes, all

111. For further information on St. Ferdinand, or Florissant as it was sometimes called, see Houck, *History of Missouri*, 2:66–67.

112. Finiels seems to have gotten his words a bit twisted around in this paragraph, for what he seems to want to say is that the nickname *Florissant* ("flourishing") came from the inhabitants' desire to improve rather than vice versa.

113. The Spanish census of 1796 (*SRM*, 2:142–43) listed 185 souls in St. Ferdinand. Assuming Finiels' figures are from 1797 and that they are more or less accurate, St. Ferdinand was growing vigorously in the late 1790s.

114. A group of hunters led by Robert Owens settled five miles southwest of St. Ferdinand in 1794 at a place called Marais des Liards, or Cottonwood Swamp. Following an influx of American farmers, the

ages, black and white, free and slave, is 180 persons. It has close to 450 head of cattle and 50 horses. It produces but little wheat, approximately 300 bushels a year. The principal crop is maize, of which it produces as much as 6,000 bushels annually, along with 3,000 pounds of tobacco.[115]

CREVE COEUR, BON HOMME CREEK, ST. CHARLES, AND DARDENNE CREEK

Continuing on to the southwest four or five leagues above Marais des Liards, you encounter Marais de Crève Coeur [Creve Coeur Marsh] on the right bank of the Missouri a bit above St. Charles; and a league above this you come upon the Petite Rivière Bon Homme [Bon Homme Creek], which flows from the south and enters the Missouri in the middle of Anse à Philippe [Philip's Bend]. The little ridge, which continues from St. Louis up to the mouth of the Missouri, swings around this mouth and heads off to the northwest, leaving a small, low plain at the confluence of the two rivers; then it approaches the right bank of the Missouri a little above its mouth and below the Rochers de l'Eau Froide [Cold Water Rocks]. There it runs atop the rocks all along the bank before leaving the riverbank at the far end of the second cove created by these rocks. At that point there is a rather extensive low point between the ridge and the river. The ridge returns to the riverbank at the next point, a little above the Isles aux Biches [Doe Islands], where it forms a hillock at the foot of the river. This hillock is called Charbonnière, and in fact it contains some fossil coal in its flanks. At this time it is hardly used, but it is a resource that will soon prove valuable. From there the ridge turns sharply away from the river and heads south-southwest, returning to the river at Anse à Philippe, a league and a half above St. Charles. Between Charbonnière and Anse à Philippe the riverbank swings about a league away from the ridge. This region is a low-lying plain nearly three leagues [62] long and at most a league wide; it is very fertile and heavily wooded, but the Missouri often covers it during flood stage. At the far end of this plain, a little above Isles de St. Charles [St. Charles Islands], is Creve Coeur Marsh, or rather pond. This is a rather large pond and contains a considerable quantity of fish of all varieties. It is also a refuge for many ducks, swans, and other aquatic birds. The proximity of the farmsteads that have gone up on the banks during the past six years will surely frighten them off, but the fish, not having the birds' ability to escape man's voracity, will remain.[116]

---

inhabitants changed the settlement's name to Owens Station, and later to Bridgeton.

115. The Spanish census of 1796 (*SRM*, 2:142–43) listed 124 persons in Marais des Liards, which indicates that it was growing at about the same rate as the neighboring community of St. Ferdinand.

116. Creve Coeur Creek now flows out of Creve Coeur Lake and enters the Missouri River directly facing St. Charles. Bon Homme Creek still enters the Missouri from the south in the middle of a bend in the river several miles above St. Charles. The Rochers de l'Eau Froide (Cold Water Rocks) are a reference to the rocky banks of the Missouri where Cold Water Creek flows into the river near Fort Bellefontaine. Lewis C. Beck remarked that "La Charbonnière [is] the name given to a coal bank on the right shore of the Missouri, near Florissant, and about 12 miles above its confluence with the Mississippi" (*A Gazetteer of the States of Illinois and Missouri*, 286). Charbonier Road still runs along the bluffs overlooking the Missouri River immediately west of Florissant.

Bon Homme Creek was soon explored by the residents of Creve Coeur and also by some Americans who likewise came to the Illinois Country to settle. This creek drains very good land near the Missouri, and that was enough to persuade the Americans to settle there. Since then a commandant, Monsieur [James] Mackay, an Englishman by birth, has been named for these two settlements.[117] He had already journeyed to the Mandans via Lakes Superior and Winnipeg [Quinijag] on behalf of English merchants in Canada before he came to settle in the Illinois Country nine years ago. Then the company created in St. Louis for the exclusive trade of the upper Missouri appointed him to lead an expedition to the Mandans, which had little success. It was on the basis of his memoranda and notes that I drafted for him in 1797 the latest map of the Missouri.[118] Creve Coeur Marsh and Bon Homme Creek still have only 80 or 90 inhabitants; they possess 130 to 140 cattle and 25 horses. When I was in the Illinois Country, they were harvesting only 2,000 bushels of maize and 200 to 300 pounds of tobacco, but since then they have turned to cultivating wheat and have been able to harvest 1,500 to 2,000 bushels.[119]

You can journey from St. Louis to St. Charles either by land or by water. This [63] village is seven leagues from St. Louis, on the left bank of the Missouri, about eight leagues from its mouth. The overland route is for travelers only and can be traversed on foot, on horseback, and even by buggy during several months of the year. The water route is for freight and, although one of the shortest in the Illinois Country, it is nonetheless difficult because it proceeds up the fearsome Missouri, which has snags from its mouth on up. Often you can make the overland trip from St. Louis to St. Charles in two or three hours. Halfway along the route, you cross two branches of Des Peres Creek, which are almost dry during the hot season but sometimes sever communications in flood time. But the real difficulty is crossing the Missouri right facing St. Charles, which is not easy even at low water. In wintertime you can often cross this river on the ice. During high water the current is so swift that sometimes you would rather not risk crossing it at all but would instead proceed to St. Louis by pirogue.

117. In 1798 Governor-General Manuel Gayoso de Lemos appointed James Mackay as the first commandant of the settlement at Bonhomme Creek and named it San Andres del Misuri, or St. Andrews. Mackay had recently returned from the upper Missouri, where he had been acting as the chief agent for the Company of Explorers of the Upper Missouri, better known as the Missouri Company. Mackay, who was a Scotsman rather than an Englishman, reported to Gayoso from St. Andrews on 28 November 1798, "On my arrival at my Post, I found all the people living in peace and plenty; indeed it is surprising to see the Great Clearing of land & the quantity of Grain raised by so small a number of inhabitants . . . ." See Mackay's appointment as Commandant of San Andres, 1 May 1798 in SRM, 2:245; and Mackay to Gayoso, 28 November 1798, in BLC, 2:588. For a biographical sketch of Mackay, see Abraham P. Nasatir, "James Mackay."
118. Finiels reveals here for the first time that he was the draftsman for the famed Evans-Mackay map that Lewis and Clark later consulted in planning for their journey to the Pacific. In a later reference in this manuscript (see note 152 below), Finiels states that he drew the map in 1798. This ambiguity suggests that he probably did it either in late 1797 or early 1798. The map had been finished by 16 January 1798. See W. Raymond Wood, "Nicolas de Finiels: Mapping the Mississippi and Missouri Rivers, 1797-1798."
119. The Spanish Census of 1796 contained no mention of either Creve Coeur or Bon Homme, but in 1800 the official census reported a population of 380 for San Andres.

You can travel from St. Louis to St. Charles by water in two or two and a half days, and sometimes even in a day and a half. You can rather easily ascend the Mississippi, in which you find Isle à Cabaret and Grande Isle before arriving at the mouth of the Missouri. At that point, the work increases. More effort is required to overcome the force of the current; snags multiply; a dozen islands and vast sandbars compel you to make considerable detours in the short stretch of river that you must ascend. First you encounter a little bayou on the right bank about a league above the mouth, and immediately thereafter you come to the Cold Water Rocks, which flank the river for a distance of a league and a half. They are covered during high water but thrust up five or six feet at low water. [64] The current has cut and molded them until they are shaped like steps; several even resemble the circular stairways found in front of grand buildings. St. Ferdinand Creek has worn its way through these woods-crowned rocks, forming criss-crossed little valleys. It empties into the Missouri a little above two islands, the largest of which was named Gayoso, who, when he was only governor of Natchez, came to visit the Illinois Country.[120] This visit demonstrated, by his neglect of the Illinois Country during his governorship, that it is insufficient to cast a quick eye on a region in order to evaluate it and determine what may be useful or not for its well-being. On the little river St. Ferdinand is a sawmill that has been a great resource in Illinois for six years. An American named Long built it on these heights. Above these rocks you can discern Portage des Sioux. This brings back painful memories, but they vanish with the assurance of security, whose price makes it all the more satisfying.[121] Next come the Isles aux Biches and immediately after them the Charbonnière, remarkable for the hillock that covers it and precious for the coal it contains. From Charbonnière to St. Charles is only two leagues, and soon you arrive at the vast sandbar at the foot of its bluff.

St. Charles on the Missouri was the first settlement to develop outside St. Louis.[122] It was founded by hunters, who always strive to get closer to their game; they pursue it step for step as it flees the settlements of its indefatigable enemy. Several farmers who had ascended the Mississippi were attracted by the beautiful plain that extends from the left bank of the Missouri for nearly twenty-five leagues. They wasted no time in joining the hunters, and soon St. Charles grew to its present size. This village was [65] nicknamed Petites Côtes [Little Hills] because of its location at the foot of a series of rather high hills that confine it against the riverbank. Because of the small space between it and the river and because of the yearly crumbling of the high bluff

120. Gayoso de Lemos's journal of his expedition to Upper Louisiana in 1795 has been translated and published in Nasatir, *Spanish War Vessels*, 235–341. Finiels' "little river of St. Ferdinand" seems to have been what is now called Cold Water Creek. There was a large family of Longs living in that area during the late eighteenth century. See Houck, *History of Missouri*, 2:71–73.

121. Finiels' "painful memories" suggest that he was alluding to the Anglo-Indian attack on St. Louis in 1780, during which Indian allies of the English, perhaps including some Sioux warriors, crossed the Portage des Sioux prior to their attack on St. Louis. This provides an alternative explanation for the name Portage des Sioux. See note 82 above.

122. Canadian trader Louis Blanchette established St. Charles in 1769. See Ben L. Emmons, "The Founding of St. Charles and Blanchette Its Founder."

behind it, it appears that the hills wish to push the village into the river. The distribution of hills in this part of Louisiana is remarkable. Nature seems to have distributed them on both banks of the Mississippi, and even on those of the Missouri, with an intentional symmetry. Almost everywhere, they alternately retreat and advance on the banks of the river in regular fashion, from a league to a league and a quarter at most. This could lead you to suspect that nature wished to distribute her favors equally on both banks in such a manner that one could not be envious of the advantages of the other. But, despite this care, you can easily discern a slight partiality in favor of the left bank if you look closely; and this partiality is even more noticeable above the mouth of the Illinois River. However, I thought that I caught a glimpse of a grander design in this rather harmonious distribution, and I shall return to a mystery that perhaps goes back all the way to the first ages of the world. This venerable antiquity will lend additional weight to my argument. And if I have gone astray with these conjectures, it may be presumed that no one will find in the folds of the thick veil that shroud this mystery any clear evidence to refute me.

St. Charles is spread out very laterally and is composed of two streets intersected by numerous cross streets. The street located on the riverbank is the most heavily settled, and the lots on the next one back are situated on the slope of the heights. Its orientation is almost parallel to that of St. Louis; it runs [66] north and south, 15 degrees west, whereas St. Louis is shifted only 9 degrees west. Like all the villages in the Illinois Country, St. Charles appears larger than it is in reality. It is very poorly built of some fieldstone houses, which can be distinguished from one another only on the basis of which is the most dilapidated. Rains render it practically uninhabitable. Its residents, more hunters than farmers, in no way participate in the civilization that exists in St. Louis. They are nearly savages, and several of them scarcely understand French. Too indolent for the effort it would require to pull themselves out of this condition, they nevertheless endure the most difficult hardships in pursuit of wild game, which often leads them into the mountains. They overcome the difficulties of the Missouri and of the Mississippi with a courage and ardor that is astonishing when you have seen them pass entire days in a lassitude that could be called softness were it accompanied by any of the trappings of luxury. Their slow, sedate pace around their village reminds one of Asiatics burdened with their climate's heat. You might consider them weak, but when necessary they are capable of the most strenuous efforts. If they were darker complected, if they were less kindly, you might mistake them for Indians. They have adopted all of their habits without possessing any of their cruelty.[123]

123. General Georges-Victor Collot, who visited St. Charles in 1795, shared Finiels' unfavorable impression of St. Charles and its inhabitants. Collot reported that St. Charles contained about 100 or 125 ill-constructed houses and observed that "it would be difficult to find a collection of individuals more ignorant, stupid, ugly, and miserable. Such are the side effects of extreme poverty, with its train of cares and evils, that it destroys not only the beauty of the person but even the intellectual powers, and blunts all those feelings of delicacy and sensibility which belong to a state of ease, and the advantages of a good education" (A Journey in North America, 1:277).

Toward the extreme north end of the village, on one of the hills behind it, you notice a stone tower that serves as a base for a windmill. This is the only one that has succeeded in the Illinois Country, and it had several false starts before it began to function. There was an attempt to build one of wood in St. Louis on the slope of the plateau where the fort is located, but in this case ingenuity tried to liberate itself by blazing a trail beyond its capacities. The blades of this mill had to turn [67] horizontally in order to grind grain; it stopped short, and all the efforts and industry of the builder could not get it to make one complete revolution. It was abandoned and is now falling into ruins.[124]

Toward the extreme south end of St. Charles two ravines have worn a bed through the village in which water from the hills flows to the [Missouri] river. The northernmost of these flows continuously over the rocks that it has exposed; it can cut no deeper but it often erodes its banks, which threatens to ruin the lots that border it.

Ascending the Missouri above St. Charles, the hills veer off toward the south a short distance from the river bank. They return to the river at the beginning of a bend, Remont à Baguette, that you encounter one league after leaving the village. The very narrow space between the hills and the river is overgrown with trees; this serves as the commons for the cattle of St. Charles. There are two islands out front of the little low point that makes up part of this commons. A sandbar that runs between them also connects them to the river bank and during low water permits cattle to seek pasture there. The hills from St. Charles up to Remont à Baguette contain vast interior quarries, but stone is only rarely extracted from them. This work is beyond the capacity of the inhabitants, and it would be difficult to transport the stone to St. Charles. The shoreline of the bend Remont à Baguette—where it begins, at the spot where the hills come down to the edge of the river—consists of a bank of sandstone, which has thus far been neglected. Another gravel bank forms the shoreline for the bed of the river. It protrudes in the form of a reef that is exposed only during low water. During high water it is covered with almost twenty feet of water. [68] In the crook of the cove the hills are some distance from the river, and two brooks flow into it a short distance from one another. Farmsteads were established on each of these brooks when I visited the area, and there is room for many more of them if settlements were extended along the Missouri.

North of the hills, a league above St. Charles toward the Mississippi, you turn sharply west more than two leagues from the river. At the spot where the hills return, you see three mounds, somewhat higher than the surrounding hills, grouped together in an almost circular shape. These are called the "Three Breasts."[125] All visitors to St.

124. At the end of the colonial era, the horse mill was still the usual device for milling flour in the Illinois Country. Water mills were less common, and, as Finiels states, windmills were very rare. Finiels, acting in his capacity as royal engineer, and Vandenbemden both signed a report of 7 July 1797 to Carlos Howard stating that the proposed stone windmill tower that Antoine Roy wanted to construct on the Mississippi would be of no military advantage to an attacking enemy and that if it were occupied by the enemy, it could be quickly destroyed with artillery. Musick, *St. Louis as a Fortified Town,* 102.

125. In his *Gazetteer of the States of Illinois and Missouri,* Lewis C. Beck remarked that "the *Mamelles,* so called by the French from their resemblance to human breasts, are the points where the bluffs of the

Charles are taken to visit these mounds, for the town has nothing else of interest to offer. Given this lack of nourishment for hungry travelers, the panorama available from their summits provides a pleasing spectacle. This spectacle is nothing more than a view of the celebrated Paillissa rocks, which rise vertically on the left bank of the Mississippi and are covered with undulating hillocks.[126] Large trees reaching to the clouds shade these as well as the low point that extends five leagues to the east, creating the confluence of the Mississippi and Missouri rivers. This view would be much more interesting if the banks of the Mississippi, Missouri, and Illinois rivers were not overgrown with trees that obstruct one's view and scarcely permit you to suspect that they exist. Perhaps we shall find another vantage point from which to admire the important courses of these different waterways which gather at this point to mingle with the Mississippi, bringing it the tribute that North, East, and West hasten to pay her.

[69] From the "Three Breasts" the hills continue up the Mississippi for twenty leagues at a distance of a league to a league and one-half from its bank. The area between them and the Mississippi from the mouth of the Missouri upriver consists of a vast low-lying plain. This plain is intersected by several streams that flow out of the bluffs and continue to the river. The first of these, the Dardenne, is scarcely three leagues from St. Charles and approximately one league above the mouth of the Illinois River. This is followed by the Boeuf, the Cuivre, and the Saline, all of which are more or less significant and provide favorable places for settlements along their banks.[127] The only persons who know this plain thoroughly are hunters from St. Charles. Salt springs have been discovered in the area near the Saline River, and some Americans had planned to settle there in order to exploit them. I do not know, however, if they have since executed this plan. All this part of Upper Louisiana between the Mississippi and Missouri rivers, although very close to the settlements of the Illinois Country, remains little known, especially the high ground in the interior. Only a few Creole hunters roam there. It is assumed that if you wished to found settlements there you would have to fight the Indians who still frequent the high, deserted ground. This area has become their hunting ground since the population of the Illinois Country pushed them away from the mouth of the Missouri.

Despite the lethargic state in which St. Charles has remained for the nearly twenty years of its existence, a small colony has sprung up on the banks of the Dardenne River. This beginning, which elsewhere suggests the vigor of a trunk that can spare

---

Missouri and Mississippi terminate. They are situated three miles below St. Charles, six from the Mississippi, and one from the Missouri river, and are upwards of 100 feet in height" (p. 248). This area is now called Elm Point.

126. The famous Piasa Bird painting, which was first described by Father Marquette in 1673, has generated much controversy and speculation. It was located on one of the Mississippi palisades (Finiels' *Paillissa* being an archaic French word for "palisade") near present-day Alton, Illinois. The painting had weathered entirely away by the time Finiels visited the region in 1797. For a recent analysis of this fascinating issue, see Jerome Jacobson, "The Riddle of the Piasa."

127. On his map, Finiels shows the first stream above the Dardenne as the Perruque rather than the Boeuf, as his text has it. Today these streams are called the Peruque, the Cuivre, and the Saline.

some of its branches without sapping itself, is in Illinois a sign of the weakness—it indicates a scarcity of arable land that is usually available. [70] When the population surpasses the number that can be employed in agriculture, it will be absolutely necessary for the surplus to search elsewhere for subsistence, which a weak and indigent Mother Nature cannot provide. With the exception of St. Louis and Ste. Genevieve, all the settlements of the Illinois Country subsist solely on agriculture and hunting. These two villages alone contain merchants, artisans, and laborers in their midst. The other villages do not yet believe that they need creature comforts [avoir besoin de luxe] and therefore disdain the arts and crafts; they supply with natural energy whatever necessity obliges them to have. They make their own carts, plows, saddles, harnesses, shoes, and rough clothing, and they build their own rustic cabins. For objects they cannot make themselves—articles of food or convenience suitable to their station in life—they go and seek them in the capital. The settlement at the Dardenne Creek had, however, still another objective, which was to establish a presence close to the mouth of the Illinois River. In that way, the portage between this river and St. Charles, which is almost three leagues in length, could be avoided.

St. Charles possesses only 450 inhabitants of all ages and colors, male and female, free and slave. They have 300 head of cattle and 60 horses; they annually harvest 400 bushels of wheat, the same amount of maize, and 2,000 pounds of tobacco.[128]

Now I will recapitulate everything that I have said thus far about the settlements of Upper Louisiana. The entire population of all ages and colors, both sexes, free and slave consists of 3,900 persons. They possess 4,600 head of cattle and 815 horses; they harvest annually 26,700 bushels of wheat, 32,600 bushels of maize, and 21,800 pounds of tobacco, and produce 120,000 pounds of lead and nearly 4,200 bushels of salt. My figures tend to be generous rather than lean.[129]

These products are the essential base upon which must be calculated the revenues of Upper Louisiana and the fortunes of its colonists. Over and above these products, all the settlements in the Illinois Country supply themselves, in greater or lesser degree, [71] with those that I enumerated when describing St. Louis. In addition,

128. The official Spanish census of 1796 (SRM, 2:142–43) listed the total population in St. Charles as 405 souls, near Finiels' number. However, in the case of wheat and maize harvests, Finiels' figures (presumably from 1797) are dramatically lower than the census of 1796. As suggested above (see notes 56 and 64), the disparity between Finiels' figures and those of the census may be because of the severe flood of 1797, which had a grave impact upon the harvests.

129. It must be remembered that Finiels was presenting statistics from the late 1790s and not from 1803, when he was drafting this document in New Orleans. In 1804, Amos Stoddard (Sketches, 226) estimated that there were 9,020 whites in Upper Louisiana and 1,320 blacks. Whatever the accuracy of these figures, it is apparent that the population of the region was growing very rapidly around the turn of the nineteenth century. Americans accounted for most of this increase. The following figures for Spanish Upper Louisiana are from the official census of 1796 (SRM, 2:142–43): human population, 3,083; cattle, 3,863; horses, 618; wheat harvest (bushels), 35,065; maize harvest (bushels), 75,418; tobacco harvest (pounds), 24,750; lead production (pounds), 219,000; salt production (bushels), 1,450. None of these figures is very precise, but salt production seems particularly inaccurate for 1796, given the facts that Finiels reports 4,200 bushels for 1797 and that the census of 1795 (SRM, 1:326) showed 5,900 bushels.

maple sugar is produced in some of these settlements, principally St. Charles. Some families gather enough for their annual needs, but it has not yet become a commercial item. This sugar could be easily gathered in large quantities, and, because of the ease with which maple trees can be grown in the Illinois Country, they should soon be cultivated as a special crop. It would have difficulty competing with cane sugar, however, for it has a disagreeable taste and is only acceptable for lack of better sugar. Perhaps refining will remedy this problem. This would be easy enough to try, for the refinery established three years ago in New Orleans has the means to do it.[130]

Before going further, we can calculate rather precisely the annual value of everything produced in the Illinois Country. These products are naturally not for export, except for some lead and salt. They are consumed in the region, and sometimes there is not even enough to go around—when Ste. Genevieve or some of the settlements in the United States on the other side of the river lose their harvests to flood waters.

26,700 bushels of wheat @ $2.00 per bushel $53,400.00
32,600 bushels of maize @ 4 escalins per bushel 16,300.00
21,800 pounds of tobacco @ 15 sous per pound 3,270.00
4,200 minots of salt @ $1.00 per bushel 4,200.00
120,000 pounds of lead @ 5 sous per pound 6,000.00
                                                                        $83,170.00

But the fur trade—that branch of Upper Louisiana's economy that is considered so productive—adds but little to the feeble production: 32,000 piastres [dollars] at most, as I shall prove further on.

Therefore $83,170.00
                                                                        32,000.00
Makes $115,170.00

A total of 115,170 piastres, of which 40,000 descend annually to New Orleans.[131]

130. There were persistent hopes in Upper Louisiana of turning maple syrup into an item of commercial importance. Many *sucreries* outside the villages did produce fine syrup, but never in sufficient quantity to make it an important item of commerce.

131. At the end of the colonial era the currency equivalents in Spanish Louisiana were as follows: the Spanish piastre or peso was equal to one American dollar; the Spanish escalin or real was worth one-eighth of a piastre; and the sou equaled one-hundredth of a piastre or dollar. Finiels' estimate of the value of the fur trade in Upper Louisiana is much too low. In this passage, for example, he states that the entire fur trade of Upper Louisiana was worth only 32,000 piastres, yet a bit further in his account he states that the trade with just the Osage tribes was worth 24,000 piastres. Fur prices fluctuated substantially in colonial Louisiana from year to year, especially during the war-wracked years of the French Revolution and the Napoleonic era. In addition, the vast majority of Upper Louisiana's furs were marketed by British firms in Canada rather than by mercantile houses in New Orleans. The unpredictability of fur prices and the local preference for the northern trading outlets may have caused Finiels to understate the value of Upper Louisiana's fur trade. Drawing upon information supplied him by the Chouteaus, Amos Stoddard reported that the average annual value of furs brought to St. Louis during the 1790s was $203,750 (*Sketches of Louisiana,* 297–98).

[72] A tabulation of the population of the Illinois Country does not offer results that are any more impressive than those of its revenues. Of the 3,900 individuals that its settlements sustain, one must subtract:

slaves[132]	700
women of all ages	1,250
older males	200
male children	500
Total	2,650

Thus you are left with 1,250 persons able to bear arms.[133] This constitutes a feeble resource for defending so vast a region, and it is even more feeble because it would have to be distributed over several areas, which would either have to be contested with an enemy or abandoned to destruction if you chose to concentrate your forces in order to defend a single place.

This brief perspective is discouraging, I admit. But it would not be impossible for the government of a powerful nation—if it has the will—to derive better results from this fine region. As I continue my examination of the colony, the means to accomplish this will perhaps become apparent. Now I am going to continue my description that was interrupted by the preceding tabulations, into which I was drawn by circumstances.

Before taking a look at the Missouri, I must call your attention to the part of the Illinois Country that belongs to the United States of America.[134] The American part, which only the [Mississippi] river separates from Spanish territory, was the root from which the Spanish part grew, but now it is dependent on the other side. Due to its location just across from the Spanish settlements, it will continue to have a profound influence on their prosperity. By origins, customs, and sentiments the American inhabitants on both sides of the river are bonded together, although they are ruled by different governments. The same blood flows in the veins of a majority [73] of the families, who are almost all related to one another; their needs and vulnerabilities draw them still closer together. They are two fragile reeds that sustain one another in order to resist the storm, which would soon have uprooted them if they had been left alone and isolated from one another.

132. Since the early days of French Illinois, black slaves had from time to time borne arms. There was in fact a cause célèbre over this issue in colonial Ste. Genevieve (see Ekberg, *Ste. Genevieve,* 348–49). A European-trained officer such as Finiels did not wish to consider the possibility of arming slaves in order to defend Spanish Louisiana.

133. For persons enumerated in the Spanish colonial census, see note 32 above.

134. American Illinois was a part of the Northwest Territory until 1800, when it was included in the newly created Indiana Territory. Illinois Territory was established independently of Indiana in 1809.

AMERICAN ILLINOIS

When you ascend the [Mississippi] river from the mouth of the Ohio to the Illinois Country, you round the upper point of Anse à Bois Brulé [Bois Brule Bend] to find yourself abreast the mouth of the Kaskaskia River. The lands on the left bank of the river from the mouth of the Ohio up to the Isles à la Course are low and covered with trees, shrubs, and weeds; they are fertile and suitable for agriculture. In the hinterland, hills rise here and there. Near the Isles à la Course, bluffs approach the river's bank, and from there up to the Isle à Roinsa they periodically advance and recede from the shoreline, remaining close to it all the way to the mouth of the Kaskaskia River. At that point they proceed up the left bank of that river five leagues in a northwesterly direction. The Kaskaskia River intersects them as it changes course, but they continue for another six or seven leagues to the north-north-west, where they swing back toward the north, remaining a league to a league and a quarter distant from the Mississippi. They do not draw closer than a league to the river until you are past the mouth of the Missouri.

The land between the bluffs and the Mississippi, from the mouth of the Kaskaskia River to [74] the mouth of the Missouri, is a fine low plain almost twenty-five leagues long. It is dotted with woods, prairies, brooks, and ponds that caught the attention of the French who settled in the Illinois Country. The fertility of this land could be the basis for immeasurable productivity if it were protected from the river's floods. The Kaskaskia, Peoria, Michigamea, and Cahokia tribes, attracted by the richness of the soil and abundance of wild game, lived here. There is no trace of these warrior tribes except for the tombs of their forefathers that are scattered here and there on the plain, which for eons was the peaceful witness to their happiness. The tombs are shaped like little rounded hills, as if to protect their venerable bones from the waters. Until now these peaceful refuges, raised by filial piety, have been respected. They attest to the universal empire of the first sacred law of nature—so religiously observed by the most barbarous nations, and so neglected by civilized peoples—which is love, respect, and gratitude for our respectable forebears. Kaskaskia was the first town founded by the French in this region.[135] Its name came from the river, and it was located on the right bank two leagues from the mouth facing the hills that border the left bank. On one of the hills facing the town a small fort was raised in order to impress the Indians, but it has since disappeared. The settlement was governed by Jesuit missionaries, and they

135. Finiels has things a little confused in this paragraph. Cahokia, founded in 1699, was the first permanent settlement in the French Illinois Country. Kaskaskia, founded in 1703, took its name (as did the river) from the Kaskaskia Indians, who abandoned their villages on the upper Illinois River near Starved Rock and migrated south with the French Jesuit missionaries at the turn of the eighteenth century. For good surveys of these issues, see Mary Borgia Palm, *Jesuit Missions in the Illinois Country, 1673-1763*; Alvord, *The Illinois Country*, 115-33; and Natalia M. Belting, *Kaskaskia Under the French Regime*, 7-23.

succeeded in giving it a certain [75] grandeur that is not yet forgotten.[136] The town was well-built then, and most of the residences were made of stone. The soil fulfilled the expectations of the farmers, hunting was excellent, and a number of fortunes were amassed upon these two foundations. The missionaries who made the colony prosper did not neglect morality, and you can still perceive vestiges of the religious spirit that they inculcated in these isolated settlers, whose imaginations had to be stimulated in order to make them forget their bitter isolation. For a long while the Illinois Country was celebrated for the gentle, peaceful disposition of its inhabitants, for their honesty, their simple customs, and the warm welcome they offered to strangers. From Kaskaskia settlements pushed out onto the plain, and as the Indian tribes atrophied, the French progressively occupied the land. The fort and town of Chartres, Prairie du Rocher, St. Philippe, Prairie du Pont, and Cahokia sprang up to grace the plain; Ste. Genevieve rose on the other side of the river; St. Louis then followed, and within the last twenty years all of the other settlements that now surround the capital of the Illinois Country.

In this way the population of Upper Louisiana developed, and at this time I do not need to present [76] any more details. However, the dissemination did not occur without weakening the original settlements, which could scarcely maintain themselves. The village of Chartres was abandoned; St. Philippe suffered nearly the same fate; Prairie du Rocher stagnated; Cahokia, the largest community after Kaskaskia, also sustained losses. The suppression of the Jesuits was also damaging, and the loss of Canada was the last blow to this part of the Illinois Country.[137] The right bank [of the Mississippi] then assumed predominance over the left bank, and many families moved to that bank, which remained French. Kaskaskia, Cahokia, Prairie du Rocher became deserts, and St. Philippe was left with only two or three families.[138] When the United States achieved independence, the Americans took possession of merely the ruins of what had been the Illinois Country. The losses were somewhat compensated for by an influx of American settlers, who replaced the French emigrants. They even

136. Kaskaskia, which served as the first capital for the state of Illinois between 1818 and 1820, was washed away when the Mississippi River changed its course in the 1880s. The remains of old Fort Kaskaskia mentioned by Finiels are a state historic site and can still be seen on the bluffs overlooking the Mississippi. The river also destroyed St. Philippe, and the village of Chartres has likewise disappeared. Vestiges of material culture dating from the colonial period can be found at all of the other village sites mentioned by Finiels.

137. Finiels correctly emphasizes the momentous changes in the Illinois Country during the 1760s in the wake of the suppression of the Jesuits, the withdrawal of the French garrison, and the arrival of their British successors. This story can be found in Alvord, *The Illinois Country,* chaps. 11 and 12, and Clarence E. Carter, *Great Britain and the Illinois Country, 1763-1774.*

138. Finiels' observation that Kaskaskia became a desert during the 1760s is an exaggeration, but substantial numbers of residents did move to the west bank of the Mississippi. For reports of the exodus of French settlers across the river, see Charles Philippe Aubry to the Minister, 12 March 1766, in Alvord and Carter, *The New Regime, 1765-767,* 185; and Capt. Thomas Stirling to Gen. Thomas Gage, 15 December 1765, in ibid., 125-26.

founded new settlements on the uplands [77] and the plain. The country would have been repopulated more rapidly if the crowd of immigrants who came west after the peace of 1783 had not stopped along the banks of the Ohio; there they found immense tracts of fertile land, which were naturally more attractive to them than the remote Illinois Country.[139]

At the present time, the American part possesses about the same population as the Spanish part; it has the same type of agriculture, the same products, and the same paucity of resources.[140] But in addition to this parity, it [the American part] has a real disadvantage—almost all of its settlements are located on the bottomland and are vulnerable to inundations of the river, which often threaten the crops and more than once have destroyed them. Kaskaskia has recovered somewhat and has regained some of its animation; Cahokia has made only feeble progress. In these two villages the French are mixed together with the Americans, but Prairie du Rocher is still inhabited exclusively by Frenchmen. They knew that strangers, with customs and mores so different from theirs, would disrupt [78] their precious tranquility, the peaceful harmony that they enjoyed. Because they own all the arable land surrounding their small village—on the plain as well as on the uplands—they chose not to sell any of their land and have thus kept the Americans at a distance. The French government could rather easily persuade these people to settle on the right bank. The least encouragement could accomplish this, and it would be so much the easier since this has been suggested to them before there was any suspicion that Spanish Illinois was changing governments once again.

The American part constitutes an important component in the whole picture of the Illinois Country. Without it the complexity that makes this region so interesting to the traveler would not exist. It has particular attractions, and their combination provides it with all its charm. The bluffs, which I have already described, offer a [79] most picturesque view of the plain, and from their heights there are delectable vistas and perspectives. In different places, perpendicular masses of rock protrude from these bluffs, which seem from a distance like vast walls covered with terraces; from them long columns of trees appear as if they wished to take flight. Here and there, deep crevasses cut through the bluffs, creating passages for the mountain streams that cross the plain to mingle with those of the river. But it is above the mouth of the Missouri, where the bluffs draw up close to the bank of the Mississippi, that a striking spectacle

139. The 1783 agreement was the Peace of Paris, which formally concluded the American Revolution. With the beginning of the preceding paragraph in the text, there is an unmistakable change in the handwriting of the text. This suggests that Finiels was dictating his copy and that he changed recording secretaries at this point in the document.

140. In 1800, the Indiana Territory, which included American Illinois, had fewer than 6,000 non-Indian inhabitants. The population of Cahokia was 719; Kaskaskia, 467; and Prairie du Rocher, 212. Bellefontaine, the largest Anglo-American settlement in American Illinois, had a population of 286. See Alvord, *The Illinois Country,* 407. Amos Stoddard reported that in 1804 Cahokia contained 120 houses, and about 45 families resided in Kaskaskia (*Sketches,* 232).

meets your eyes. An immense panorama of rocks is deployed along the bank for more than four leagues, after which it disappears at the mouth of the Illinois River. These rocks, which have been given the name Paillissa, attain in several places heights of 130 to 140 feet above the river.[141] Their walls are almost always rounded, and they often appear as a succession of pointed towers that from a distance might be taken for some old, redoubtable fortress. [80] This shape piques the curiosity of the traveler, who is compelled to find a reason for the configuration's uniformity. Undulating hillocks surmount these rocks, sometimes rising thirty to forty feet above their summits. Some of these have massive, ancient trees; others are covered only with grass five or six feet high. It is on these Paillissa heights, near the Illinois River, that you discover the fine perspective that is incomplete from the "breasts" of St. Charles. You can from there admire the confluences of the Mississippi, Missouri, and Illinois rivers, get drunk on an indescribable spectacle, and lose yourself in the profound meditations that it inspires.

This is not the refined nature that we generally see displayed before us in Europe, which embellishes with her most brilliant gifts the spectacle that here strikes our astonished gaze. It has a special quality that nature knows so well how to convey, and vary, and adapt to places and circumstances. In all countries you find rocks heaped up in more or less picturesque fashion, shaped [81] in more or less bizarre forms. But here there is a prevailing tone, a consistency, a certain quality that suggests a great undertaking of which these rocks are only the death's-head. Nature seems to have placed them there only in order to challenge the human mind, inviting you to try to comprehend her. The profound solitude that engulfs you on these heights; the majestic and imposing silence that reigns as the murmuring waters of the Mississippi swirling around the rocks present the only intrusion; the wild and rustic appearance of these summits, which the luminous forest renders even more savage and desolate, darkens thoughts provoked by the spectacle of the rocks. Finally, you feel a need for a diversion from the melancholy notions that grip your imagination; you gaze across the clumps of woods and murmuring waters at your feet. Off in the distance to the southwest a streak of dark blue against the trees reveals the course of the Missouri. Here and there its waters appear through the clearings, and soon, as far as the eye can see, the highlands along its banks are deployed. [82] Returning to the Mississippi, you can follow its waters for a great distance. They recede to the east-southeast, embracing a multitude of islands and twisting every which way to elude the sandbars that seem to want to block them. If you swing your eyes back toward the west and the north, your gaze is consumed by the vast plain that proceeds up the Mississippi from St. Charles; prairies, clumps of woods, ponds, and streams dissect it, and the irregular loops of the river seem to want to imprison it. Moving northward, the left bank

141. Concerning Finiels' use of the word *Paillissa,* see above, note 126. This part of Finiels' account, which was based upon his recollections of the view from the Illinois bluffs, evoked some of his most romantic sentiments.

of the river, which was almost at water level at the mouth of the Illinois, seems to rise up in the distance. To the eye that likes to discern forms, it presents the famous Cap au Grès, which all travelers admire. This dominates the Mississippi eight leagues above the mouth of the Illinois River and graces the American bank for five leagues with a series of rocks just as interesting as those of the Paillissa.[142]

At the crest of Cap au Grès the land descends toward the east and slopes gently toward the Illinois River, which ascends to the northeast. How beautiful, from Paillissa heights, appears the [83] little Illinois River, which is not more than two hundred toises wide during most of its course. Its gentle, voluptuous contours seem to embrace the fine plains that it drains from near Lake Michigan to the Mississippi as it descends, just a feeble stream compared to the two rivers with which it mingles it waters. You might say that nature wished to depict the image of the sweet and peaceful life, which sages spend in repose and in agreeable and eternal calm, in contrast to the frightening scene of a long career continually fraught with excess, violent storms, and passions.

All of American Illinois from the mouth of the Illinois River to more than twenty leagues above it is a good location for settlements that would be [84] very advantageous. The lands between Cap au Grès and the Illinois River are high and as fertile as any in this region; they are drained by numerous streams and creeks, some of which flow into the Illinois and some into the Mississippi. There are vast plains, sometimes covered with fine woods and sometimes with immense pastures. The banks of the Illinois never erode like those of the Mississippi and Missouri, and during high water it is navigable almost all the way to Lake Michigan;[143] during low water, you can ascend about ninety leagues from its mouth. This is the usual route of Illinois traders; they prefer to take their furs to Michilimackinac, where they receive the most in return, and at lower prices than in New Orleans.[144]

No doubt when rumors begin to circulate about the impending return of the French to the Illinois Country, the U.S. Congress will cast anxious glances toward that part of its territory where it has not encouraged much population growth. It will soon begin to sell land, and this [85] will rapidly create a large population on the banks of the Mississippi and Illinois rivers; this deserted area will teem with settlers. France will see a proliferation of settlements across from her that will outflank hers,

---

142. Although Finiels did not label Cap au Grès on his map, he is clearly referring to the bluffs along the east bank of the Mississippi above present-day Pere Marquette State Park in Jersey County, Illinois.

143. In this paragraph, Finiels is obviously referring to the famous Chicago portage between the headwaters of the Illinois River and Lake Michigan. However, another favorite route between the upper Mississippi valley and Lake Michigan was via the Wisconsin and Fox rivers, across present-day Wisconsin. This latter route led to the establishment of the famous trading outpost of Prairie du Chien, on the east bank of the Mississippi just above the mouth of the Wisconsin River.

144. It was a notorious fact that fur traders from St. Louis often preferred to trade with British Canada rather than with Spanish New Orleans (see Foley and Rice, *The First Chouteaus,* 37). On the whole issue of Anglo-Spanish rivalry in Upper Louisiana, see the many authoritative works by Abraham P. Nasatir, including "Trade and Diplomacy in Spanish Illinois, 1763-1792."

extending from the Ohio all the way up the Mississippi to the Falls of St. Anthony.[145] Indiana Territory, which they have recently named this part of the Illinois Country, will be all the more imposing because it will have secure and easy communications with Kentucky. Further on, I will examine the consequences of these settlements; for the moment I return to Missouri.[146]

MISSOURI

The Missouri River is one of the most interesting regions of Spanish Illinois. It could furnish a considerable portion of Upper Louisiana's produce if its great resources were augmented by a one-sixth increase in the fur trade with the Indians who inhabit its banks, and the tribute from the various streams that flow into it from the south, the north, and the west were added. I must address the situation from this perspective.[147]

The Indian trade [86] is an issue of great urgency and competition among the inhabitants of Illinois.[148] It alone has enough sway over them to shake them annually out of the diversions in which they seem to be habitually buried. Hardly has the ice disappeared, freeing traffic on the streams, than large pirogues, light flat-bottomed barges, and birchbark canoes are made ready.[149] Soon they are filled with trade goods, which have become indispensable to the Indians because of their contact with white men. *Engagés* press around these frail vessels; they stretch their arms, which are numb from six months of inactivity, but which soon recover their suppleness, elasticity, and vigor.[150] Farewell songs ring out; paddles whip the waves into a froth, leaving behind a long wake that is quickly swallowed up by the next; a din from the splashing paddles rises in the air to mingle with joyful shouts. The frail vessels finally [87] triumph over the waters; they soon disappear in the winding river and lose themselves in the distance among the islands that intersect their course. White hunt-

145. Minneapolis now stands at the Falls of St. Anthony.

146. As previously noted, the Indiana Territory was created in 1800. Finiels was correct in predicting that the United States government would begin to sell public land in the Illinois area, but it did not begin to do so until 1814, after the land claims of the older residents had been resolved and Illinois Territory had been carved out of the Indiana Territory (1809). See Alvord, *The Illinois Country,* 453–55.

147. There is a substantial literature on the fur trade of the Missouri valley during the late colonial era. A recent work dealing with that subject is Foley and Rice, *The First Chouteaus.* A convenient bibliography on this subject may be found in W. Raymond Wood and Thomas D. Thiessen, eds., *Early Fur Trade on the Northern Plains.* Among the various source materials available, Nasatir's *Before Lewis and Clark* is indispensable.

148. The standard works on the American fur trade are Hiram M. Chittenden, *The American Fur Trade of the Far West;* Paul C. Phillips, *The Fur Trade;* Harold A. Innis, *The Fur Trade in Canada.*

149. Finiels' reference to birchbark canoes ("canots d'ecorce de bouleau") may be the earliest mention of this sort of vessel being used in the Missouri River fur trade.

150. *Engagés* were men hired (i.e., "engaged") for fixed terms, usually one to three years, to work at the tasks specified in their contracts of engagement. These contracts, of which there are thousands in various depositories, often pertain to fur-trading operations, but also deal with numerous other sorts of labor-intensive activities, such as lead mining.

ers usually get a jump on the season; they preempt the ice and spend the winter on the streams that they think will offer the best hunting. Sometimes they go it alone; often they join Indians with whom they have cultivated friendships and hunt with them. Some of them trade their booty right on the spot; others take it back to their village, or ascend the Illinois River and trade at Michilimackinac for merchandise that arrives every year from Canada.

Some *habitants* have obtained the exclusive right to go to certain Indian tribes, while other tribes may be visited by all traders.[151] Ambition, and a certain ancient inclination that the Illinois settlements have to be entirely devoted to hunting and trading, means that each year a crowd of traders visits the Indian tribes. Their exertions and fatigues are incredible, and often they find themselves frustrated of their fondest hope. [88] Despite their efforts they might arrive too late, or the Indians will have had bad luck hunting, or they will be indisposed. Mistreated, the *habitants* are compelled to make bad business deals, but nothing discourages them. The fur trade in Illinois has the same allure as the mines in Peru and Mexico: everyone wishes to profit from it, but no one thinks through the means to do it; no one weighs the disadvantages against the dubious results. It is pursued up rivers that bristle with difficulties, dangers, and pitfalls; it is pursued across deserted and waste regions. It is like a miner hot on the trail of uncertain veins that he follows into the bowels of the earth, at the risk of perishing a thousand times should the perilous route, which he has had the audacity to chart in his head, collapse.

But let us not anticipate the thoughts that this subject brings to mind; they will fit in naturally after we have described the arena of so much struggle and effort. For some time now, the English have been attempting to vanquish us by overcoming unbelievable obstacles [89] and by trying to shroud their success in shadows of impenetrable mystery.

The Missouri empties into the Mississippi from the right bank at 39 degrees north latitude, nearly four and a half leagues above the city of St. Louis. First it ascends to the west some leagues from its mouth and then turns sharply south at Anse à Philippe. At that point it again heads west up past the Osage River, from where it tends a bit northward up to the mouth of the Platte River. There it begins to head more directly northwestward, running between 47 degrees and 48 degrees north latitude and approximately 111 degrees west of the London [Greenwich] meridian up to the point occupied by the Mandan Indians. There the river heads a bit more northward [actually, westward] and approaches the Rocky Mountains, in the midst of which all

151. The Spanish colonial government required all traders to be licensed. Theoretically, the commerce was open to all Spanish subjects, but in practice the licensing requirement limited the actual number of participants to a favored few whom the Spaniards used as quasi-governmental agents. By tradition the lieutenant governor in Upper Louisiana reserved a portion of the trade for himself, and the common practice of granting licenses to the highest bidder permitted a small number of influential traders to monopolize the most lucrative trading positions. Despite periodic attempts to liberalize Spanish trading policies, the closed system generally prevailed throughout the colonial era.

Indians agree is its source, which has been explored by no European. The map of this river that I drafted in 1798 based on the memoranda of Messieurs Mackay and Evans gives a very precise rendering of the section of the river that is best known at this time.[152] [90] The Mandan tribes are located at the edge of this region, but these tribes are more than five hundred leagues from St. Louis, and the area between the mouth of the river and their settlements could provide an immense region for lucrative commerce. It will become a source of abundant harvests that will require the government's most serious attention, both in order to maximize profits and so as not to lose any of its products.

What I am recounting here about the Missouri is based upon reports of traders who travel it every year. Among them there are always some intelligent persons, observant persons, who can render an exact account of what they have seen. I have assembled as many of these reports as possible, carefully compared them, scrutinized them closely, rejected all those that seemed untrue, and accepted only those whose internal consistency gave me a clear opinion about what had been seen firsthand.[153]

Thirty leagues above the mouth of the Missouri, reckoning that distance through the river's numerous twists and turns, [91] you arrive at the Gasconade River flowing in from the right bank. This is the first river of consequence one meets after leaving the Mississippi. Before coming to this river, you pass numerous small streams and bayous on both banks; they are of little consequence, and most of them have no names. The rivers are the Bon Homme on the right bank at Anse à Philippe, the Femme Osage on the left bank, the Dubois on the right bank, the Tuque [Togue Creek] and the Choret [Wolf Creek], which are close together on the left bank, and the Berger on the right bank. Above the last you find a large island, La Pensée, which creates, between itself and the left bank, a narrow channel of the same name that is more than five leagues long. The Rivière à la Outre empties in about the middle of the channel, and there are also two bayous, one on either end of the channel.[154]

A league above this channel on the right bank is the mouth of the Gasconade River.[155] The Missouri's course, from its mouth up to [92] this point, is littered with islands of various sizes, sandbars, and fallen trees and stumps, all of which make navigation very difficult. Some claim that the Gasconade River is navigable with

152. Finiels again acknowledges his role in the preparation of the Mackay-Evans Map, but he changes the year from 1797 to 1798. See note 118 above. John T. Evans, who, along with Mackay, provided the information upon which the map was based, was a Welshman who came to North America in 1792 in search of a supposed tribe of Welsh Indians said to be inhabiting the American wilderness. In 1795, he signed on with Mackay as a member of the expedition dispatched up the Missouri by the Missouri Company. See Nasatir's "John T. Evans."

153. Nasatir's long introduction to *Before Lewis and Clark* provides a splendid account of the numerous traders from Spanish Illinois who had ascended the Missouri River during the eighteenth century.

154. Most of the streams mentioned in this paragraph have kept their French names as given by Finiels. His island of La Pensée is probably what is now called Rush Island; the Loutre River flows into the Missouri from the north just above the island.

155. *Gasconades* being tall stories told by the Gascons, it would seem that the name of this river derived from the deceptive character of its mouth, which seduced *voyageurs* by its tranquil appearance.

hunting canoes for more than sixty leagues from its mouth. I scarcely believe it, however, for that river, which is barely twenty-five or thirty toises wide, is filled with rapids for almost its entire length. I presume that if its appearance at its mouth persuades you to ascend it, you would soon become discouraged by the difficulties of the constant rapids and that its name derives from the frustration of shattered hopes. Moreover, that river is not inhabited by any Indian tribe; it is thus useless for trading purposes, and the only interest one might have in ascending it is the hope of finding cedar. This wood is becoming very rare in the Illinois Country because of the enormous consumption since the settlements began and because of the recklessness with which it was destroyed around the settlements. [93] Several of the small rivers that I've mentioned still offer this wood, which is precious because of its durability.[156] But they are difficult to ascend, and it is even more difficult to fetch the logs out to the settlements on the Mississippi.

Ascending ten leagues above the mouth of the Gasconade, a group of five small islands announces the arrival of the Osage River, whose mouth appears just after passing the islands. In this stretch you pass by the Rivière à Monbrun, the Grande and Petite Rivière aux Vases, and the Sandstone and Bear rivers. These, as well as the two or three bayous appearing on either side of the river, are all of small consequence.[157]

The Osage River is large and important because of the trade that is conducted with the Indian tribe from which its name is taken. It is about the same width as the Illinois River, and it ascends 110 to 120 leagues westward from the Missouri. However, it is in fact much longer than that because of the multitude of twists and turns and because of the large radius of its bends.[158]

The Big Osage village, [94] which is only 60 leagues from its mouth as the crow flies, is 115 leagues by river.[159] Portaging, which could lessen the distance, is not practical during the season when you ascend this river, for the banks are low and swampy. The largest of the bends might be avoided by creating a channel between Gravois Creek and a bayou that empties into the Osage River above the big

156. The French Creole practice in the Illinois Country of constructing their houses with palisaded exterior walls and encircling their residential properties with palisaded fences drove up the price of cedar, which is rot-resistant even when in contact with the soil. In the 1790s, cedar was worth three times as much as oak in the Illinois Country (see Ekberg, *Colonial Ste. Genevieve*, 284–85). Finiels' observation that the Gasconade might become an important source of timber proved to be remarkably prescient. In 1819, Major S. H. Long noted that several sawmills along that stream were already supplying settlements on the Missouri with lumber (*Account of an Expedition from Pittsburgh to the Rocky Mountains*, vol. 14 in *Early Western Travels*, ed. Reuben G. Thwaite, 136–37).

157. Some of the streams mentioned in this paragraph now have different names, but Auxvasse Creek and Little Auxvasse Creek still enter the Missouri from the north, just below the mouth of the Osage River. On the meaning of *aux Vases,* see above, note 38.

158. A comprehensive recent study of the Osages is Willard H. Rollings, "Prairie Hegemony: An Ethnohistorical Study of the Osage from Early Times to 1840." For an account of Spanish-Osage relations, see also Gilbert C. Din and Abraham P. Nasatir, *The Imperial Osages,* which contains a comprehensive bibliography of both primary and secondary materials on the Osages.

159. For the location of the Osage villages, see Carl H. Chapman, "The Indomitable Osage in Spanish Illinois (Upper Louisiana), 1763–1804."

rapids.[160] This route would be only 5 leagues long and would cut 20 off the river route. Many points might also be eliminated by using very small canals, several of which already exist in the Mississippi; but such work could be undertaken only after more thought and after weighing the costs against the potential real benefits.

Although much narrower than the Missouri in width, [95] the Osage River, from its mouth up to the Little Turkey Creek (approximately 70 leagues), is strewn with islands and sandbars; there are several rapids, and in some places rocks that could be dangerous.[161] Numerous bayous and small rivers flow into the Osage and considerably enlarge it. The Rivière à Marie [Maries River], two leagues above its mouth on the right bank, is the first of these. Then you ascend 20 leagues and pass only three small bayous. Next, Little Saline Creek comes up on the left bank after Roche DeBout [Standing Rock]. Then, successively, Gravois and Little Gravois creeks, Grand Glaize Creek, Niangua Creek, Rainy Creek, the Vermillon, the Grande Rivière, the Pomme de Terre, Turkey Creek, Brush Creek, the Bois Blanc, Angry Creek, La Fourche, the Manigua [Monegaw], the Pichard, and finally the Little Osage River on the left bank.[162] Facing the mouth of the last, a quarter of a league inland, is the Big Osage village. This is a bit above the new Fort Carondelet, which was built eight years ago by Monsieur Auguste Chouteau, who then possessed exclusive trading rights with the Big [96] Osages.[163] Two leagues further inland, close to the left bank of the Rivière du Champ des Marmitons [Marmaton River], which also flows into the Osage River from its right bank, is the Little Osage village, whose trading rights are combined with those of the Big Osage village.

These two tribes constitute a group of about 1,200 men.[164] The river upon which they have lived for a long time bears their name. The Osages are not the best hunters, but they have acquired through war and their substantial numbers a reputation that intimidates the weaker neighboring tribes. They are generally strong, tall, and robust, but cruel, untrustworthy, and troublesome. Each year their hunt takes them

160. Much of Gravois Creek is now part of the Lake of the Ozarks, but before the creation of the lake, the creek flowed into the Osage River at Horseshoe Bend in Morgan County. The large bends mentioned by Finiels are now called Horseshoe and Shawnee bends.

161. Little Turkey Creek flows into the Osage River near the upper end of Lake of the Ozarks in Benton County.

162. Although Finiels does not have all of the tributaries of the Osage River enumerated in precisely the correct order, his listing is generally accurate, and many of the names are still the same, or least similar enough to be identifiable.

163. Halley's Bluff in Vernon County appears to have been the site of the long-lost Fort Carondelet. See Chapman, "The Indomitable Osage," 300–307. The story of the Osages, Chouteau, and Fort Carondelet can be found in Din and Nasatir, The Imperial Osages, 255–90, and Foley and Rice, The First Chouteaus, 46–64.

164. Finiels' estimate of 1,200 men in the two Osage tribes is the same as that given by the lieutenant governor of Upper Louisiana, Zenon Trudeau, in 1798. See Trudeau to Gayoso de Lemos, 15 January 1798, in BLC, 2:539. They may have been relying on the same sources, or perhaps one of them got his information from the other. The Osages were universally viewed as the most intractable of the Indian tribes in Spanish Illinois. Auguste Chouteau and his brother Pierre were particularly adept in their relations with the Osages; see Foley and Rice, The First Chouteaus.

up the Arkansas and St. Francis rivers, into the hinterlands behind Cape Girardeau
and New Madrid. Their hunts are notorious for their more or less outrageous depredations, which injure these various settlements a great deal. As swift afoot as deer,
which they track in the hunt, [97] the Osages never spot a loose horse without feeling
a passionate desire to steal it. This is despite the fact that they have repeatedly promised most solemnly to respect the property of whites. They disdain depending upon
the strength and speed of these animals by fleeing on their backs; rather, they run
behind the horses, spurring them on with their own speed, and soon they are both
beyond pursuit by whites. From time out of mind, the Indians have made springtime
the season for war. It is the season to savor the vengeance that seems to slumber in
their breasts during the rest of the year. They are peaceable during hunting season,
harvest season, and their periods of rest in the villages; no passions seem to inflame
them; their souls seem to be completely at ease. Then, hardly does spring arrive,
before the yeast of hate, fury, and vengeance begins to ferment in their blood. They
tremble with impatience and the need to shed human blood; they gather around [98]
various chieftains; they fan out through forests and across deserted plains; they take
to the waterways to find distant enemies and strike them down. The Osages
rigorously maintain the traits characteristic of almost all the Indian tribes; despite the
efforts that have been made to weaken them, they continue to make the European
settlements uneasy. Only seven or eight years ago Monsieur Auguste Chouteau was
able to provide some relief for these settlements. He succeeded in acquiring influence
with the Osages that contained them while he traded with them. Since then, this trade
has passed into less able hands, less skilled at managing savage minds, and they have
already returned to harassing the Illinois Country.

In the best years, the Osage tribes produce 600 bundles of peltries at 100 pounds
apiece. In the Illinois Country a pound of pelts has a fixed and unchanging value of
forty sous without consideration of [99] fluctuations at New Orleans. The 600 bundles are therefore worth 24,000 piastres, which is the most ever made in trade with
the two Osage tribes.[165]

Seventy leagues above the mouth of the Osage River, the Kansas River flows in
from the right bank of the Missouri. After the Osage, the Kansas is the first river up
which trade may be conducted with the Indians. Along this 70-league section, the
Rivière à la Mine [Lamine River] comes into the Missouri from the right bank 20
leagues above the Osage; next, the Rivière Chératon [Chariton River] comes in from
the left bank 5 leagues above the Lamine; then the Grand arrives, also from the left
bank, 9 leagues above the Chariton; and, finally, from the right bank Prairie Fire
Creek comes in 26 leagues above the Grand. This substantial distance is deserted, and
although crossed by three very navigable rivers, the Grand in particular, no Indian

165. Once again Finiels' statistics agree exactly with those of Lieutenant Governor Zenon Trudeau
(*BLC*, 2:539). Since bundles of furs weighed 100 pounds and pelts were valued at 40 sous per pound, a
bundle of pelts was worth 40 piastres (dollars).

tribe has chosen to settle there. This is no special advantage, however, because the lands are vast, high prairies. These are more appropriate for wild, nomadic animals than for human settlements, [100] and humans would find nothing in the area to satisfy their indispensable needs.

The Kansas is a fine river and is navigable for more than 100 leagues into the hinterland. Forty leagues from its mouth its banks are quite wooded; the remainder of its course crosses only high prairies, whose soil is generally good and suitable for agriculture. The Kansas' village is located eight leagues from the mouth of the river that carries their name. This tribe consists of approximately 400 warriors; they are reputed to be better hunters than the Osages and just as fearsome if judged by the pillaging that they would conduct as far as Illinois if the distance were not so great. Hunting used to take them over to the Arkansas River along with the Osages, but the latter have by force turned that area into an exclusive preserve and will not permit them to enter it. The Kansas would perhaps range even more widely there than the Osages, [101] for they have never been constrained by the same limits.[166]

The Kansas are the only Indians in Missouri for which there is no exclusive trade license. It is shared by the merchants of St. Louis and Ste. Genevieve and is divided on a predetermined basis. This demonstrates the necessity of regulating that type of commerce and shows the disadvantages of leaving things to chance. Each year the total trade is divided into six lots. Then there is a drawing by all the merchants of both towns, and those who obtain a lot are excluded from the next year's drawing until each of the others has received a lot. The merchants all contribute an equal share of the trading equipment. Experience has shown that this association is basically nothing more than an exclusive company, even though trade with that tribe appears to be unrestricted.

In the best of times, the Kansas supply no more [102] than 180 bundles of peltries each year. This amount, according to the price I quoted when speaking of the Osage trade, returns only 7,200 piastres. The most that any one of the merchants can accumulate after waiting several years is 30 bundles or 1,200 piastres. This is not much, if you consider that a pound of peltries is sometimes worth only 30 or 32 sous in New Orleans, which often equals the profit that can be made with Indian trade goods that are transported so far and at so great an expense.[167]

Seventy-five leagues above the Kansas River, the famous Platte River flows into the Missouri from the right bank. This river is as wide as the Missouri, and it could easily fool a navigator if he did not know that the latter descends from the northwest. The Platte is not very deep and flows over a bed of sand, gravel, and often rocks; its

166. Again, Finiels' numbers in this paragraph and the two following are the same as those cited in Trudeau's letter of 15 January 1798. The best account of the Kansas Indians is William Unrau, *The Kansas Indians: A History of the Wind People, 1763–1873*.
167. Finiels continues to evaluate peltries at the fixed price of 40 piastres per bundle (i.e., 40 sous per pound) in Upper Louisiana.

swiftness makes it difficult to ascend. Its watershed consists of low-lying prairies that are very fertile. Some leagues from it, [103] small hills rise on both banks. There the high prairies begin, and they offer no hope of productive agriculture.[168]

Three tribes are located near the Platte River. Close to its confluence with the Missouri, the Ottoctatas [Otos] occupy the river bank, and their village overlooks the river's mouth.[169] This tribe is said to have 400 warriors, who are known for their bravery and skill as hunters. Twenty-five leagues above the mouth of the Platte River you find the village of the Grand Pawnees, which has 800 warriors.[170] This tribe does not possess the courage of the Ottoctatas; they are weak and effeminate. The rigors of the hunt are beyond their strength, which has been sapped by sloth and a sedentary lifestyle; they produce virtually no pelts.

Five leagues above this village of sybaritic savages, the Rivière des Loup [Loup River] flows into the Platte from the left bank. The Panimaha [Skidi-Pawnee] tribe lives on its banks. It has 600 warriors, who are [104] redoubtable in war; they are a poor resource for trading purposes, however, and are almost as inept at hunting as the Grand Pawnees.

Eighty leagues above the mouth of the Platte River is the Mahas' [Omahas'] village, and seventy leagues further upstream that of the Poncas.[171] The Maha tribe can raise 600 warriors. They are both warriors and huntsmen; they are ferocious; and they are governed despotically by a chief, who is as cruel as he is barbarous. His tyranny extends to the whites who trade in that region. His dominion over his tribe is based upon methods that all tyrants make use of in order to subjugate ignorant and naive peoples. Numa used them to make the Romans happy, but how many fierce men must also endure the chains that they employ in order to control their blind subjects! This Indian chief seems to have had in his hands the power of life and death; all who resisted him were struck down as Mahomet struck [105] down Leida and

168. The mouth of the Platte River was generally considered to be the line of demarcation between the upper and lower Missouri. According to Finiels' calculations in this document, the mouth of the Platte River was about 185 leagues above the mouth of the Missouri. The Soulard map of 1795 (reproduced in Moulton, *Atlas of the Lewis and Clark Expedition,* map no. 4) shows this distance as 250 leagues. Jean-Baptiste Truteau's memoir of 1796 (*BLC,* 2:378) gives the distance as 200 leagues. James Mackay's table of distances up the Missouri done in 1797 (ibid., 489) showed the distance as 171¼ leagues. The disparity between Finiels' figure and Mackay's is a bit puzzling since it would seem that Finiels relied heavily on information collected from Mackay, who had traveled the Missouri River in person. Finally, William Clark reckoned the distance from the mouth of the Missouri to the mouth of the Platte as 210 leagues (Reuben G. Thwaites, ed., *Original Journals of Lewis and Clark,* 6:5).

169. The Otos were of the Siouan linguistic family (John R. Swanton, *The Indian Tribes of North America,* 287), whereas the Pawnees were of the Caddoan linguistic stock and closely related to the Arikaras (ibid., 273, 289). Information about their village on the Platte River probably came from Jean-Baptiste Truteau.

170. The population figures for various Indian tribes given in this and the following two paragraphs are the same as those in Zenon Trudeau's letter (cited above, note 164).

171. The Mahas, or Omahas, were, like the Otos and Poncas, part of the Siouan linguistic family. See Alice C. Fletcher and Francis La Flesche, *The Omaha Tribe;* James H. Howard, *The Ponca Tribe.*

Palmyra.[172] The Mahas set aside a certain day for the destruction of anyone who was brave enough to question his power. A subtle poison, cleverly poured into the food of the unfortunate proscribed person, ensured that the chief's prophecy was fulfilled.[173] Several such assassinations lent credence to his claim that he be regarded as a terrible deity, and since then he has been obeyed as if he were one.

The Ponca village contains only 400 warriors. This tribe spends its time hunting, and its customs are less harsh than those of the Mahas.[174]

Trade with these five tribes was consolidated and conveyed as an exclusive privilege to a company that was created nine years ago in St. Louis, which was called "The Trading Company of the Upper Missouri."[175] This company was not supposed to confine itself to trade with the five tribes that I have just described. Its goal, with the concurrence of the government, was to penetrate as far as possible up the Missouri in order to trade with the tribes whose names were unknown and whose very existence was [106] uncertain.[176] High hopes were especially pinned on the Mandans, who were rumored to have contacts with the English from Canada. They were supposed to be located 600 leagues from St. Louis, and trade with them was going to be all the more lucrative because of their location. It was sincerely hoped that through them fine peltries—more precious and valuable that those coming from the lower Missouri— would be discovered. With this in mind, the company made enormous efforts to reach them.[177]

172. Numa Pompilius, the second king of Rome (traditionally 715–673 B.C.), was "probably a historical figure, although most of the reforms ascribed to him were the result of a very long process of religious and cultural development" (*The Oxford Classical Dictionary*, 2d ed., 741). According to tradition, he claimed that he was inspired directly by the gods. Leida (Lydda), in Palestine, and Palmyra, in Syria, were cities that may have resisted Moslem power during the seventh century, but Finiels' reference here is uncharacteristically arcane. Finiels was not a pedant, but occasionally he liked to demonstrate that he had a classical education in the best upper-class tradition of the eighteenth century.

173. Poisoning among the Plains Indian tribes was not confined to the Omahas. On this interesting topic, see Annie Heloise Abel, ed., and Rose Abel Wright, trans., *Tabeau's Narrative of Loisel's Expedition to the Upper Missouri*, 136, note 105.

174. Trudeau's letter cited above does not provide a figure for the number of warriors in the Ponca tribe. Perrin du Lac's account from 1802 (*BLC*, 2:706) credits the Poncas with 300 warriors. The Poncas were of the Siouan linguistic family, as were the Mandans, who lived further up the Missouri (Swanton, *Indian Tribes*, 291).

175. Jacques Clamorgan was a driving force in the creation of the Company of Explorers of the Upper Missouri, commonly called the Missouri Company. In 1794 and 1795, the Missouri Company dispatched three major trading expeditions up the Missouri to initiate trade with tribes along the river's upper reaches. None succeeded financially, but the final one, the Mackay-Evans expedition, yielded dividends in the form of important new information about the upper Missouri country, some of which Finiels utilized in the preparation of this manuscript.

176. In this section, Finiels obviously drew upon Trudeau's letter to Gayoso dated 15 January 1798 (*BLC*, 2:539–40). For information concerning the founding of the Missouri Company, see *BLC*, 1:84–92, and also Nasatir's "The Formation of the Missouri Company."

177. For general information about the upper Missouri tribes, see George Peter Murdock and Timothy J. O'Leary, *Ethnographic Bibliography of North America*, 5:1–162; Roy W. Meyer, *The Village Indians of the Upper Missouri: The Mandans, Hidatsas, and Arikaras;* Frank H. Stewart, "Mandan and Hidatsa Villages in the Eighteenth and Nineteenth Centuries"; and Wood and Thiessen, *Early Fur Trade on the*

These attempts met the same fate as all those that pursue unknown trails without having reckoned the difficulties and costs. Equipment that might have produced good profits with the known tribes was absorbed by the scale of the project and by the sacrifices necessary to conciliate new tribes and establish new outposts. The company soon went broke, but its disaster provided us with our best information about the upper Missouri. These merchants, [107] motivated by greed to pursue their own interests, wished to accomplish for the colony what the government should have done before them. The company would then have had the data to calculate its operations more advantageously, and both government and company would indisputably have been able to reap the profits that they had promised each other. I'll return later to the company's operations, and we'll see how the fur trade has collapsed in the settlements of the Illinois Country.

Ten leagues above the Poncas comes the White River, and 70 leagues further on the Cheyenne River.[178] Sixty-five leagues above the latter you find the Cannon Ball River, and 35 leagues beyond that the village of the Ricaras.[179] This is the first tribe since leaving the Poncas, a distance of 180 leagues, and it is settled on the banks of the Missouri. Ten leagues above the Ricaras you find the Mandans and their allies.[180] This point, according to the best reckoning of *voyageurs,* is 540 leagues above the mouth of the Missouri. Thus the trip from St. Louis to the Mandans can scarcely be accomplished [108] in less than three and a half months in the best of circumstances, and usually requires more than four. On the basis of several trips, it has been determined that you can barely average more than four leagues per day on the Missouri.[181]

Let me now summarize all of the data that can be assembled on this river. I much regret that I cannot speak from firsthand experience. I'm forced to compensate for this with the attention that I devoted to this subject when I was in the Illinois Country and the care with which I've sifted through the reports that I've been able to gather.[182]

Northern Plains.

178. The distances between the various rivers came from John T. Evans, identified in note 152 above. Evans's report can be found in *BLC,* 2:498. The White River joins the Missouri in Lyman County, South Dakota. See Moulton, *Journals of the Lewis and Clark Expedition,* 3:76, note 2. The Cheyenne River is also located in South Dakota. See ibid., 3:130, note 2. The Cannonball River is the current boundary between Sioux and Morton counties in North Dakota. See ibid., 3:183, note 1.

179. The Ricaras, or Arikaras, were the Mandans' closest downriver neighbors. They were of Caddoan linguistic stock and were a comparatively early offshoot of Pawnee groups to the south. See Douglas R. Parks, "The Northern Caddoan Languages: Their Subgroupings and Time Depths." Finiels places the Arikaras ten leagues downriver from the Mandans, probably using Evans as his source (see *BLC,* 2:496). Lewis and Clark, in contrast, found the tribe substantially further down the Missouri at a location between the Cannonball and Grand rivers.

180. The Mandans were of Siouan linguistic stock (Swanton, *Indian Tribes,* 276), and their role as traders has been described in Wood and Thiessen, *Early Fur Trade.* Their culture is described in Alfred W. Bowers, *Mandan Social and Ceremonial Organization.*

181. Lieutenant Governor Zenon Trudeau reported that the Mandan tribe was "supposed" to be 500 leagues distant from St. Louis, so in this instance Trudeau and Finiels used different sources. See *BLC,* 2:539.

182. As Nasatir remarked in his introduction to *BLC* (1:109), "By the turn of the century, the Missouri River was well known to the St. Louis traders as far as the Mandan nation." While in St. Louis in

Tradition has it that there is a long chain of very high rocky mountains that run northwest-southeast in the northern part of New Mexico; these are considered an extension of the Cordillières. They are approximately 170 leagues to the west of the Mandan village. This chain of mountains must be dissected [109] internally by valleys and deep ravines within its rocky interior. The Missouri River rises in the midst of these valleys and ravines between 43 degrees and 44 degrees north latitude; it then flows northward through the mountains to 49 degrees north latitude. There, finding an outlet, it descends eastward out of the mountains onto the immense plain that lies at their feet. Traversing this plain, it carves out the bed that carries its waters down to the Mississippi.[183]

This river has a fearsome reputation where its waters strain against the flanks of the mountains and are compelled to struggle constantly against the rocks that cross their course. The falls by which it descends onto the plain are not, it is said, any less wondrous; their dizzy height stuns your gaze; their swiftness is a kind of impetuous fury, with the waters leaping out onto the plain as if they are indignant with the constraints just overcome; the thunder in the air, the echoes reverberating through the flanks of the mountains, provide a spectacle that makes the famous Niagara Falls [110] pale in comparison, if you believe the astonishment and surprise that sweeps across Indian faces when you question them about the sources of the Missouri. From these falls to the Mandan village must be 200 or 250 leagues. Scarcely has the Missouri proceeded some distance onto the plain than it loses all of the fury with which it descended upon the plain. It flows peacefully on to the Mandan village, and if it sometimes returns to its impetuous and threatening ways, this is only because melting snows add a mass of additional water to its current. At the foot of the Rocky Mountains [Montagnes de Pierres] the Missouri crosses a wooded plain. The mountains themselves are covered with trees, and it is assumed that ancient forests extend from there all the way to the shores of the Pacific Ocean. Vast prairies, ponds, and marshes occupy the region between these forests and the Mandan villages. [111] There are few hills in this area. It is drained by several rivers, of which the principal is the Yellowstone, which flows from the southwest; it empties into the Missouri more than 80 leagues above the Mandan village. Certainly the Rocky Mountains contain many ermines and wild cats, whose beautiful fur is spotted like a leopard. On the left bank of the Missouri, not far from the mouth of the Yellowstone River, another fine large

1797-1798, Finiels would have had the opportunity to have spoken to many persons who had themselves ascended the Missouri. Among his informants may have been any or all of the following: Jacques d'Eglise, Jean-Baptiste Truteau, Joseph Garreau, Francisco Dérouin, James (Jacques) Mackay, John T. Evans, and René Jusseaume. These men appear in BLC and may also be found in Wood and Thiessen, Early Fur Trade.

183. Cordillières was a name originally applied only to the Andes Mountains, but it later came to include the Sierra Nevada and the Cascade and Rocky mountains as well. The distance of 170 leagues between the Mandan villages and the Rocky Mountains was obtained by Finiels from John T. Evans (see BLC, 2:497). Finiels' latitude for the sources of the Missouri is correct, although at its most northerly point the river only reaches 48 degrees north latitude.

river flows in from the northwest. This is called Rivière du Foin, and it serves as habitat for untold numbers of beavers and otters, which have thus far lived in peace.[184] The Indians, however, will soon discover the value of their pelts, and the timid animals will soon come to experience terror.

The Indian tribes that inhabit the extensive plain and the Rocky Mountains remain little known. [112] The few visits made to the Mandans have only established that they exist and the names of some of the others. These are the Hocats, the Cheyennes, the Caninawis, the Shiwitoons, the Crows, and the Sioux of the Grand Detour and the plains.[185] The last are a large and ferocious tribe and must be a branch of the tribe that inhabits the upper part of the Mississippi. They may be considered the Tartars of this part of the world and are nomads of the plains lying north of the Missouri and the Grand Detour. In springtime and autumn they come hunting along the banks of the White River. From there, they always interdict communications with the Mandans by harassing traders; they pillage, ransom, and sometimes massacre them if a means is not found to avoid their surveillance.[186]

The Mandans, as well as the Manitaris [Gros Ventres (Big Bellies) of the Missouri, or Hidatsas] and their friends the Watasoons [Ahnahaways], inhabit five villages on the banks of the Missouri a short distance from each other.[187] Three of these villages [113] are on the right bank and two on the left bank of the river. They are located at approximately 47 degree 48 minutes north latitude and 111 degrees west longitude from the Greenwich meridian. These five villages, according to all reports, are located in an area that is rather attractive, agreeable, and healthy. They are on a high plain that is level and fertile and that extends in all directions, so that you have an immense view embracing the countryside as far as the horizons. These tribes cultivate the surrounding lands, which are the most fertile lands anywhere along the banks of

184. John Evans wrote, "They call it Riviere dufoin (Hay River) they say it is a large and fine River in which there is More Beaver and Otters than in any other part of the Continent." See *BLC,* 2:498. William Clark named it Martha's River, but neither the French nor Clark's name endured. Today the stream, which is located in Roosevelt County, Montana, is known as Big Muddy Creek. See Moulton, *Journals of the Lewis and Clark Expedition,* 4:86, and 88, note 4. Evans also reported, "There are . . . found on the Rocky Mountains, Ermines, and kind of Wild Cat, whose skin is of a great Beauty, it is spotted as that of a Leopard." See *BLC,* 2:498.

185. The Shiwitoons (Shevitoons, Shivitauns) are a seldom-mentioned, rather mysterious tribe. They appear in James Mackay's journal (*BLC,* 2:494) and on a map done by John T. Evans (Moulton, *Atlas of the Lewis and Clark Expedition,* map 30). This leads to the conclusion that Finiels' reference to the Shiwitoons was based on information he had received from Evans and Mackay in St. Louis.

186. Finiels' remarks concerning the Sioux of the Grand Detour also seem to be based on information received from Mackay (see *BLC,* 2:494–95). This Grand Detour, which is located in present-day South Dakota, should not be confused with the Great Bend in present-day North Dakota, where the Missouri River turns southward after flowing in a basically easterly direction. On the issue of the various "Grand Detours" of the Missouri River, see Melburn D. Thurman, "The Little Missouri River: A Source of Confusion for Plains Ethnohistory."

187. The Gros Ventres of the Missouri River and the Ahnahaways were, like their Mandan neighbors, of the Siouan linguistic stock. Unlike the Mandans, however, they were part of the Hidatsa tribe. Swanton, *Indian Tribes,* 275; W. Raymond Wood, "Origins and Settlements of the Hidatsa"; Wood and Thiessen, *Early Fur Trade,* passim.

the Missouri. They raise maize, beans, pumpkins, squashes, and so forth. Surely they must have received the seeds from some European country, for these plants do not seem to be indigenous to this part of America. They are no strangers to making pottery; they have fire-resistant clay pots in which they prepare their food. It is possible that they learned this by themselves, or perhaps we again see some European influence. They possess some guns, [114] powder, and shot; they say that they received them in exchange from other tribes who in turn got them from whites. Probably English traders have already penetrated into several areas of this region, or perhaps Spaniards out of New Mexico have done so.[188]

The Mandans, their friends, and other less-well-known tribes to the west are, according to the reports of traders who have visited them, generally as good and docile as the Sioux are intractable and ferocious. They have always appeared to welcome friendships with Europeans, but it is to be feared that closer contact with whites will rapidly change the primitive goodness that once characterized most of the Indian tribes who had no contact with them. It is unfortunate that European contact with these tribes must be initiated by the most immoral Europeans. Because these simple and ignorant men assume the superiority of [white] men whose color, skills, and industry amaze them [115], they are stunned by the disgusting spectacle of their debauchery and gross passions, which the Indians assume are the usual customs of whites.

The Indians are given liquor that intoxicates their feeble reason and makes them susceptible to pleasures that they lack the strength to resist; seduction is the entire objective of the whites. How can the Indians avoid acquiring vices and their pursuant needs in exchange for peltries? We deceive them; they perceive this and in turn deceive us. They see us as greedy and avid, and they soon imitate us. The child of nature, aping the European and believing himself thus improved, is soon nothing more than a degraded creature; he cannot shed his shame, for to do so he requires examples that are missing and knowledge that he can never acquire.

The Missouri is more than 350 toises wide at the place where the Mandans have selected to live. Although [116] from there upstream it is not as wide as it is farther down, no doubt it can be ascended much higher than the Mandans; you can penetrate easily into the Rivière du Foin and the Yellowstone; you can in several places approach the famous Rocky Mountains, about which conjectures are all the more uncertain because they are based upon vague descriptions, gesticulations, and confused mutterings of Indians. Descending from the Mandans to the Platte River, the Missouri runs southeast. Its waters flow mostly over a bed of gravel or rock, and mountains of sand

188. Once again, it is apparent that Finiels' information in this paragraph came largely from Mackay and Evans (*BLC*, 2:494–96). There was no doubt that traders from British Canada had traded with the Mandans and associated tribes, and Finiels knew this from having conversed with Mackay and Evans. The native agriculture and pottery were ancient elements in the Missouri valley and owed nothing to European influences.

and rock enclose it on both banks. Occasionally they draw so close that they seem to compress the river, reducing its width to less than 400 toises; other times they are more or less distant from the banks. Thus there are sometimes rocky, sterile shores and sometimes level shores, which are a bit more fertile but are covered with woods. Beyond the woods, [117] the countryside is empty; there are immense savannahs covered with high grass on which countless bison [*boeufs et vaches sauvages*] graze. Here and there you find clusters and clumps of trees along the banks of the various tributaries of the Missouri. The river's course from the Mandans down to the Platte River is cluttered with thickly wooded islands. Ancient wild vines tightly interlace the trees on these islands, making the woods so dense that it is difficult to penetrate them. There are many vast sandbars along the banks or even in the middle of the river; these greatly increase the number of turns that must be negotiated in order to ascend it. However, you find fewer snags and logjams than farther downstream. The banks are firmer; they erode less easily; and the trees upon them very rarely fall in and add new obstacles to those that the river naturally carries and that already much [118] impede navigation. In this section between the Mandans and the Platte River, the river is generally 900 to 1,000 toises wide; it is less deep than down below, but there is always enough water to carry the usual trade boats. As you approach the Mandans the current slackens, and you can proceed to that tribe without being impeded by the rapids, falls, and cataracts that you find in most rivers on this continent. The traders, it is true, always complain about the ferocious winds that assail them with impetuous turbulence. They are then compelled to seek shelter, which they often can't find, on the banks; frequently they must unload their trade goods in order to secure them against the fury of the waves.[189]

However incomplete the foregoing survey of the Missouri may be, it is adequate for the present time to give a rather precise notion of the benefits you might expect to derive from the fur trade. Before [119] analyzing its present condition and its potential, I believe I must return to the Mandans in order to present some details about their contacts with both the English and the Spaniards. The former believe that they can seize what the negligence of the latter has left to their discretion. It is to be feared, if things remain for long as they are, that the English will begin to think of themselves as the owners of something that they have so patently usurped, that they will succeed in persuading the Indians of this, and that they will take vigorous measures in order to take possession of the fur trade.

189. A French toise equals 6.38 English feet. Although, as we have observed in earlier footnotes, Finiels relied heavily upon information from James Mackay and John T. Evans in describing the upper Missouri valley, in this paragraph his measurements do not correspond to those given by Mackay and Evans. Evans, for example, gives the width of the Missouri at the Mandan villages as 500 toises (*BLC,* 2:498). At Fort Mandan, Lewis and Clark found the Missouri to be 500 yards (i.e., 235 toises) wide (*BLC,* 1:237), and at the mouth of the Osage River they found the Missouri to be 875 yards (i.e., 411 toises) wide (*BLC,* 37). The Missouri River can, of course, vary considerably in width over even relatively short distances, but it does seem that Mackay, Evans, and Finiels exaggerated the width of the river.

More than twenty-five years ago, Englishmen from Canada cast envious glances at the trade that could develop, via the Mandans, with the tribes that border the Rocky Mountains.[190] This was the first tribe that could be easily reached, and they hoped to use it as a means of acquiring all the trade along the Missouri [120] between that tribe and the mountains that contain the sources of the Missouri. It was not simply upon direct trade with the Mandans that the English hoped to accrue future profits based on their contacts; they knew that that tribe was in itself a small resource. But they thought highly of the trade that might be opened through the Mandans with the tribes of the Rocky Mountains. They spared nothing in order to succeed, and their skill in speculation, as subtle as it is sure, is well known; they know how to calculate accurately the importance of trade after making persistent efforts to ensure that they will reap the profits from it.

Let us follow for a moment these audacious traders whose penetrating vision runs from the icy banks of the St. Lawrence River to the most remote wildernesses of western America, more than 1,200 leagues [121] from Montreal and Quebec, in order to generate profits for the mother country. We shall be amazed by the labor, the superhuman efforts, and the bravery that that great journey entails.[191]

It is only half accomplished, however, by those financially involved—the merchants and traders; nonetheless, it is surprising. It shows the enormous, burning ambition of that nation, whose eyes take in all the resources of the universe; it demonstrates the shrewdness with which the English know how to penetrate every route so that all of the world's riches may flow to them.

The Montreal merchants travel every year to Grand Portage at the extreme north end of Lake Superior, which is about a 500-league journey. They carry all the trade goods known to be necessary and indispensable to the Indians; they exchange these annually for peltries that are the products of the Indians' winter hunt. You must know the geography of America in order to comprehend such a journey. It is not my intention to present here the details of its difficulties, heartbreaks, and [122] obstacles. I

190. The origins of the trade route from British Canada to the Mandans via the Great Lakes and the Assiniboine and Souris rivers are discussed in Innis, *The Fur Trade in Canada,* 166–262; see also the introduction by Thiessen and Wood in *Early Fur Trade.* Finiels' remarks in this paragraph are further documentation that the British North West Company was aggressively expanding its interests toward the upper Missouri River tribes in the late 1770s.

191. Much, though not all, of the information that Finiels presents in these several pages concerning the British trading network that stretched from Montreal all the way to the upper Missouri came from John T. Evans and James Mackay. See especially Mackay's journal in *BLC,* 2:490–94. Finiels' information, however, is much more detailed than that contained in Mackay's journal. This is either because Mackay and Evans gave additional information to Finiels in person in St. Louis, or because Finiels had access to other sources. For informative modern discussions of this fur-trading network, see Wood and Thiessen, *Early Fur Trade,* and Eric W. Morse, *Fur Trade Routes of Canada, Then and Now.* The first published account of the British-Canadian trade network from Montreal, through the Grand Portage on Lake Superior and westward toward the headwaters of the Missouri and the Pacific Ocean, appeared in Alexander Mackenzie's *Voyages from Montreal Through the Continent of North America* (1801). It is unlikely that Finiels, living in New Orleans, would have had access to this work before writing the present document in the early summer of 1803.

will only say that they make this trip in birchbark canoes, very light and fragile, especially when you are familiar with the route they must traverse. These canoes are more or less freight canoes, and they can carry up to 10,000 pounds. At every portage from one lake to another or from one river to another, the trade goods must be unloaded. Sometimes carts make the portages easier; often they are not available, and, after having carried the merchandise, the *engagés* must complete the job by transporting the canoe on their heads.[192]

At Grand Portage, the merchants meet English traders, who proceed west by an equally long and arduous route. The traders bring the peltries they collected from the Indians at the last trading, and they exchange them for trade goods that the merchants have brought. Then they all return by their respective routes in order to seek further work and more fuel for this commerce.

The English traders also come to Grand Portage [123] in birchbark canoes, whose capacity is, however, limited to 2,500 pounds at most.[193] This is because they have less manpower, because they must traverse shallower water, and because their route is even more strewn with obstacles than that from Montreal to Grand Portage. In these frail canoes they cross a surprising multitude of lakes, ascend and descend numerous rivers, are constantly stopped in their laborious work by rapids, and cross innumerable portages, all of which are conducted with brute strength. They carry the trade goods on their shoulders to the closest lake, to a neighboring river, or around some rapid. Then the canoe is reloaded and the voyage is resumed, only to have the same process repeated at the next obstacle.

The traders returning west usually head for the grand portage at Lac la Pluie [Rainy Lake]; from there they proceed to Lac des Bois [Lake of the Woods] and then to Lake Winnipeg [Ouinipig], which is the largest and most westerly of them all. There are 72 portages between [124] Grand Portage and Lake Winnipeg, which are at least 250 leagues apart. Some of these portages are a league in length, many are shorter, and some are only 60 to 80 feet.

The land between Grand Portage and Lake Winnipeg is high and interspersed with rocks and mountains. It is almost entirely non-arable and sterile and is traversed from southeast to northwest by a string of small lakes, which are connected by small creeks. These delineate the traders' route from Grand Portage to Rainy Lake. Around these small lakes roams an Indian tribe called the Bungi, or more com-

192. The most detailed examination of bark canoes is in Edwin Tappan Adney and Howard I. Chapelle, *The Bark Canoes and Skin Boats of North America*. See also a discussion of the trade canoes used on the waters of western Canada in Morse, *Fur Trade Routes*, 6–8, 22–24. Finiels' claims for the carrying capacity of the enormous *canoes de maître* (sometimes called Montreal canoes), which had beams nearly 6 feet wide and were up to 40 feet long, are exaggerated little, if any. These remarkable birchbark vessels contained not a scrap of metal.

193. The smaller canoe described in this paragraph was known as the north canoe, which had a carrying capacity of between 2,500 and 3,000 pounds and which was light enough to be carried by two men.

monly the Sauteur.[194] They hire themselves out to the traders to assist in making the portages; they periodically gather around these places during their wanderings. More nomadic, more wretched even than the Sioux, they have no established settlements and they cultivate nothing. The hunt takes them hither and thither over the broken surface of that poor land. Part of the year they pursue [125] reindeer, which provide their sole subsistence. Wretched creatures, made ferocious by misery and a bitter climate, they have no idea of what we call pleasure. During part of the year, they cease their exertions by making war on the Sioux, who inhabit the upper tributaries of the Mississippi and who are a bit less ferocious and miserable wretches than they.

Once they reach Lake Winnipeg, the traders cross the extreme southern end from east to west, which is a distance of about 40 leagues. At the western end they enter the Assiniboine River and ascend it for nearly 200 leagues via one of its southwestern tributaries called the Catepoi [now the Qu'Appelle] River. Then they come to the westernmost outpost of the Canadian merchants, which is the rendezvous for the fur trade in that remote part of America. As I mentioned, this outpost is 200 leagues from Lake Winnipeg, which means that the traders travel a total of almost 500 leagues to get there from Grand Portage, and just as much to return.[195]

[126] The sources of the Assiniboine River are located in the Rocky Mountains much further north than the headwaters of the Missouri. It flows generally in an easterly direction; it traverses immense plains, which are magnificent and fertile, at about 51 degrees north latitude and empties into Lake Winnipeg at its far southwestern end. The Turtle Mountains separate the headwaters of the Missouri and Assiniboine rivers, and they are inhabited by the Indian tribe after whom the latter river is named.[196]

Several times during the last twenty years [1783–1803], English traders from an outpost on the Catepoi River have penetrated to the Missouri and the Mandan villages, which Europeans had never previously seen.[197] Twelve years ago they built a

---

194. *Bungi* (more often *Bungee*) and *Sauteur* were alternative names for various groups of the Chippewa, or Ojibwa, tribe, which was of the Algonquian linguistic stock. See James H. Howard, *The Plains-Ojibwa or Bungi, Hunters and Warriors of the Northern Prairies.*

195. Finiels' "westernmost outpost" was certainly Fort Espérance, located near the confluence of the Assiniboine and Catepoi (or, more commonly, the Qu'Appelle) rivers (Daniel J. Provo, *Fort Esperance in 1793–1795: A North West Provisioning Post*). James Mackay, one of Finiels' principal informants, had passed through Fort Espérance in 1787 on his way from Canada to the Mandan villages (see *BLC,* 1:94). In the 1790s and early nineteenth century, the more usual route to the Mandans from Canada was via another tributary of the Assiniboine, the Souris River (see also Wood and Thiessen, *Early Fur Trade,* passim).

196. Finiels' geography is more or less correct in this paragraph, except that the Assiniboine River in fact flows into the Red River of the North, which in turn flows into Lake Winnipeg. Turtle Mountain is a dome-shaped highland on the North Dakota–Manitoba boundary.

197. Finiels obviously knew nothing about the expeditions that members of the La Vérendrye family made from Canada to the Mandan villages in the late 1730s. See G. Hubert Smith and W. Raymond

fort near these villages, and since then have maintained a continuous presence there. When the Spaniards visited there in 1796, a British flag was flying overhead. The overland distance between the Catepoi River and the Mandan villages on the Missouri is at the most 80 leagues, proceeding more or less due [127] south; there is no water link between these two rivers. Thus trade goods must be transported on horses or mules supplied for a price by the natives of the region. This route crosses vast plains and extensive marshes. The plains are dissected by valleys and streams, along whose banks are thin clusters of trees, which include a small variety of poplar [aspen?]. During the winter this trip is made by dog sleds, and trade goods are transported the same way. The trip requires ten to twelve days in summer; in winter it takes at least sixteen to eighteen days.

While the English were thus furtively approaching the Mandans, the Company of the Upper Missouri was being established in St. Louis; it contracted to combine the Mandan trade with that of the five tribes living near the Platte River.[198] That premature contract ruined the company because it was in too much of a rush to fulfill it. To be sure, the company had easier [128] access to that area than the English, but it did not have the powerful resources they possessed. And perhaps one might reproach its members for lacking the breadth of imagination required for speculative enterprises; this permits adverse events that have been foreseen to be compensated for with well-managed resources, which, so to speak, will lead to a happy conclusion.

In 1794, the company began to prepare an expedition to the Mandans. In fact, the expedition departed the same year under the leadership of Monsieur Truteau, who was experienced with navigation on the Missouri.[199] Monsieur Truteau had scarcely passed the Poncas when he encountered an errant group of Sioux, who were hunting on the White River and who compelled him to winter with the Poncas; the gifts that he was forced to distribute consumed his trade goods. The Ricaras were not as yet as close to the Mandans as they are today. Monsieur Truteau decided to wait at their village for the assistance that the company [129] had promised to send. In fact, assistance was sent, but the leader of this expedition was ineffective; the Poncas detained him, and once again all the trade goods were consumed.[200]

Wood, *The Explorations of the La Vérendryes in the Northern Plains*. Welshman John T. Evans was the "Spaniard" mentioned by Finiels later in this paragraph as having visited the Mandan villages in 1796 (*BLC*, 2:496). Evans appropriated the North West Company Post built there by René Jusseaume in about 1794.

198. Concerning the founding of the Missouri Company, see *BLC*, 1:84–92, and Nasatir, "The Formation of the Missouri Company," 10–22.

199. Jean-Baptiste Truteau, a French-Canadian trader who came to St. Louis in 1774, also served intermittently as the local schoolmaster until his death in 1827. For biographical information, see Nasatir, "Jean Baptist Truteau." A portion of Truteau's journal is reprinted in *BLC*, 2:376–82. Douglas R. Parks of the American Indian Studies Research Institute at Indiana University is editing for publication a translation of Truteau's complete journal that has been translated from the French by Mildred Wedel of the Smithsonian Institution.

200. In 1795, the Missouri Company sent a trader named Lecuyer up the Missouri River to provide Truteau with assistance. The Poncas relieved Lecuyer of 8,000 piastres worth of trade goods before he

In order to compensate for these losses, the company launched a third effort in the summer of 1795. It equipped a boat under the leadership of Messieurs Mackay and Evans, but they departed too late in the season and got no further than the Mahas before they had to winter over.[201] Monsieur Mackay made use of this occasion to establish the company's projected outpost with the Mahas. He used most of the trade goods to maintain his men, in construction costs, and in gifts to assure the Indians' goodwill. The next spring, Monsieur Evans left the Maha outpost with the remains of their trade goods to try to penetrate as far as the Mandans. The terrible Sioux again appeared and descended on him forthwith; he was lucky to escape by promptly retreating to the Mahas. In June, Monsieur Evans struck out again [130] and arrived without mishap at the Ricaras. They had moved their village ten leagues below the Mandans in order to escape harassment by the Sioux, whose hunting ground was close to the Ricaras' former village. The Ricaras wished to detain him with the pretext that they needed his trade goods. Finally, on 20 September he was able to leave for the Mandans. He arrived on 23 September and was very well received by the small confederation formed on that part of the Missouri. These friendly tribes were overjoyed at seeing white men and expressed the most sincere attachment to their great Spanish father. They allowed Monsieur Evans to take possession in the Spanish king's name of the fort that the English had built and seemed pleased to see the Spanish flag flying there.

To these fruitless attempts, to these small successes were confined the enterprises that the company had dreamt of to yield such rich results! Messieurs Mackay and Evans returned to St. Louis the next year [131] with very few peltries. After their return, the company no longer had the means to outfit new expeditions to the upper Missouri tribes. It gradually dissolved, and today its stock is held by Clamorgan, Loisel, and Company, which is unable to undertake anything by itself.[202]

An isolated event also contributed a great deal to accelerate this company's ruin. It sealed its ruin by preventing it from recouping its losses through new enterprises, which surely would have been better planned if there had been more experience. This was the death of Monsieur [Andrew] Todd, an English merchant from Canada, who had come to the Illinois Country with plans more grandiose than had ever been conceived by his compatriots.[203] These were an extension of the views that the English had always entertained concerning trade with all of the Indian tribes from that

---

reached Truteau. See Zenon Trudeau to Carondelet, 3 July 1796, in *BLC,* 2:440-41.

201. Important extracts of the journals of James Mackay and John T. Evans are published in *BLC,* 2:490-99. See also Gwyn A. Williams, *Madoc: The Making of a Myth.*

202. Concerning Clamorgan, Loisel, and Company, see *BLC,* 1:108-15, 2:571-79; Abel, ed., *Tableau's Narrative,* 16-20.

203. Andrew Todd, an influential British trader from Canada, had switched his allegiance to Spain and moved his headquarters from Michilimackinac to New Orleans in return for numerous trading concessions granted by the governor general of Louisiana, the Baron de Carondelet. Todd died unexpectedly of yellow fever in 1796. For information concerning Todd, his grandiose plans, and his death, see *BLC,* 2:481-82, 524-25, 541-42; and Foley and Rice, *The First Chouteaus,* 55-56, 77-78.

region of America. At the very time that the Company of the Upper Missouri was being founded, he obtained exclusive rights to the trade of the [132] upper Mississippi above the Missouri, together with the privilege of receiving directly from England all the merchandise necessary for this trade. Simultaneously, he contracted with the Company of the Upper Missouri to supply at St. Louis all of the merchandise that it required for its trade. By means of this double commerce, England would have assured itself the most profitable part of the Illinois Country trade and would also have obtained a splendid market for its trade goods under the aegis of the Spanish government itself, without even mentioning the various commodities that would have come into Upper Louisiana under the cover of that legal trade. These facts make it clear that the profits from all of this would have gone exclusively to England and that the majority of the peltries would have passed through Canada, with New Orleans handling only a token amount. This was necessary to keep up appearances, so as not to challenge too openly the government, which was weak enough to grant terms that were as advantageous to England as they were disadvantageous to Spain and her colony.

[133] In 1796, Monsieur Todd descended to New Orleans in order to set his enterprises in motion, and he became one of the victims of the epidemic [of yellow fever] that for the first time demonstrated to the citizens the unhealthiness of their climate. The death of this man, who was the only axle capable of keeping this monstrous scaffold of speculation rolling, shattered these grandiose trading projects, which had intoxicated so many men for three or four years in the Illinois Country. Since that time, the province has reverted to torpor; it has resumed its old habits of weakness, ignorance, and indolence that have characterized it since its origins.

The trade of the upper Mississippi, like that of the upper Missouri, has therefore produced nothing for Spanish Illinois. The English, however, are neglecting neither region.[204] It is very likely that they've returned to the Mandans since the events I've described and that they've profited from a spurt of activity [by the Spaniards], which seemed to upset their plans but which did not persist, in order to persuade the Indians of Spanish impotence and attach the Indians to themselves by ties of dependency that had [134] been developed. We know that the English visit the east side of the upper Mississippi annually. It's true that they must cross American territory to get there, but that's not much of an impediment to them. They easily obtain permission from the American commandants at Michilimackinac to trade in the part of the Mississippi valley that belongs to the United States. From there they have no trouble in penetrating Spanish territory, which has been totally abandoned for five or six years.[205] If you

204. Abraham P. Nasatir is the foremost authority on the bitter rivalry between Spain and Great Britain. Of his numerous publications on this subject, see especially *BLC*, 1:98–115; "Anglo-Spanish Rivalry on the Upper Missouri"; and *Spanish War Vessels on the Mississippi*.

205. Traders coming out of British Canada used Prairie du Chien, located on the east side of the Mississippi a short distance above the mouth of the Wisconsin River, as a jumping-off point for penetrating Upper Louisiana. See John Long, *Voyages and Travels*, ed. Milo M. Quaife, 184–90; Peter L. Scanlan, *Prairie du Chien: French, British, American*.

reflect on these activities, on this coordination of efforts to seize the Indian trade of northern and western Louisiana, and that they [the English] are doing much the same thing in Florida, you see one of the reasons why France had so much trouble reacquiring Louisiana. This point should not be elaborated at this time; it is easy to comment upon if you appreciate the magnitude of the interests, for both England and America, that are related to keeping this province permanently in Spanish hands.

The only means to regain the rights that the English have usurped from the Spaniards, because of the government's neglect and lack [135] of attention to that lucrative branch of commerce [i.e., the fur trade], is to return to the tribes with sufficient forces to intimidate them and with abundant trade goods in proportion to their needs. You must visit them regularly and never neglect them. The assurance of having all their needs met will encourage them to settle down and make them more eager to pursue the hunt. They are very much creatures of habit, and once you have developed a relationship with them they are loath to terminate it. The quality of merchandise carried to them is of critical concern for assuring regular and continuous trading with them. Guns, powder, agricultural implements, and so forth must be of good quality and capable of withstanding a variety of uses. The French have often been remiss in this regard; their trade goods were much inferior to those of the English in both quality and appearance. Consequently, the Indians always preferred English goods in all regions where they competed with those of other nations.[206] You can only deceive these creatures once. [136] They are ignorant in comparison with Europeans but are perhaps much superior to them in possessing more delicate and refined instincts in all matters concerning their personal interest and well-being.

The men employed to deal with the Indians—perhaps to negotiate with them, or arrange treaties, or to reside in the outposts established near their villages—must be firm, prudent men, possessing good morals in the Indian sense of them.[207] Bravery is one of the surest ways to capture the friendship and admiration of these men, who have always considered it one of the principal virtues. You must adhere exactly to what you have promised and be equipped with plausible excuses in case circumstances prevent you from following through, in order to demonstrate that you have not deceived them. In all dealings with them you must convey the impression that you respect them without fearing them; you must show them affection and evince a generous compassion [137] for their wretchedness. There is no being, however coarse and simple he may be, who doesn't have a more or less strong component of self-esteem and vanity, and it is often only a matter of knowing how to handle him skillfully in order to gain his confidence and loyalty. Once you learn the customs, habits, and character of the Indians, you can manage them with surprising ease. Their customs are not difficult to study. They are simpler and less complex than has been suggested

206. It was a well-known fact that the British supplied better trade goods at lower prices than either the French or the Spaniards could. On this subject, see Foley and Rice, *The First Chouteaus,* chap. 4.

207. The unrivaled masters at Indian trade diplomacy were the Chouteau brothers, Auguste and Pierre, of St. Louis. See Foley and Rice, *The First Chouteaus.*

in most descriptions presented to the public. You must be wary of exaggerations that present Indian customs as either too exalted or too debased. Two or three traits are deeply engraved in them, but all other facets of their character are devoid of passionate commitment. They possess a calm indifference that would suggest their souls are asleep. Yet on certain occasions they display an energy of which they did not seem capable if you observed them only during the numerous tranquil periods, [138] which they seem eager to prolong.

One of the surest means of obtaining and maintaining their friendship is generosity, but you must understand their meaning of the word. It is not the abundance, quantity, or size of gifts that earns you the title "generous man"; rather, it is the manner in which you give that establishes their opinion of you as a liberal or stingy person.[208] A few examples will permit you to understand better the kind of attention they require. A commandant who wants to give them some bread must be sure to give each of them an entire loaf; no matter how small it is, they will be content. If, on the other hand, he hands out slices, even though they may be larger than a loaf, they will take umbrage and claim they're being starved to death. This little mistake is enough to upset them. If you serve them brandy in a large glass filled only half full, they'll accuse you of being stingy; [139] a small glass filled to the brim that contains much less than half a large one will satisfy them and will not cost you their esteem. If you give them gunpowder in containers proportioned to the quantity, if they are full, your gift will have full value in their estimation; if there are empty spots, it will lose its entire value.

The Indians are eager for gifts; they will humble themselves in order to get them; and you acquire a very poor idea of their scruples if you witness only the moments when they come to solicit them. All governments distribute them each year, but this means of cultivating their goodwill demands prudence and caution so that they do not abuse it and so that you receive credit for it. If you intend to give gifts, do not give them all at once. They will surely make further demands upon you, which they always do even if the gifts are generous. If you hold back some, you will be able to please them by adding to your [140] original gifts those that you kept in reserve. They will flood you with thanks for such generosity, and you will maintain your sway over them. These little details, calculated on the basis of a precise knowledge of their character, may seem trivial, but they are more essential than you might think. For having neglected them, hatreds and aversions have been generated in the hearts of several Indian tribes; they have often preferred those who understood minor nuances and adhered to them.

You can now understand Upper Louisiana's fur trade and envision the means that

208. Concerning relationships between fur traders and Indians, see Lewis O. Saum, *The Fur Trader and the Indian*. For a recent discussion of the meaning and importance of gift-giving in Indian cultures, see William Cronon and Richard White, "Indians in the Land." On gift distributions in Upper Louisiana, see Pierre Chouteau to James Wilkinson, 12 April 1806, in *BLC*, 2:767–71.

might improve that essential branch of commerce. The trade of the upper Mississippi is reduced to a few individual efforts, to a bit of trading done by white hunters and small traders who rarely risk ascending as far as the Des Moines River. Since the decline of the Company of the Upper Missouri, the trade of the Missouri is reduced to that conducted directly with the Osages, and to that with the Kansas (who continue their hunting, [141] as I explained in the section concerning the two rivers), who sometimes penetrate as far as the Mahas. The profits from the two principal trade networks that I have discussed are scarcely more than 32,000 piastres annually, as I tabulated it in the enumeration of all products from the Illinois Country. Clandestine trading conducted by individual traders is of little consequence; it is largely subsumed under the two principal trade nets, for most of the small traders are usually obliged to get their supplies from the storehouses of the major owners.[209]

This overview of the fur trade's present condition in Upper Louisiana—its breadth, the obstacles that inhibit expansion and success, its low returns—should not discourage the government. Nor should the government underestimate this branch of commerce, which is so attractive in several respects and which is very precious both for the colony and for the metropole.[210] It only proves the ineptness of the present government and alerts the one to come, promising it ample recompense for the wise and prudent measures that it will take in order to give the colony the vigor of which it is capable, and assure the metropole the advantages [142] that it has a right to expect. I will return to this subject when I deal with the commerce of Upper Louisiana.

Having already described the best-known parts of this subdivision of the colony, I believe that before going further I must say a word about the character, customs, and morals of its inhabitants. A topographical description of a region and of its waterways, knowledge of its lands and their products, these provide only a static and imperfect portrait. It is the virtues, vices, passions, and morals of its people that provide the life and vitality necessary to bring it to life. These qualities are not least useful in determining the means by which to promote the colony's prosperity.

MORALS, MORES, AND CUSTOMS

The population of Spanish Illinois is at this time composed of 3,900 to 4,000 persons, as I pointed out earlier. These are subdivided into whites, mulattos, and Negroes; in the last two categories some individuals are free and the remainder are slaves.[211]

209. Concerning the fur trade up the Missouri River in late colonial times, see Foley and Rice, *The First Chouteaus,* chap. 4; *BLC,* 1:108–15. Again, in this paragraph there is a distinctive change in the handwriting, which suggests that Finiels had again changed secretaries.

210. When Finiels was drafting this document in New Orleans in June 1803, he believed that France would soon take up the reins of government in Louisiana. News that Napoleon had sold the Louisiana Territory to the United States did not reach New Orleans until August 1803. See Lyon, *Louisiana in French Diplomacy,* 243–44.

211. When Finiels wrote "at this time," he was actually referring to the late 1790s when he had been a

Whites constitute the largest class, which is the way it should be in the entire colony, whose future does not demand a great deal of manpower. This class is very mixed. Presently, it is composed of [143] Creoles, Canadians, Frenchmen whom the Revolution has driven there during the last ten years, and Anglo-Americans from Kentucky who have been immigrating for the last seven or eight years and who themselves are a mixture of English, Irish, German, Swiss, and Dutch.[212]

The Canadians came first to mix their blood with that of the Louisiana French. They hired themselves out in Canada with merchants of the Illinois Country for periods of three, four, or sometimes six years.[213] During that time they worked only for their masters, whatever their occupations were. Until the time when the Anglo-American immigration began, the laborers and artisans in the Illinois Country were exclusively Canadians. They are very industrious in their country, where they practice most of the crafts that are common in Europe and which are of prime importance in society. When their terms of employment were up, they always stayed and settled in the Illinois Country, where they gradually increased the population and practiced their trades for their own profit. It is rare, and perhaps without precedent, for a young Creole, whatever the needs of his family, to take up a manual art or a craft as a vocation. Several artisans, despite having made very advantageous offers, [144] have been unable to find any apprentices. The proud Creoles consider it beneath them to practice the most useful professions. They prefer to gain their livelihoods hunting, which flatters their pride with its independence, or in rowing as hired laborers [engagés] on trading or commercial bateaux. This is arduous work, harder than any known occupation. But for a long time it has been associated with a certain point of honor, which makes it attractive to the youth and entices the children of even the best families to prefer it to other occupations. Farming, hunting, fishing, fur trading, extended river trips, excursions in the woods, and commerce are the sole occupations of the white population in the Illinois Country. And whenever they are not working, they spend their time lazing and loafing.

There are only a few free Negroes and mulattos.[214] They serve as hunters,

---

resident in Upper Louisiana. Immigration had substantially increased the population in the region between 1797 and 1803. The official census of 1800 listed Upper Louisiana's population (including New Madrid) as 6,911 souls, and Captain Amos Stoddard, the first U.S. commandant in Upper Louisiana, estimated the region's total population, black and white, to be 10,340. See SRM, vol. 1, facing p. 414; and Stoddard, Sketches, 226.

212. Finiels here uses the term Creoles in its original sense, i.e., persons born of European parents in colonial Louisiana, but note that on p. 109 he uses the term to refer also to slaves owned by the French.

213. Many of the French Canadians who migrated to Upper Louisiana came first as engagés employed in the fur trade. The thousands of contracts of engagement preserved in Canadian archives contain many surnames that eventually became important family names in the Illinois Country. See, for example, the notarial records in the Archives Nationales du Quebec a Montreal. Concerning French-Canadian colonization of Illinois, see Renald Lessard, Jacques Mathieu, and Lina Gouger, "Peuplement colonisateur au pays des Illinois."

214. The Upper Louisiana census of 1800 (SRM, vol. 1, facing p. 414) listed a total free black and mulatto population of 77.

boatmen, and riverboat skippers; some of them conduct trade up the rivers. In general they are very useful to the residents, who use them as resources whenever they need them. These persons have slightly lower status in the Illinois Country than in the more densely populated colonies of the Antilles, Africa, [145] and India. More obvious because of the sparse population, they are kept in place by the customs of the whites, upon whom they model themselves. They do not scandalize—with their eyes, their vices, and their excesses—the way they do in hotter climates. Their customs are distinguished from the whites only by their morality, which is a little less rigid, and because they are more relaxed about the severe laws imposed by decency. But they are more active and vigorous than the whites; they endure hard labor more courageously, and they could become as good warriors as they are hunters.

Black slaves constitute about one-sixth of the population.[215] When a *habitant* owns two or three to use in agriculture, he thinks he is in a position to undertake anything. The black slaves are almost all Creoles [i.e., American-born], with the exception of those whom the Anglo-Americans have recently brought in. They retain absolutely none of the customs of their native land, which they have totally forgotten. Generally they are spoiled and corrupt, and they lie and steal. During the French regime, the slaves possessed some virtues, and the missionaries paid as much attention to their morals as to those of the whites. The slaves performed their duties conscientiously, [146] promptly, and in good humor. The Spanish regime has destroyed all of this by its bias against their masters and by its lack of laws, police, and a system for making the slaves adhere to their duties.[216]

When the Illinois Country was populated exclusively by Canadians, the *habitants* all possessed the same manners, and you might even say the same characteristics. Since the arrival of the Anglo-Americans, several nations have added nuances of their various traits. They brought different manners, habits, and ideas, but these foreign elements are not yet well enough established to convey to the general mass a character that can be defined as a whole. My remarks here will deal only with the population as it existed before this immigration, which was in full swing at the very time [1797-1798] that I was exploring this interesting part of Louisiana.[217]

My description thus far of the Illinois Country has already offered some glimpses

215. The 1800 Spanish census listed 1,191 black and mulatto slaves—approximately one-sixth of Upper Louisiana's 6,911 residents. The slaves were very unequally distributed, however, and the populations of some communities such as Ste. Genevieve had a substantially larger percentage of slaves.

216. In 1781, Lieutenant Governor Francisco Cruzat issued new ordinances governing slave conduct in an effort to curb the abuses of unruly slaves in St. Louis. See "Ordinance Regarding Slavery," 12 August 1781, in *SRM*, 1:244-45. For information concerning slavery in Spanish Louisiana, see Hans W. Baade, "The Law of Slavery in Spanish Louisiana, 1769-1803"; Ekberg, *Colonial Ste. Genevieve*, 204-11; Stephen Webre, "The Problem of Indian Slavery in Spanish Louisiana, 1769-1803," 121-22.

217. On American immigration into Spanish Louisiana, consult Lawrence Kinnaird, "American Penetration into Spanish Louisiana," in *New Spain and the Anglo-American West*, ed. George P. Hammond, 211-37; Kinnaird's dissertation, "American Penetration into Spanish Territory, 1776-1802"; Gilbert Din, "The Immigration Policy of Governor Esteban Miró"; and Din, "Spain's Immigration Policy in Louisiana and the American Penetration, 1792-1803."

into the character of the inhabitants. And it provides a partial basis for understanding their customs, habits, and attitudes. Mostly French, they [147] have been stamped since the days of the first settlements in Louisiana with an imprint that advantageously distinguishes that nation from all other peoples in the universe. The most obvious proof of this is the affection, not yet extinguished, which they have effortlessly generated in the hearts of all the Indian nations. At the same time, the English, Anglo-American, and Spanish nations have succeeded only in inspiring fear and alienation.[218] For a long time isolated and inaccessible, the residents of the Illinois Country have maintained some of the primitive traits they brought with them. They were then slowly molded with a distinctive character that acquired its most prominent aspects from their surrounding environment.

The first colonists in the Illinois Country were almost all settlers from Lower Louisiana, and their character had already been somewhat modified by their sojourn there.[219] Among the founding personalities were several persons who possessed good European upbringings. Their budding settlements contained missionaries—educated, enlightened, and learned—who oversaw with infinite care [148] the training of the young and gave them some of the education they thought necessary for their well-being. Education in the arts and sciences, which enlarged the human spirit and promoted happiness in many societies of the ancient world, was unable to impede, as one might have expected, the rapid [downward] pace that seemed to accelerate because of progress in the arts and sciences. We have lost out in educating ourselves, in enlightening our minds too much beyond that which is necessary in order to control our passions. And if we dare to be sincere and appraise the results of this vast and sublime knowledge, the acquisition of which makes us so proud, we should acknowledge that all we have really gained in Europe from this growth of knowledge boils down, as far as morals are concerned, to the art of mitigating our vices, of putting an attractive veneer on the many treacheries that have become, due to the poverty of our spirits, the current coin of good society. When all is said and done, we do nothing but disguise the ugliness, while we have lost between us that mutual trust, the product of pure morals, without which there can be no refinements in society, no true pleasures. We can no longer even dream of this felicity.

The man who has received some education, [149] who knows the sciences and cultivates the arts, when he is relegated to the wilderness under the eyes of nature and

218. It had become an eighteenth-century cliché—or truism—that the French generally got along better with the Indians than did the English or Americans. For modern assessments of this complex topic, see James Axtell, *The Invasion Within: The Contest of Cultures in Colonial North America;* Robert F. Berkhofer, *The White Man's Indian: Images of the American Indian from Columbus to the Present;* Olive Dickason, *The Myth of the Savage;* Cornelius J. Jaenen, *Friend and Foe: Aspects of French-American Cultural Contact in the 16th and 17th Centuries;* and Gary B. Nash, *Red, White, and Black: The Peoples of Early America.*

219. Finiels here contradicts his earlier observation that most of the early settlers were French Canadians, which they were. See pp. 108–9 above.

is far removed from societal influences, assembles them all for their true purpose—the felicity of the human species. No longer having any reason to disguise himself, he feels more strongly the pull of virtue, whose seed nature has sown in his heart. His knowledge then serves only to temper the savagery and original rudeness of nature. He remains close to her and instills in his morals, his thoughts, and his actions the sweetness, gentleness, and affability that should always be the fruit of our knowledge. His demeanor becomes sincere as soon as he no longer needs to conceal his passions, which are rarely aroused in the silence of the forest. They remain simple and unaffected; they command trust; they possess the charming allure of genuinely rural habits, the unique perfection of rustic and shy customs natural to creatures left alone in the wilderness. Thus proceeded the retro-march of the customs and character of the inhabitants of Upper Louisiana after they settled there. They [150] shed old vices and clothed themselves in new virtues, and in appearing to degenerate they made giant steps toward achieving happiness.[220]

The inhabitants of the Illinois Country, although originally French, first lost some of their national character in the swamps of Lower Louisiana. Then, when they ascended the Mississippi to settle in its solitary valley between the mouths of the Missouri and Kaskaskia rivers,[221] their customs were further influenced by the environment, becoming yet more simple. For a time they even combined the purest morals with the best rural good humor. These pastoral customs slowly eroded with the growth of population and the extension of the settlements, which crossed the Mississippi and developed on the west bank. Education waned with the departure of the Jesuits,[222] and ignorance compounded declining morality. Some of the more isolated settlements became more wild and almost unsociable. Then in more auspicious times foreigners [151] arrived in the Illinois Country, bringing knowledge that had been lost and refinement that had disappeared. Let me describe some of the principal circumstances that bore on these changes.[223]

Solitude; isolation; religion, which is always strongest when we are isolated and remote; hunting; the fur trade; long sojourns in the forests and on wild rivers; proximity to the Indians—these are the important factors that altered the native traits of the colony's first settlers. Whether the inhabitants lost or gained more in this process would be futile to discuss at this point. Nonetheless, the result was a rather interesting mix, basically something that a philosopher might see as the point at which the

220. The proto-romantic ideas of Jean-Jacques Rousseau are apparent in this paragraph and the preceding one. See the Introduction above for a discussion of this subject.

221. Technically, the only permanent settlement established *west* of the Mississippi during the French regime was Ste. Genevieve, founded c. 1750. See Ekberg, *Colonial Ste. Genevieve,* chap. 1. By the time Laclede founded St. Louis in 1764, France had already agreed to transfer Louisiana to Spain.

222. Concerning the suppression of the Society of Jesus in the Illinois Country and their departure in 1763, see Mary B. Palm, *Jesuit Missions in the Illinois Country, 1673–1763,* chap. 8.

223. Although on the whole the Anglo-Americans, who began arriving in the Illinois Country in substantial numbers in the 1790s, may have been more literate than their French Creole counterparts, Finiels' assertion that the Americans were more refined is certainly debatable.

human species should have stopped in order to have the best chance of obtaining happiness, since it is a fact that Louisiana's adolescence was the most felicitous time that the region has experienced thus far.[224]

From the beginning, solitude and isolation destroyed in the settlers of Upper Louisiana that French vivacity, which originates in activity, in intellectual give-and-take, in quick repartee, in a populous environment. Their imaginations stagnated without the kaleidoscope of events [152] in city life. They became more grave, slow, deliberate, and less accomplished than Frenchmen are accustomed to be; this had a baleful effect upon society. It would be virtuous if inaction and silence stimulated thinking, but in these vast wastelands illiterate men have no food for thought; there is no visual stimulation when the scene never changes. And you might say that if they weren't talking they were likewise not thinking. However, because imagination is never totally asleep, theirs were being stimulated by stories and songs, which crowded their memories. Each one more amusing and absurd than the next, the stories and songs lessened their boredom on long trips, sparked their courage, and strengthened their sinews. Although the discordant verses vanished among the trees of the forest or fell on the deaf ears of the river, they helped them forget the arduous work required to overcome its strong currents and to attain the goal toward which they were painfully advancing.[225]

The proximity of the Indians, the ease of communicating with them, the need [153] to hunt with them and live in their villages in order to trade—these had no small influence on the character of the colonists. They were compelled to adopt many Indian customs and clothing styles: the breechclout took the place of culottes; leggings replaced stockings; doeskin moccasins succeeded European shoes; a loose-fitting tunic covered the rest of the body; a blue kerchief wrapped about the head completed the costume. When cold weather renders this dress inadequate, a cloak of bergopzoom or rough blue fabric, fitted with a hood, protects the body.[226] Some persons don fur hats that cover their necks and ears and a pair of fur mittens attached by a long string that passes over the shoulders like a stole; the mittens hang down on either side in case your hands need protection, but when not required they are out of the way without any danger of being forgotten or lost. With this simple outfit you can move easily through the woods, tracking deer, wildcats, and wild turkeys, and your body learns to endure the fatigue. Female costumes have the same simplicity: [154] a skirt of blue gingham and a short calico vest in the summer or wool in the winter; a

224. The influence of Rousseau's romantic notions is again apparent in this paragraph.
225. A wonderful collection of early French folktales carefully passed down from generation to generation by French-speaking residents of Missouri can be found in Rosemary Hyde Thomas, *It's Good to Tell You: French Folk Tales from Missouri.* For the river songs, see Marius Barbeau, "Voyageur Songs of the Missouri."
226. *Bergopzoom,* a woolen fabric, took its name from the town in the Netherlands, Bergen op Zoom, where it was first woven. Estate inventories from colonial Ste. Genevieve (originals in Ste. Genevieve County Courthouse, microfilm in Missouri Historical Society, St. Louis, and Western Historical Manuscripts Collection, Columbia, Mo.) provide a good idea of the variety of clothing that was worn in the community, including articles of Indian clothing like *souliers sauvages,* moccasins.

sort of long cotton cloak (called a *pelisse*); a blue or sometimes white kerchief knotted over the forehead, the other two corners of which hang down behind the head; this constitutes daily dress. Calico dresses with dyed designs, and some silk dresses in the antique style that suggest a bit of opulence, make up holiday clothes. They clothe faithful and modest wives, tender mothers, sensible daughters, naive and sincere sweethearts. There is no attempt to accentuate beauty; they leave that to a gay vivacity, which gives them an animated expression; to a timid modesty, which covers them with a charming patina of innocence; to a kindness blended with light touches of charity; to a contentedness of spirit, which provides a certain serenity; and finally to a healthiness, which combines all these expressions with brilliant highlights of freshness, in subtly associating them with the lilies and carmine of nature's fresh sketches, with which art does not challenge.

Forced to gain their subsistence [155] by hunting and their comforts by trading, they soon became accustomed to the rigor of these occupations; ascending roaring rivers further toughened them. From this has resulted a predilection that no young man can resist without facing the scorn of his comrades, and which has become a focal point of their rivalry from boyhood onward. In order to be respected, you must acquire the reputation of being a good boatman; to be a man you must have made three expeditions, paddle in hand—one to New Orleans, one to Michilimackinac, and one up either the Missouri or the Ohio. Then you can boldly go a-courting, which would be contemptible if you had not shown the strength and the courage necessary to endure the hardships of these three trials.[227]

In withstanding these trials they acquire the demonstrable bravery that makes them so fit for the kind of warfare that characterizes this region. They have well proven this, notably when they marched to the aid of Fort Niagara, which the English besieged in 1757. They would surely have saved that fort had Monsieur Aubry [Marin], who commanded the fort, known how to make use of his advantages and profit from their bravery.[228]

These occupations—plus the constant thievery and depredations of the Indians— have prevented them from pursuing agriculture.[229] They turn to it only out of necessity or old age and never by preference. And then they practice it only long enough to

227. The 1779 muster roll of the Ste. Genevieve militia company (AG, PC, legajo 213) lists occupations, and that of *voyageur* constitutes the largest category. Describing Canadian *voyageurs*, Father Pierre-François Charlevoix (quoted in W. J. Eccles, *The Canadian Frontier* [Albuquerue, 1983], 91) remarked, "The journeys they undertake; the fatigues they undergo; the dangers to which they expose themselves; and the efforts they make surpass all imagination."

228. Captain Pierre Pouchot, not Aubry Marin, was commandant at Fort Niagara, and the British under William Johnson besieged and seized Niagara in 1759, not 1757. Nonetheless, it is true that Frenchmen from the Illinois Country served as irregulars under Aubry Marin in the battle for Niagara on 25 July 1759. See A. G. Bradley, *The Fight with France for North America,* 350-51, and Milton W. Hamilton, *Sir William Johnson, Colonial American, 1715-1763,* chap. 21.

229. Amos Stoddard (*Sketches,* 211) remarked, "It has been the misfortune of most of the first settlers in Louisiana, particularly the French, to neglect agriculture, and to turn their attention almost wholly to the Indian trade, which at best only afforded a precarious subsistence." Yet, as Finiels' report points out, serious agriculture was practiced in the Illinois Country.

gain their subsistence and pay off their debts. [156] Requiring rest after the onerous hardships of hunting and fur trading, they become homebodies, indolent and even lazy. They spend a considerable amount of time lazily smoking cigars.[230] When summoned forth by the dance, however, which they love yet more passionately, they stream out of their cabins; dancing is one of the first things they think about upon returning from an expedition. While en route, they yearn to return to their peaceful households only for the festivals that they contemplate as events to signal their return. Often after a week of revels the young men are left with nothing but memories to show for what they earned during four or five months of labor and deprivation.

In the Illinois Country, religion once exercised an imperial power that was not abused. The Jesuits, satisfied with their dominant spiritual position, turned their religious authority to moral issues; when they were recalled [1763], these mission-aries, who had never dishonored their mission with bigotry or fanaticism, were sin-cerely missed. Far from their order's circles of intrigue, with ambitions curtailed by lack of resources, these ministers of religion found in the wilderness of the Illinois Country an island of calm from the stormy passions that disrupted their order in Europe. They left a legacy of morality etched deep in the hearts of all these simple and trusting beings. If they suffered some setbacks during that era, it was with the traders, who often forgot [157] their principles when they lived among the Indians, whose freer morals suited the passions of the traders better than the rigid austerity of the missionaries.[231]

Thus the people of the Illinois Country had their golden age like all other peoples, like all other new societies on earth, and the memory of this has not yet vanished. Less than twenty-five years ago, an educated traveler eulogized these *habitants*.[232] He praised their affability, their gracious, frank, unaffected welcome, their generous hospitality, their charity, the gentle, polite, simple, and natural qualities of their society. These virtues have not entirely disappeared, and traces of them still remain. But, it must be admitted, these characteristics have changed much in the last twelve or fifteen years; the colors have faded, vanishing more each day, and the tableau consists now only of some sketchy outlines.[233]

---

230. There is no doubt that Frenchmen in the Mississippi Valley had a fondness for tobacco, which was raised in the Illinois Country, but probably it was more often consumed in clay pipes than rolled into cigars. See De Lassus de Luzières' "Observations sur les abus qui s'opposent aux progrès et au parfait succès du bonheur des Illinois" (attached by him to the New Bourbon census of 1797 [AGI, PC, legajo 2365]), in which he complained that everyone in the Illinois Country, Indians and blacks as well as whites, smoked pipes and carelessly dumped their ashes, which then started forest fires.

231. The Jesuits, with their establishment at Kaskaskia, were the largest missonary order in the Illinois Country during the French regime, but the important mission at Cahokia was founded and operated by Seminarians. Concerning the Jesuits in the Illinois Country, see Palm, *Jesuit Missions of the Illinois Country*.

232. Finiels provides no hint of the identity of his "educated traveler."

233. Whatever the defects of Finiels' nostalgic romanticism in this paragraph, he is correct in suggest-ing that society in the Illinois Country underwent a dramatic transformation beginning c. 1790, as Anglo-Americans began to flood into the region and contacts with New Orleans became more regular.

Morality is certainly no longer as clean and pure as it was long ago in the Illinois Country. Religion and hospitality remain, however, even though a taste for luxury developed with the advent of commerce and foreigners. The total idleness that characterizes the youth during part of the year leaves them with nothing but gaming and drinking for recreation; this is the usual manner of killing time during idleness.[234] People have become more self-centered with the growth in population and the admixture of foreigners. This has sharply eroded the strict principles of honesty that guided the first colonists. Intrigues and commercial cunning are increasing; they've [158] replaced the forthrightness of earlier transactions, and soon business affairs will become as crafty as they were once open and honest.

Young women and maids already disdain the costumes of their mothers and have relegated them to old age for covering their wrinkles and the ravages of time. Embroidered muslin, tarlatan, fine and brilliant silk, and lawn cloth have replaced modest cotton, printed calico, and bergopzoom. Elegant corsets gallantly delineate waistlines that were once covered by jackets and suggest the seductive figures that they scarcely conceal. Long tresses of hair are no longer restrained with cotton kerchiefs; they float in voluptuous swirls or are artfully braided. Ribbons and flowers are skillfully added in order to draw out more advantageously divers nuances, and coquetry is beginning to eradicate all traces of the tableau that delighted our hearts when we glimpsed the modest beauties that once adorned the wilderness.[235]

The men have not yet become so elegant. Many of them continue to wear clothes that are practical in the woods, and they shed them only reluctantly. These clothes are becoming unfashionable in the capital [St. Louis], however, where some dandies can already be seen. Soon they will be driven from the towns and will be found only in the villages, woods, and hunting canoes. There they will be hidden from a society whose sense of refinement is becoming offended by their rusticity.

In general the men are good [159] husbands, fathers, and sons, but their minds are limited and uncultured.[236] They lack the means to receive an education that would give them a less rustic appearance and that would allow them to acquire better manners, which are generally stiff and awkward. Their ignorance also makes them vain and presumptuous, for being unaware of everything they might learn, they reckon that they already know everything; they are curious, indiscreet, and importunate, and

234. Perrin du Lac, a Frenchman who traveled through the Illinois Country just after the turn of the nineteenth century, commented that the youth of Ste. Genevieve spent their time "exclusively with hunting, horseback riding, and dancing" (*Voyages dans les deux Louisisanes*, 172).

235. Concerning the issue of clothing in the Illinois Country, see above, note 226. Peter Kalm's observation that French-Canadian women, who were, after all, the ancestors of most of the women in the Illinois country, flirted within the bounds of propriety calls into question Finiels' remark that coquetry was replacing the former modesty of the French Creole women. The latter idea appears to have been rooted in the romantic notion of the virtues of a bygone era. Kalm's comments can be found in *Peter Kalm's Travels in North America*, ed. Aldolph B. Benson, 2:402–3.

236. Throughout the colonial era, a substantial majority of the French Creoles in the Illinois Country remained illiterate. See Ekberg, *Colonial Ste. Genevieve*, 278–83.

their high opinion of themselves makes them very haughty. They lie easily, but rather for fun than to deceive; this they owe to the Canadians who have settled among them. These fellows' penchant for tall stories is so well known in Louisiana that everything that seems dubious or imaginary is referred to as Canadian.

Lacking education and manners, their conversation is monotonous rather than entertaining; most often it revolves around farming, hunting, fur trading, and absurd Indian tales. They are superstitious and credulous, which is the usual effect of religion on weak minds that have not had a chance to mature through study and experience. All these defects are the inevitable result of their environment; we see endless examples of this in less civilized nations. Many European peasants are even less civilized than the inhabitants of the Illinois Country. The latter are generally more disposed to improve themselves [160] than our peasants, and a concerted effort might well succeed in turning the *habitants* into interesting and agreeable persons.[237]

They are coolly brave, patient under duress, and inured to the toughest work. They passionately love their former Fatherland, and if compelled to reside under another government, centuries would pass before they forgot the blood that flows in their veins.[238] Quarrels and lawsuits are rare among the whites, and disputes are often resolved with one word from the commandant. Thefts and murders are committed almost exclusively by Indians or slaves; complaints were increasing, however, that Indians and slaves were readily finding "fences" [*receleurs*], and even encouragement, among lower-class whites. This class is the scourge of all societies, and it can rarely be altogether eliminated no matter how pure the morality.

The women are clearly superior to the men. They possess better judgment, greater firmness, a more supple, finer tact, more delicate taste, and a grace in manners that stands in marked contrast to the brusque, awkward comportment of the men. Respectful daughters, faithful wives, good, hardworking mothers, they fulfill all the sacred tasks of nature that the Creoles of the Caribbean are reproached for neglecting. And there are few women in the Illinois Country who have not given suck to eight, ten, twelve, or up to fifteen children.[239] The households are unified, tranquil,

237. Finiels refers here to peasants in France, who may well have been more imprisoned in poverty, illiteracy, ignorance, superstition, and provincial isolation than the *habitants* of the Illinois Country. See, for example, Robert Mandrou, *De la culture populaire en France aux XVIIe et XVIIIe siècles*.

238. Earnest Liljegren concluded, "The conditions which fostered sedition in Lower Louisiana were not to be found in the Illinois country. . . . On the whole the people had a keen interest in the French Revolution and hoped to be reunited to France, but they were not prone to assume a rashly belligerent attitude. Had the Spaniards been driven from Lower Louisiana, they would have readily acquiesced; or, if a determined force had appeared from the United States, they would have capitulated. In the interim, there was little to lose by waiting and pledging loyalty to His Catholic Majesty" ("Jacobinism in Spanish Louisiana, 1792–1797," 87).

239. Fertility rates were high in the Illinois Country, but infant mortality was also very high. See Ekberg, *Colonial Ste. Genevieve*, 269–73. A recent account of the roles of French Creole women in Upper Louisiana is Susan C. Boyle, "Did She Generally Decide? Women in Ste. Genevieve, 1750–1805." Concerning the legal status of women in colonial Louisiana, see Vaughn Baker, Amos Simpson, and Mathé Allain, "*Le Mari Est Seigneur:* Marital Laws Governing Women in French Louisiana."

and [161] peaceful, and it is largely to their good conduct that this is generally the case. I have already mentioned that they are beginning to dress in good taste. They are much alike in appearance, very white and fresh complected, nicely shaped, and there is more than one head among them that a painter would not mind using for a model; perhaps not for Beauty herself, but surely for any one of those graces who customarily accompany her.

The women tend the poultry yards and gardens. Interested in maintaining the latter, their delicate hands do not shrink from cultivating it themselves. Straw hat on the head, spade and cultivator in hand, sometimes they prepare the soil for the seeds or nourish the budding plants; sometimes they attack the voracious weeds that would choke out the vegetables destined to fill the cellars, in which they last throughout the winter. The burning heat of the sun does not discourage the young beauties, so jealous of their fresh complexions. They can be pardoned their elaborate evening toilette when they've spent the entire morning in the garden, heedless of the allures that they willingly sacrifice in order to fulfill their duties. Happy they would be if the alarming advance of luxury could stop at this point. Decadence has not yet crept in when garden work is allied with the refinements of the toilette. At this time, there is an approximate balance between [162] the good and the bad, but this is a delicate balance; a few more steps, and the side of the scale that carries duties and virtues will tilt upwards.

Creole fathers and mothers in all the colonies have been reproached for badly spoiling their children—giving in to all of their whims and demands, even the most excessive and ridiculous of them—and making them willful, despotic, and tyrannical toward their slaves. In this regard, the people of the Illinois Country are not as culpable as those of Lower Louisiana, and the children there are generally better brought up. While still deserving the title "worshipful mothers," which all Creole mothers have acquired, those of the Illinois Country supervise their children much more closely. There are just as many families in which the children are rather strictly reared as there are in which the families have become slaves to their children's whims. This is one more item of praise to add to the interesting balance sheet of their virtues.

Thus the inhabitants of the Illinois Country, like all human societies on the face of the globe, present an admixture of qualities and virtues, defects and vices. For the moment, however, the balance probably leans more toward the former than the latter. Their climate is alternately hot, often oppressively so, and cold, usually bitterly so, and this prevents the growth of those burning and tumultuous passions that consume the Creoles who reside in the tropical colonies. Love, [163] and jealousy, vengeance, and hate, which ravage the torrid zones, never flare up here into a frenzy, made dangerous by its excess. Examples of disasters provoked by love, of emotional outbursts in which irrational jealousy can transport a man overcome by a puerile imagination, are rare. Only one case has occurred in St. Louis; there was one other case in

Ste. Genevieve, where a very respectable woman had these weaknesses in conjunc-
tion with all the virtues generally cherished and esteemed there.²⁴⁰

These people's language has necessarily changed somewhat. However, it is not as
corrupt as one might expect after having observed several French provinces in which
the language is unintelligible to a French person. The Canadians have provided
several expressions peculiar to their country, and the people of the Illinois Country
have also borrowed some Indian idioms that seemed to be more expressive for convey-
ing their thoughts or describing interesting events. They usually receive a rudimen-
tary education in the principal villages of the colony; schoolmasters teach them
reading, writing, and arithmetic. Because in this region there is little social distinction
between the *habitants,* each of whom wishes to do what his neighbors do, almost all
children spend three or four years in school. If they don't acquire an exact knowledge
of the language, they retain enough of it [164] so that they don't change it very
much.²⁴¹

Daily life for the inhabitants of the Illinois Country, in their villages as well as in
their capital, is an amorphous mixture of city and rural customs; everyone is more or
less an urbanite and a peasant at the same time. City habits begin where plowing and
hunting leave off, and the morning farmer is sometimes the evening dandy, striving to
be socially adept.²⁴² Creoles of both sexes love dancing, horse races, sleigh rides,
fishing, and excursions in the woods; they avidly pursue all the pleasures that the
resources of the area offer. But despite this there is not much social life. Socializing is
usually done within the family, especially in St. Louis, where social life is becoming
much more fragmented than in the other villages of the colony.

This sketch of the manners and character of the Illinois settlers pertains to the
general population. But, because the Illinois Country is divided into several rather
distinct parts, there are some traits that pertain to each particular settlement. These
are immediately apparent to the traveler who examines them, which must be done in
order to complete the portrait of this region.

At Cape Girardeau the white population is entirely agricultural; hunting is done
only for recreation and is not related to commerce. The Shawnees and Delawares
who live in the area practice agriculture as well as Indians can, [165] although they love
to return to hunting, which is their customary and favorite occupation. Monsieur

240. The specific cases in St. Louis and Ste. Genevieve to which Finiels refers have not been identified.
In Ste. Genevieve, the most flagrant known case of adultery in colonial times is that of Charles Vallé, son
of the community leader, François Vallé I. Charles discredited himself by conducting a notorious liaison
with a black slave woman, and he eventually had to flee the town (see Ekberg, *Colonial Ste. Genevieve,*
192–94).
241. Concerning the language of the Mississippi valley French and French Creoles, see William A.
Read, *Louisiana French,* and John Francis McDermott, *Glossary of Mississippi Valley French,*
1673–1850. On schools, see Ernest R. Liljegren, "Frontier Education in Spanish Louisiana."
242. The large residential lots in the towns of the Illinois Country—upon which were often located
barns, stables, corn cribs, slave quarters, and so forth—meant that there was a strong rural ambiance
within the confines of the communities.

[Louis] Lorimier, their leader, collects all the proceeds of this hunting; his storehouses are always stocked with Indian trade goods, and he provides the exclusive market for all their furs.[243]

Agriculture is practiced at the Saline settlements, and at the little village near the Grand [Saline] there are a few hunters. The principal occupation of both groups [farmers and hunters] is salt production.[244]

New Bourbon is mostly agricultural, although a few young men are hunters and some of the residents are lead miners.

At Ste. Genevieve there are farmers, merchants, hunters, traders, miners, and some workmen and craftsmen. This town owes its position to its antiquity and to the fact that after St. Louis it is the largest Spanish settlement in Upper Louisiana.

At Carondelet the residents farm and hunt. This village is too poor and too small for any other sort of enterprise to develop.

St. Louis contains the largest population in the Illinois Country. It has the most complex social structure and affords opportunities for the largest variety of occupations. It has farmers, merchants, traders, some hunters, and the largest possible collection of workmen and artisans [166] given the slow and laborious march of progress in this region.

St. Ferdinand and Marais des Liards are almost exclusively agricultural, and St. Charles contains about equal numbers of farmers and hunters; the latter also has some traders and businessmen.

All these settlements also have, because of their mobile population, a supply of *engagés* for water travel. There are also skippers who are experienced on the Mississippi, the Missouri, the Ohio, the Illinois, and the other rivers that are tributaries of the first two.[245]

Cape Girardeau still consists of only a few farmsteads grouped on several points of land; most of the proprietors are Anglo-Americans. They have only recently arrived in the colony and thus retain the manners that they brought with them from Kentucky. Because of their location, their settlements escape the notice of travelers, who can see little but the residence of Monsieur Lorimier, where they must disembark.[246]

At the Saline and New Bourbon the *habitants* have a shy, rustic, wild, and embarrassed demeanor, which is the result of being isolated and seldom visited by strangers.

Only at Ste. Genevieve do you begin to find some urbanity, unaffected politeness, and openness, which offer to the traveler some promise of comfort and hospitality.

243. Concerning Lorimier and the two Indian bands associated with him, see above, notes 24, 26, 27.
244. In the paragraphs that follow, Finiels summarizes his earlier comments on Upper Louisiana's various settlements.
245. *Engagé* was a word often, though not always, used interchangeably with *voyageur* because, in the French-speaking parts of North America, men who were hired (i.e., *engagé*) under contract were often employed as boatmen or canoemen.
246. In 1804, Amos Stoddard observed, "Not more than three or four Frenchmen live in this district; the rest are English Americans" (*Sketches,* 214).

The residents of Carondelet, St. Ferdinand, Marais des Liards, and St. Charles are reserved, [167] withdrawn, and not very sociable. This is especially true at St. Charles because the Missouri has for a long time been a big obstacle, blocking communication with the other settlements. Its residents, more interested in hunting than farming, have taken on a wilder aspect than in any other settlement of the Illinois Country. Strangers seem to bother these men, and they would rather flee than socialize.

St. Louis is, however, the center of manners, urbanity, and elegance in the Illinois Country. If the traveler does not find in its customs that delicacy and refinement which he often unfairly demands and expects to find everywhere because he is accustomed to them in France, it is not the fault of the residents. He must consider that these remote settlements are in an impossible situation for acquiring amenities, and he must credit the residents for their good will, which is apparent enough at St. Louis to be worthy of this indulgence. People are more polite, gracious, and obliging in St. Louis than in Ste. Genevieve, but it doesn't take long to determine that they are more sociable in Ste. Genevieve than in St. Louis; as always, appearances differ from reality.[247]

In Ste. Genevieve people often gather in the homes of the commandant or other important residents. Everyone is welcome at these affairs provided you have a good reputation. Sometimes there is dancing, but more often they play games that everyone enjoys. The more comical the better, for [168] laughter and gaiety are what they usually enjoy most. In the midst of a rollicking, boisterous tumult the soirees unfold, and everyone retires still in stitches from pranks that in other places would scarcely be condoned in children.[248]

In St. Louis dances are held throughout most of the year, but with more pomp and pretension. Every Sunday and holiday are devoted to activities that the Creoles find infinitely appealing. Dances begin three hours after dinner and finish at 10:00 p.m.; they last all night only during Carnival. Meanwhile the older folks play cards, and, in order to see how much more sophisticated St. Louis is than Ste. Genevieve, it suffices to observe that some of them play whist.[249]

I've already remarked that townspeople spend part of each day in rural activities, and that for the remainder of the day they completely forget they are farmers. This mixture of activities is indispensable in a region that requires individual energy not just to live well but even in order to obtain the necessities of life. I've already conveyed

247. Henry Marie Brackenridge remarked, "St. Louis, however, was always a place of more refinement and fashion, it is the residence of many genteel families, both French and American" (*Views of Louisiana, Together with a Journal of a Voyage up the Missouri River in 1811,* 124). For a description of life in colonial St. Louis, see Foley and Rice, *The First Chouteaus,* chap. 2.

248. After the parish church, the commandant's house was the center of public life in colonial Ste. Genevieve. It was the place, for example, where political assemblies were held when important community issues were discussed (see Ekberg, *Colonial Ste. Genevieve,* 376–77).

249. Brackenridge remarks about dancing in Ste. Genevieve, "The minuette was the principal dance. I think it is in some measure owing to this practice, that the awkward, clownish manners of other nations, are scarcely known among the French" (*Recollections of Persons and Place in the West,* 29).

an idea of these difficulties when I described St. Louis; here I will only add what is needed to complete the picture.

Hard currency is extremely rare in the Illinois Country.²⁵⁰ To compensate for this, deerskins have been generally adopted as the standard currency, and their value is fixed and steady at forty sous per pound. Thus [169] when you talk about paying twenty or thirty piastres for any object whatsoever, without saying anything more, it is understood that payment will be in skins. Two-and-a-half pounds of deerskins equal one piastre, and on this basis all accounts are reckoned and paid, unless there is an express agreement that payment will be made in some other fashion.²⁵¹ In specie the piastre is worth twenty sous more, is therefore worth six francs [instead of the usual five], and is usually valued at three pounds of deerskins; this value has made them a trade item that strangers must heed. The general lack of specie in the Illinois Country means that all exchanges, commercial or otherwise, have been reduced to bartering. This is advantageous to anyone who has the facilities needed to acquire those goods, and it can much reduce daily expenses in this region.

In examining this state of affairs as it has developed naturally in the Illinois Country, one is astonished to see how the residents have begun to imitate, obviously without suspecting it, the most carefully calculated affairs of the most advanced nations; how they imitate the world's most important commercial nations in order to compensate for the lack of specie and to lubricate the wheels of commerce. In fact, the Indians are the true bankers of this region: their peltries are the bills placed in circulation, and their hunting provides security for the fictitious specie [i.e., peltries] upon which the merchants base their business. To assure the strength and stability of this system, [170] which is advantageous to everyone, it has been sufficient to set the value of the piastre [in specie] at twenty sous more and to fix the value of skins permanently at forty sous. Authority and credit have accomplished nothing, and confidence is greater because the system emanates from bows, arrows, gunpowder, lead, guns— these are the items that secure this singular banking system, into which anyone can dip and renew his fortunes. If this system were due to the careful calculations of some individual, it would serve to cover his name with immortal glory. But if it derives from a natural concatenation of things, you can only admire nature's instinct, which sometimes leads us to simpler and better solutions than those produced by much thought and research.²⁵²

250. Concerning the scarcity of hard currency in Spanish Illinois, see Foley and Rice, *The First Chouteaus*, 40, 41, 82, 177.

251. Deerskins were an enormously important part of the economy of colonial Louisiana. See Daniel Usner, "Frontier Exchange in the Lower Mississippi Valley: Race Relations and Economic Life in Colonial Louisiana, 1699–1783." Concerning the relative values of various commodities and currencies, see Ekberg, *Colonial Ste. Genevieve*, appendix H, 475. In 1763, deerskins were, after indigo, the largest export product of Louisiana (*Executive Documents of the House of Representatives, 1887–1888*, 180).

252. Finiels here espouses a laissez-faire economic philosophy, emphasizing—as had Adam Smith and the French physiocrats—that the economy is healthiest that emanates from a "natural concatenation of things." In other passages, however, he seems more inclined to favor at least some government regulation

Thus the Illinois Country should and can dispense with hard currency as long as an abundant fur trade continues. It is for this part of Louisiana what the mines are for Mexico and Peru. It is the true basis for future prosperity; all other branches of commerce that contribute to it are nonetheless secondary to it. Because of it, Upper Louisiana is a region utterly independent of Lower Louisiana, and it should be independently organized and developed through different means. [171] Then the government could succeed in turning it into the splendid place that nature seems to have intended. To accomplish this, you don't have to turn things upside down; they simply need to be developed and perfected.[253]

Necessities of life in the Illinois Country seem to the stranger at first glance to be exorbitantly priced, while at the same time they seem very cheap to the residents who are familiar with the region's economy. This situation requires some explanation, which may seem tedious but without which you cannot get a precise idea of how to live economically and avoid unnecessary expenditures. This is good enough to provide me with an excuse, and I shall continue: A chicken, for example, costs 50 sols, and a dozen eggs the same. Neither the season nor availability has any bearing on these prices. Whether you pay in cash, skins, or merchandise, the prices remain unchanged. If a stranger pays in piastres, which I did for some time, his expenses are quadruple those of the resident who nonetheless claims to be paying the same price—and this is how it works: All those who can do so have brought from New Orleans coffee, sugar, and other goods that have fixed prices (as they all do) and that are in demand in the Illinois Country. Coffee costs 1 piastre per pound, and sugar 50 sols. [172] For those who bring them up from New Orleans, coffee costs 24 to 30 sols and sugar 12 to 16 per pound. Therefore in paying a pound of sugar for a chicken and a pound of coffee for two dozen eggs, both of them come to 12 to 16 sols, which was the usual price in Europe before the Revolution. The same is true for many other indispensable commodities, which are brought up and which increase as much, if not more, in price between New Orleans and the Illinois Country. It is with these commodities that you procure and pay for all of your needs—bread, meat, cattle, often houses and real estate, wages of *engagés,* and so forth. By this means almost everything is reduced one-fourth in price.[254]

Labor is likewise acquired very cheaply by this means. It would be exorbitantly high if you were obliged to pay wages in cash. But laborers willingly take commodities for wages, or if they prefer peltries you can obtain these just as advan-

---

of economic affairs.

253. Finiels' dream of an autonomous Upper Louisiana was impractical because New Orleans remained the indispensable market for products from the Illinois Country.

254. The marketing system was subject to greater fluctuations than Finiels' statements imply. Commodity prices did not remain constant. For example, when François and Jean-Baptiste Vallé of Ste. Genevieve had their factor in New Orleans, Berte Grima, ship coffee and sugar to them in July 1795, the coffee cost 22 sols per pound, and the sugar 24 sols per pound. François Vallé Papers, Missouri Historical Society, St. Louis, box 3.

tageously with the same commodities. Thus, without necessarily being a merchant, you can have your own storehouse (which is often used only for making payments) that in effect serves as your strongbox. The art of [173] living well in the Illinois Country boils down to knowing when to exchange cash for merchandise.[255]

The products of the region—such as wheat, maize, and tobacco—have also become currencies, and you can pay with these things as well as with trade goods. Wheat is worth 2 piastres per bushel, maize 50 sols, and tobacco 12 sols per pound.[256]

As soon as you become known in the Illinois Country, you can also pay for all your needs with IOUs [bons], which circulate freely and are not discounted by bakers, butchers, farmers, or merchants. Some of the latter with the largest stocks of merchandise accept them eagerly because they take them in exchange for merchandise and the issuers redeem them with peltries. Furthermore, this facilitates small purchases and benefits commerce, for without it, it would be difficult to sell some articles that can be unloaded with IOUs.[257]

This custom—ingenious result of necessity, of a lack of currency, of difficulty finding markets, and of a total lack of resources—permits you to see what commerce is like in a region where you must use similar means to subsist. The daily and most abundant aspects of consumption are necessarily absent when every resident is involved in exchanges that [174] alone allow him to sustain his family and have a few small luxuries. Thus commerce is reduced almost entirely to fur trading. Besides peltries, merchants are obliged to take in payment all sorts of products and convert them to peltries before dispatching them to New Orleans, which is the only market where cash can be obtained; and this occurs only if in the meantime those peltries are not committed to fulfilling other contracts.[258]

The bitter, long winter in the Illinois Country occasions an enormous consumption of wood. The price per load, which contains as in New Orleans a half-cord, is one piastre, or two-and-a-half pounds of skins. Although this price appears to be only half that in New Orleans, it is in fact excessive because you must keep a fire going day and night during that season, which begins at the end of October and sometimes lasts into May. During the heart of winter, which I have spent in the Illinois Country, I used at least 160 cartloads, and many households larger than mine got by with hardly less

255. On paper, wages were twice as high in the Illinois Country as in New Orleans (see Ekberg, Colonial Ste. Genevieve, 162–63).

256. The prices that Finiels quotes for grain and tobacco tend toward the high end of a fluctuating scale, probably because Finiels resided in the Illinois Country immediately after the 1797 flood, which destroyed many crops. See Ekberg, Colonial Ste. Genevieve, 474.

257. Most business transactions in Upper Louisiana were paper transactions because of the scarcity of hard currency. See Foley and Rice, The First Chouteaus, 39–41, 82, 177.

258. All businessmen of any significance in Upper Louisiana had agents in New Orleans who handled their affairs there; moreover, these businessmen often traveled in person to the capital to handle financial affairs. During the late colonial period, the only substantial amount of specie was kept in the Spanish royal treasury in New Orleans.

than 300, 400, or 500 cartloads. It's true that the resident who has merchandise can much reduce this expense through his system of payment. Moreover, a person can fetch his own wood if he has a cart and [175] slaves. Most of the forests are still in the public domain, and everyone has a right to cut what he needs in these forests.[259] Despite this, when there is a wet winter, wood becomes scarce because of bad roads. It's not yet being brought in by water, but it won't be long before this will become necessary.

Forests are getting thinner and harder to find, especially near St. Louis. When the Mississippi is solidly frozen over, some residents take their carts, cross it, and cut wood in the deserted forests on the other bank. This resource is only temporary, however, for the Americans are starting to keep an eye on this infringement of territory, which will cease as soon as the population begins to grow. Beyond the demand that a variety of building occasions—including the indispensable picket fences—the liberty that each person has to collect his own wood causes enormous waste, which is destroying the forests. No sense of economy, no thought of replanting has yet been conceived for this region. The notion that forests are inexhaustible since they once were all-surrounding has from the beginning inspired an unpardonable carelessness in this regard. If a Creole is in the woods with his axe and wants to eat some [176] pecans, persimmons, or wild cherries, he does not take the trouble to climb the tree and collect the fruit branch by branch. Rather, with a laziness that is as ignorant as destructive, he sets about a larger project—he sinks his axe in the trunk and fells the tree in order to be able to eat the fruit at his leisure. Thus it is that colonies' riches and resources, abundantly provided by nature, are abused, and no thought is given to the privations that this will create in the future or for later generations.[260]

These, then, are the rustic, plain men who combine virtues and qualities with a rough, coarse appearance. This, together with their defects, is a consequence of their environment and a generally savage life style. The Spanish regime, which is more lax in the Illinois Country than in Lower Louisiana, has accustomed them to a sort of independence; moderation and leniency should be employed to enlighten them about self-interest and extract them from the inertia into which they have fallen. Before demanding production beyond their present capacity, you must provide them with markets and with some means to expand and increase their fortunes. They are human beings, and their hearts are not devoid of ambition; they will ardently pursue a goal sketched out for them by an able hand.[261]

259. Forests and pasture land, as opposed to arable land, tended to remain in the public domain during the colonial period. The extravagantly inefficient fireplaces made deforestation a serious problem in the Illinois Country, as they did in eighteenth-century Europe.

260. In De Lassus de Luzières' "Observations sur les abus qui s'opposent aux progrès . . .," he lamented the waste of firewood and recommended regulations to conserve the forests.

261. Finiels' ruminations about economic theory provide an interesting mix of notions, suggesting that individual self-interest and free markets be directed by the "able hand" of enlightened government.

The Spanish government has never stationed anyone but a lieutenant governor in the Illinois Country, and he is usually a captain from the fixed regiment of Louisiana.[262] At the same time, [177] he is an agent of the intendant and military commissioner and has responsibility for all military, civil, judicial, and financial affairs. A secretary, storekeeper, and interpreter are the only positions under him that the government authorizes and supports. A few years ago, they added a surgeon attached to the hospital of the garrison, which is supposed to consist of forty men but is rarely that large. Commandants of the other settlements dependent upon St. Louis, which is the usual residence of the lieutenant governor, are usually local militia officers and are generally natives of the settlements they command.[263] Since the lieutenant governor appoints them, he always solicits village opinion about the choice for leader. In this fashion, good men live tranquilly, peaceably, and submissively under the authority of one of their fellow citizens, whom they often regard as their father. Lawsuits, disputes, and quarrels are resolved by the commandant at no cost. The respective parties come before him and present their cases. If it is a serious matter, the secretary records the proceedings, which might be used as an official transcript in the future; but usually the commandant resolves things without that formality, and everything is forgotten. Men who are accustomed to this patriarchal system will only reluctantly accept a more severe and demanding government. But they would be delighted to accept one whose appearance closely resembled their present one—especially if it were offered to them by France.

CLIMATE AND PRODUCTS

The Illinois settlements may be thought of as located between 37 and 40 degrees north latitude.[264] The [178] region's temperature should be moderate enough so that one wouldn't need to explain excessive heat and cold. However, the situation is quite the opposite. The cold is just as bitter as that in Holland, and the heat just as burning as that which annually dessicates most of the fertile plains of the Antilles. It is hard to find a satisfactory explanation for the intense heat in the Illinois Country during the

262. Upper Louisiana's Spanish lieutenant governors between 1770 and 1803 were Pedro Joseph Piernas, 1770–1775; Francisco Cruzat (first term), 1775–1778; Fernando de Leyba, 1778–1780; Francisco Cruzat (second term), 1780–1787; Manuel Pérez, 1787–1792; Zenon Trudeau, 1792–1799; and Charles (Carlos) Dehault Delassus, 1799–1803.

263. Finiels' claim that local commandants were usually drawn from the militia companies of the Illinois Country must be qualified. Commandants were, in fact, frequently outsiders assigned by the Spanish governor in New Orleans. Concerning the issue of local government in Spanish Illinois, see Ekberg, *Colonial Ste. Genevieve*, 335–77. Finiels was, however, correct in predicting that the Creoles would be reluctant to accept a change in governments. They experienced numerous problems in adapting to the American system following the Louisiana Purchase. See William E. Foley, *A History of Missouri, Volume I: 1673–1820*, 71–88.

264. A latitude of 37 degrees north falls near New Madrid, Missouri, and 40 degrees north falls near Hannibal, Missouri. Therefore, Finiels defined the geographical limits of the settlement in Spanish Illinois broadly, for there were no white settlers as far north as present-day Hannibal.

months of June, July, August, and September. During those months, it is the same as in New Orleans, although that city is 9 degrees further south than St. Louis. According to all the colonists who have come from St. Domingue to Louisiana, the heat in New Orleans is just as intense as that which seems so devastating at Cap Français [on St. Domingue], although that city is itself 10 degrees farther south than New Orleans.[265]

Thus during almost one-third of the year it is just as hot in the Illinois Country as in New Orleans, and in New Orleans as at Cap Français. During the months of June, July, August, and September, a difference of 10 to 19 degrees latitude signifies no noticeable change in the scorching temperature of these three far-flung places, but in the winter there are striking differences between them. The progression of change, however, cannot be reckoned by corresponding temperature changes in such places as Europe, Asia, or Africa.

In fact, the winters of Cap Français, which are what one would expect [179] given its location, and those of New Orleans and St. Louis might seem proportional to the distances between them if you were considering only those three cities. But in comparing the winters of the two Louisiana cities, New Orleans and St. Louis, with those from corresponding latitudes in the three other sections of the globe, you are astonished by the enormous differences between them.

It is usually colder in New Orleans during the months of January, February, and March than it is during winter in any similar latitude in the Old World. Sometimes there is snow, and it often freezes during these three months. The Cape of Good Hope on the other hand, which is 4 degrees of latitude closer to the South Pole (known to be colder than the North Pole), is never cold enough to require heating during the months of May, June, and July, which is winter there; there is never any snow, much less ice. It would be even more striking if I were to compare winter temperatures from New Orleans and all places of 30 degrees latitude in Africa, Asia, and even in South America; Buenos Aires, at 35 degrees south latitude, never has winters like those in New Orleans.[266]

But the cold spells in St. Louis, which is about 39 degrees north latitude, during the months of December, January, February, and March, are just as surprising, if you compare them to those in Lisbon, the islands of [180] Majorca, Minorca, and the Peloponnesus, Turkey, Asia, and so forth, which are at the same latitude. I've already mentioned that the cold in St. Louis is equivalent to that in Europe at 52 degrees north latitude, while in some French provinces at 42–43 degrees latitude the winters are so mild that you find snow only on the high mountain peaks. I'll never forget the surprise of several Languedociens who came to settle in Lorraine when, for the first time, they

265. In this section, many of Finiels' observations about specific conditions in Upper Louisiana have some basis in fact, but his explanations about climate and weather tend to be conjectural and fanciful.
266. The Cape of Good Hope, at 35 degrees south latitude, is 5 degrees closer to the South Pole than New Orleans, at 30 degrees north latitude, is to the North Pole.

saw water condensed in light flakes, which fluttered in midair or which struck them in heavy, solid masses.[267]

Thus the summers of Cap [Français], New Orleans, and St. Louis are all equally hot, while the winters are very different. In the latter two cities, nature, in contrast to the way she acts in the Old World, seems to contradict herself throughout the year.

Louisiana is not the only place in America where there are these variations in temperature compared with corresponding latitudes in the three other large divisions of the globe. The same situation characterizes the entire United States from the Mississippi to Penobscot Bay, which is at 40–42 degrees north latitude. The heat there is as intense as in the Antilles, and the cold as penetrating as in most of our frozen northern regions.[268]

Not enough thought has been devoted [181] to the temperature variations that characterize this part of America; too few observations have been made to provide a sound basis for hazarding guesses as to what causes them. In almost all of these places, they are attributed to geography. The chain of lakes that extends from the St. Lawrence River toward Hudson's Bay plays a prominent role in explaining the extraordinary cold of Louisiana. But it is just as surprising that several of these lakes freeze as solidly as they do. Lake Erie is located at only 41 degrees north latitude; Lakes Ontario and Huron at 43 degrees; and Lake Michigan begins at 41 degrees. To be sure, it sometimes freezes at these latitudes in Europe, but never as persistently, solidly, and for as long a period as in the different regions of Canada that I've just mentioned.[269]

Moreover, these temperatures, extraordinary enough in their own right, are subject to a multitude of variations that range from one extreme to another in the same day. They change constantly and seem to be in perpetual motion, making them singularly strange. Summer and winter days often alternate from hot to cold, from dry to wet, from calm to stormy. The progress of summer itself is not always even; it can begin early or late and conclude the same way. Cold mixes easily with heat, and heat with cold. Several [182] summers have been very pleasant in New Orleans, such as in 1802. It preceded a severely cold winter for that region, although it is not unusual to spend winters there without markedly cold weather. That of 1802 was rather more warm than chilly. Everything was sprouting in January and February, and there was scarcely any frost in March, which is often the coldest month of winter. On the other hand, the winter of 1803 was persistently bitter, and several times the ice was nearly an inch thick.[270] In the Illinois Country, rainy winters are mild winters; then spring comes

267. St. Louis lies at 38½ degrees north latitude, while 43 degrees north latitude falls at the Pyrenees Mountains. Finiels fails to distinguish clearly between coastal and continental climates, nor does he seem to have any awareness of the climatic effects of the Gulf Stream.
268. Penobscot Bay lies between 44 and 45 degrees north latitude.
269. Lake Erie lies between 42 and 43 degrees north latitude. Lakes Huron and Ontario lie at about 45 degrees north latitude. Chicago lies a little north of 41 degrees north latitude.
270. Finiels lived in New Orleans between 1798 and 1804, and therefore knew firsthand what the

very early; hot spells arrive in February, and vegetation seems to be several months ahead of nature's usual schedule. On other occasions, frost comes as early as October, and cold weather arrives rapidly; by the end of November it is already extreme, and during December the river freezes solidly. The ice remains until the end of March, and often all the houses keep fires going during the month of May. Residents are obliged to struggle against the last remnants of cold, which seem to leave the region only reluctantly.

In examining the configuration of lands that constitute the center of the [North] American continent, you begin to suspect that part of the rigor of the winters, as well as the fluctuations in temperature, are due to the high terrain that serves as a barrier to the many lakes strung out from East to West. Niagara Falls clearly proves that Lakes [183] Erie, Huron, Michigan, and Superior are nearly 300 feet higher than Lake Ontario.[271] The latter is itself much higher than Montreal, for the entire range of the St. Lawrence River between Lake Ontario and that city is straight and turbulent; that stretch is full of falls and rapids, indicating a considerable descent. From the Great Lakes to below Cape Girardeau, the terrain slopes downward very noticeably, which reveals the velocity of the Mississippi; it is much swifter from its source to Cape Girardeau than from Cape Girardeau to La Balise.[272] A further demonstration of the Mississippi's greater drop over that stretch is that its course is much less tortuous than it is farther down. Descending headlong with the power that the descent conveys to its waters, it has overcome obstacles presented by the densest soils and rocks and has blazed a direct route to the South. But scarcely does it enter the alluvial lands of Lower Louisiana than it quickly slows down; it often detours across loose and erodable soils, taking from the right bank in order to deposit on the left and then, a bit further on, redepositing on the right. The current is no longer hurried onward by its slope. Thus it travels twice as far, while cavorting across these vast plains, to get to the Gulf of Mexico than if this enormous basin of lowlands were sloped more. Two [184] leagues below Cape Girardeau, the highlands, veering westward, form bluffs almost 160 feet high. At the foot of these bluffs begin the Lower Louisiana lowlands that slope only slightly all the way to the sea. From this configuration it is easy to gain a favorable impression of the Illinois Country, and it is also easy to see that the lands of Lower Louisiana depend indirectly upon those of the Illinois Country, even though they are the immediate result of the winds.[273]

---

weather conditions had been like during that time period.

271. The elevations of the Great Lakes are as follows: Lake Superior, 600 feet; Lakes Huron and Michigan, 581 feet; Lake Erie, 571 feet; Lake Ontario, 246 feet. Finiels was using French feet, which equal 1.063 English feet; therefore, his comment that Lake Erie is "nearly 300 feet higher than Lake Ontario" is reasonably accurate. It is 306 French feet. Of course, that fall is not entirely a result of Niagara Falls, for there are also sharply descending rapids above the falls.

272. La Balise was at the mouth of the Mississippi, where the French had earlier established a small fort. Laussat's *Memoirs of My Life,* 11–14, contains a good description of La Balise as it was in 1803.

273. Although Finiels' general topographical description in this paragraph is essentially correct, he exaggerates the extent to which a geographical line of demarcation near Cape Girardeau could be construed as a physical boundary between Upper and Lower Louisiana. The wind-deposited soils that

The southern summer winds that raise temperatures in Europe cool the air in Louisiana during that season, while during the winter they warm it. In summer, northern winds make the sun hotter, and in winter they make the cold more bitter. The reasons for this seem rather plausible after what I've just said. In summer the southern wind crosses vast expanses of sea before arriving in Louisiana; it arrives charged with water vapor and is thus less hot than the local winds; in winter it arrives after having passed over less cool regions, which are not frozen over, and it arrives in Louisiana bringing milder temperatures than those that come from the North. In summer the north wind brings hot air that has passed over terrain heated by the fiery sun, and thus it raises temperatures in these regions [of Louisiana]. In winter it blows across snow and ice and brings a northern climate to regions that nature would seem to have intended, on the basis of their latitude, to be warmer during that season.

[185] Thus you must attribute to the winds, in addition to the geography of these lands, the daily temperature variations in Louisiana. And you must confer to the north wind all honors for bringing to this province winters that are just as bitter. The same mechanism explains the sizzling summers of Upper Louisiana. South and southwest winds, which generally prevail during the summer, arrive there only after having passed over all of Lower Louisiana, and their fiery air is responsible for scorching the earth in Illinois during that season.[274]

The Illinois Country has yet another obvious climatic characteristic, which is the progressive development of the growing season in the respective settlements. These are located only eighteen to twenty leagues apart by the usual routes, but are much closer as the crow flies. And yet trees only starting to bud in St. Louis are already far enough along in Ste. Genevieve to turn the forest's somber hue a brilliant clear green that brightens the crests of the trees. At the same time, the leaves are out in Cape Girardeau, and at New Madrid blossoms have arrived. Vegetables, plants, and flowers follow the same pattern. In the capital [St. Louis] you are still deprived of these products of nature when in New Madrid you can savor almost all their favors, and yet only a degree and a half of latitude separates these [186] two towns.[275]

Louisiana's climate, even in the region closest to the mouth of the Mississippi, has for a long time been considered healthy and moderate. In the last twelve to fifteen years a great revolution has occurred in temperature and salubrity. The older residents claim that summers are hotter and winters colder, and they complain about many fatal diseases that did not exist in decades past. At New Orleans, the year 1796 was marked by an epidemic that was as frightening as it was unexpected, and which

---

Finiels speaks of are the well-known loess deposits of the Mississippi valley.

274. Finiels' analysis of weather conditions in both Upper and Lower Louisiana is an admixture of conjecture, fancy, and a few more-or-less accurate observations. His attempts to supply detailed and dogmatic explanations of weather conditions with little knowledge of the subject make him appear, in this instance, almost medieval in outlook.

275. Although there is some variance between the growing seasons in St. Louis and New Madrid, Finiels has exaggerated the difference; moreover, St. Louis and New Madrid are separated by two degrees of latitude rather than one and a half degrees.

baffled the medical doctors. In 1799 an even more serious epidemic returned and wreaked further ravages. Since then, every year has been more or less disastrous; each summer brings more fears and fatalities. Even autumn, winter, and spring are not free of dangers. Pleurisy, pneumonia, sore throats, whooping cough, and scarlet fever have arrived and gripped these seasons, which were formerly regarded as a refuge from the fury of summer illnesses; they've mowed down many children and adults. Each season now seems to present its own special dangers, as it likewise brings forth its respective flowers, fruits, plants, and vegetables.[276]

In the Illinois Country, however, the climate is generally healthier. This is especially true in the Spanish part and particularly [187] in the higher locations, such as St. Louis. During the summer, this capital is usually attacked by fevers, but these are almost always recurring fevers, and, if cared for, they disappear after several attacks. Not very dangerous in themselves, they do nonetheless lower your resistance, leaving you for some time during convalescence in a sort of melancholy stupor. This stupefaction seems to be due only to the difficulty that the humors have in settling down. An emetic, medicines, and some good quinine rarely fail to be effective, and moderation completes the cure. Putrid, malignant fevers sometimes arrive, making simple illnesses dangerous and aggravating them according to the particular circumstances of each summer. You must also be on guard against colds, pneumonia, and pleurisy, which are easily contracted in this part of Louisiana during the rainy, wet periods of spring and autumn; they are due to variations in the weather. You can avoid them only by paying attention to the way you dress and guarding against the foolish mistake (only too easily committed) of exposing yourself to the fickle effects of the air.[277]

St. Ferdinand, Marais des Liards, and Carondelet have climates similar to St. Louis. They experience the same illnesses, which are characterized by more or less the same symptoms. St. Charles and the settlements that surround the [188] various communities on the lowlands along the banks of the Mississippi, the Missouri, and other rivers are susceptible to more malignant fevers.[278] This is perhaps due to lack of medical attention. Or perhaps it is because the farmsteads are owned either by Creoles, who do not take very good care of themselves, or by Anglo-Americans, who are

---

276. Finiels' generalizations in this paragraph are certainly suspect, but it is true that 1796 was the first in a series of years when yellow fever wreaked ravages in Lower Louisiana (Charles Gayarré, *History of Louisiana*, 3:375).

277. Mosquito-borne diseases such as malaria and yellow fever were less virulent in Upper Louisiana than in the lower portion of the province, but they were a serious problem in the Illinois Country. See Ekberg, *Colonial Ste. Genevieve*, 240–68. Finiels' "recurring fevers" were surely malaria. Amos Stoddard commented that in Upper Louisiana "the heats produce lassitude and languor, and exercise becomes irksome. In this state of the bodily system, people who live on the borders of great water courses are seized with diseases, generally of the intermittent kind" (*Sketches*, 237).

278. It was commonplace in the Illinois Country to associate wet and swampy areas with disease, but the diseases were never linked with the mosquitoes that proliferated in those places. Finiels' contemporary and countryman Constantin-François Chasseboeuf, Comte de Volney, was an avid observer of climate, both in Europe and America. Volney traveled extensively in the eastern half of North America, but he came only as far west as Vincennes and the Wabash River valley. See his *A View of the Soil and Climate of the United States of America*, 253–61.

known for a curious negligence in treating illnesses, for excessive drinking, and for their bad diets even when they are in good health; when they become ill they reluctantly change their diets.[279] It should be noted, however, that all the low areas in the Illinois Country, those that are at river level and vulnerable to being inundated during floods, are usually much more dangerous than those that are located above the flood line.

Ste. Geneviève is more susceptible than St. Louis to fevers that may have bad consequences. New Bourbon, which is higher and breezier, is less troubled by fevers; and living is not terribly dangerous at either of the Salines. Everything suggests that Cape Girardeau is quite healthy despite the annual fevers that attack the Anglo-American families living there. We can thus conclude that with regard to health, Spanish Illinois is clearly superior to Lower Louisiana, even though it [189] is not exempt from danger. It will become even healthier when some experienced medical doctors settle there. The persistent lack of such skilled persons in the settlements of Spanish Illinois is yet further evidence of their healthiness.[280]

The Anglo-American settlements in the Illinois Country do not enjoy nearly the same advantages as the settlements on the right bank of the Mississippi. That lovely plain, which is so delectable when the prairies and woods are in bloom, conceals dangers in its bosom. These are not always avoidable, and sometimes the plain witnesses a grim harvest of deaths. In 1797, a malignant fever ravaged New Design and several other parts of the plain. It's a rare year when the fever does not snatch some victims from the love of their grief-stricken families, for such losses strike more often on the left bank of the Mississippi.[281]

Smallpox often plays havoc in these settlements, as it also does in the neighboring Indian tribes.[282] Even St. Louis is not immune. For the half-century since its founding, St. Louis seemed to be exempt from nature's law that governs almost all human

279. Frenchmen seemed to agree that the Anglo-American diet was injurious to the health. Volney, for example, remarked that if one were seeking "a regimen most destructive to the teeth, the stomach, and the health in general, none could be devised more efficacious for these ends than that in use among this people" (ibid., 257).

280. Medical doctors, midwives, and medicines were in chronic short supply in the Illinois Country during colonial times. De Lassus de Luzières complained bitterly about that situation in his "Observations sur les abus qui s'opposent aux progrès . . . ."

281. Finiels' claim that in the Illinois Country the west bank of the Mississippi was healthier than the east bank is questionable. Nonetheless, it was true that St. Louis had a higher location than either Cahokia or Kaskaskia, both of which were situated on the flood plain, and was therefore less susceptible to mosquito-borne diseases. Finiels thus looked at diseases in Upper Louisiana from a geographical perspective. Amos Stoddard raised the question of the etiology of diseases in the Illinois Country from another perspective—population differences: "The endemics in Upper Louisiana are almost exclusively confined to English Americans, who were born and educated in more northern climates; and even these after a residence of one or two years in the country, generally enjoy a good degree of health" (*Sketches,* 237). Stoddard seems to have been referring to the "seasoning" period that newcomers to the Mississippi Valley experienced as their bodies adjusted to the malaria parasite. The complex issue of malaria's effects on different areas and population groups might be clarified with a comprehensive study of mortality for all of the colonial communities in the Illinois Country.

282. Concerning smallpox in Spanish Illinois, see Houck, *History of Missouri,* 2:62, and Ekberg, *Colonial Ste. Geneviève,* 258–60. Also see note 106 above.

beings—to experience one time during their lifetime the effects of that cruel disease. Finally, however, she [Mother Nature] withdrew that precious favor, especially for women, and the capital [190] of the Illinois Country now shares and fears the dangers from which she seemed immune for so long. Constant breezes, frequent fluctuations from wet to dry and from heat to cold, create and aggravate the problems, along with numerous incidents and illnesses. This is not because the entire region is unhealthy, but only because some particular localities are; this includes most places where temperatures fluctuate.

It is not only upon man that this fickle climate wreaks destruction. Plants and animals are also subject to it, and there are few products of Upper Louisiana that escape its effects. I've already presented the nomenclature of these different things in the special sections devoted to each community in the Illinois Country; I'll not repeat them here. But I will make some indispensable remarks in order to explain the hopes that are based upon these products and to demonstrate their vulnerability if human skill does not succeed, so to speak, in bending nature to its will.

In enumerating a colony's principal sources of prosperity and riches, you must always calculate the number of cattle that can be raised and fed on the land. Cattle speed up work, increase the amount that can be accomplished, assure subsistence, and facilitate transportation, thus encouraging inland settlements [191] in all those areas remote from the rivers. Settlers never dare to venture far from the rivers if they don't have a sure means of transporting their goods to the riverbanks. However well-endowed Upper Louisiana may be with navigable rivers, if its settlers can expand only along waterways, their communities will never have cohesiveness, staying power, strength, or vigor. For the most part isolated because the river banks are only sporadically suitable for cultivation, the settlers cannot help each other. They languish, each in isolation, and although the colony seems to be growing, in reality it is making but little progress.[283]

In this state of affairs, communications are tedious and difficult, for you must endure the capricious meanderings of the rivers; you must overcome obstacles created by their uneven beds, seizing the moment of high water. And, while it is easy to travel downstream, it is difficult coming back up, which means that you lose in arduous labor precious time that might have been spent on agriculture. Overland routes, on the other hand, shorten distances. They are passable during some seasons, most especially when the rivers are either dried up with excessive heat or locked up with bitter cold, rendering [water] transportation impossible. [192] But overland transportation is futile unless you have quantities of draft animals that can be employed without using those that are indispensable for tilling the soil. This has been a persistent problem in the Illinois Country. The animals are frequently attacked by dis-

283. Given the increases in Upper Louisiana's population that occurred while Finiels lived there in 1797-1798, his comments here seem unduly pessimistic.

eases and die in droves; they are victims of burning heat, which brings droughts, shortages of fodder, and illnesses; or they are victims of bitter cold, which strikes down the mothers with their young, thus inhibiting reproduction, which should be increased to its maximum.[284]

Fickle weather is one reason that Upper Louisiana has been producing only small numbers of cattle, which have multiplied little since the founding of the colony. Each year there are about the same number, and that is almost always inadequate for subsistence and agriculture. Once again, we find in this shortage of animals one reason for the continuing lethargy of the settlements in the Illinois Country. It's true that Indian raids have contributed much to inhibit the multiplication of livestock, but if cattle had been more numerous St. Louis and Ste. Genevieve would have developed more quickly. These two towns would have soon created [193] overland communications; the region between them would be settled, and forty years ago they would have been as large as they are today.[285] You can't deny that Mexico, Peru, and all the other Spanish settlements on the [American] continents owe what little vigor they have to their abundant livestock. They alone have given these colonies the capacity to transport goods to all regions and from one ocean to another; they have made it possible to transport to the coasts all the goods and products of the interior.

The flora of Upper Louisiana are just as threatened by the constant seasonal changes. Harvests are precarious; they are as unpredictable as the weather, and the farmer in this region of fickle and capricious climate can only rarely count on harvesting the fruits of his labors. Torrential rains often drown the seeds in the fields; they rot in the persistently damp soil, and the reproductive germs decompose. The despairing farmer rushes to plant fresh seeds in the wet soil; he suffers the same fate several times, and then there is no more harvest to anticipate.[286] Sometimes a propitious spring raises fond hopes in his heart; the soil sufficiently [194] irrigated by gentle, infrequent rains preserves without damaging the seed entrusted to it; a temperate warmth incubates the seed, which soon pushes its fragile stem to the surface. Then the farmer's contented eye follows the progress of growth that promises a rich harvest. Nonetheless, having become wary through experience, everyday he watches the skies anxiously. He observes them remain clear and calm, while the sun becomes increasingly tropical, doubling the intensity of its rays. The earth slowly dries and loses all of its nourishing nectars; it no longer possesses the vitality to sustain the plants, which have not yet fully matured. The dazzling greenery, which had embellished and enlivened the scene, slowly fades to yellow before maturity time. In vain,

---

284. Finiels correctly assesses the difficulties of overland transportation in Upper Louisiana, but, as previously noted, he exaggerates the shortage of livestock in Spanish Illinois. See note 93 above.

285. Concerning the overland route between St. Louis and Ste. Genevieve, see note 71 above.

286. Lieutenant Governor Trudeau wrote in 1798 (*BLC*, 2:535) about agriculture on Ste. Genevieve's Grand Champ: "Freshets of the river frequently inundate it, destroying in an instant the fruit of a year of toil. The most notable *habitants* have assured me that they are accustomed to lose two out of five harvests regularly . . . ."

the farmer calls for help upon the generous clouds, which alone contain the element that can convey vigor to the plants and fertility to the soil. If the clouds seem sometimes to harken to his wishes, this is only in order to mock his patience. They dissolve under the burning rays of the sun, which returns with greater intensity after having dissipated them; they evaporate together with the farmer's hopes, which had been raised only momentarily.

Sometimes growth, accelerated [195] by an early hot spell, doesn't allow the sap to spread throughout the plants, and they shoot up quickly and deceptively. But cold weather, sharp and biting, soon arrives to strike them down, and they perish at the very moment they seemed most vigorous. Other times, violent spring storms alone are enough to wreak havoc and devastation; the earth becomes littered with vegetal debris; fruit trees, uprooted by sudden winds, lie side-by-side with slender plants whose fragile heads have been severed by hail. The fruits of long labor are then lost in an instant.

When these constant changes in the weather do not succeed in totally destroying the harvest, they nonetheless affect to some degree the quality of the crops; this is a consequence of the plants' irregular growth as they are abruptly and alternately stimulated or retarded. You are tempted to believe that nature, after having tried everything to prevent their growth, renders them to mankind only reluctantly; that despite herself she must obey certain immutable laws that have imperiously ordered her to produce. In fact, even those crops that escape the uneven seasons have neither the perfection, nor the savor, nor the exquisite taste that they acquire in other countries. The cereal grains, [196] vegetables, and fruits cannot compete in excellence with those produced by the temperate climate of the Old World. Perhaps they could do as well as in some of the other climates of the world. But, as I have pointed out, this depends upon human effort alone, upon the ability to harness nature, contain her daily digressions, blaze a trail for her, and by dint of effort prevent her from deviating from it.

These then are the obstacles you face in Upper Louisiana if you wish to succeed in any agricultural enterprise. It is wrong to point exclusively to the inhabitant's sloth as the reason that the colony has languished since its beginnings. That sloth exists, to be sure, but it is due to many factors that can be eradicated, and it would disappear along with them. I have already described some of them. In addition, however, you must reckon the uncertainty of the harvests, which generally makes the *habitants* hostile to unrequited labor, the fruits of which are never certain. Furthermore, you must consider their ignorance and lack of experience, which means that they have been unable to compensate with industry for those things that nature obstinately refuses to give them. This is in contrast to most other colonies, where the need to cultivate products more valuable than those produced in the Illinois Country has forced them to toil and succeed. [197] This demonstrates that it is sometimes possible to command nature and compel her to lavish on man what she did not seem disposed to grant him.[287]

Is it not then groundless to call the climate of Upper Louisiana the happiest and most beautiful on the face of the earth? It is scorching for more than four months of the year; it freezes when the sun approaches the Tropic of Cancer and heads back toward the equator. During the intermediate seasons, the weather is fickle and subject to constant changes. Springtime is often merely a continuation, and autumn a fore-taste, of winter. Sometimes this is reversed, with spring anticipating summer, and summer continuing far into autumn. Often spring is characterized by continual rains, violent storms, and cloud-filled skies. Heaven's flanks then harbor lightning and hail; the atmosphere becomes unstable, and violent north winds rush forth. They rend the skies, leaving havoc and terror in their wake. Other years, there are persistent droughts; scarcely has spring arrived when it is already as hot as in the midst of dog days, and most days, so smiling in [198] temperate climates, are only a prelude to the scorching days that will arrive in the coming season. Autumn, although it is usually the best season of the year, having the most even temperatures, is nonetheless subject to the dominating variations that constantly affect the climate in the Illinois Country. Rains, droughts, prolonged hot spells, premature frosts often throw it off course. These perpetual changes have an impact on all flora and all fauna; they disturb man's health, producing rather serious illnesses, which shorten the lifespan that nature has determined for most persons. This means that they don't live as long as one might expect in a more stable climate.[288]

I have exaggerated nothing in all that I have just reported concerning the climate and the products of Upper Louisiana. Naturally, I have described what has transpired during the time since Upper Louisiana was founded; and I have described those things that must be known in order to get a good idea of the climate, which is not adequately defined by merely stating that it is the finest and happiest on earth. A climate's beauty inheres in the constancy of the seasons, [199] in the measured pace with which they succeed one another while each maintains its appropriate qualities. A pleasant climate is usually healthy, without violent shocks that bowl over everything on the earth's surface. It delivers, effortlessly and tranquilly, all the products that can be cultivated at its particular latitude. In Europe, Asia, and even Africa it is not difficult to find climates

287. Finiels seems to be comparing Spanish Illinois with the French West Indies, where "products more valuable" (i.e., sugar) had made the islands an economic success. With regard to Upper Louisiana, Amos Stoddard argued that "until greater industry and enterprise be excited, we shall hardly know what the soil is calculated to produce" (*Sketches*, 237).

288. In discussing the climate of Upper Louisiana, Amos Stoddard, unlike Finiels, emphasized the dis-tinctions between coastal and continental climates. In reference to the settlements of the Illinois Country, Stoddard remarked, "The winters among them are much more severe than in the corresponding latitudes on the sea coast. They generally set in about the twentieth of November, and continue till near the last of February"; and regarding summers, "If the cold in these regions in winter is greater than that in the same parallels of latitude on the sea coast, the heat in summer bears a proportionate increase" (*Sketches*, 236).

that possess all of these virtues, and these can truly be called the happiest and most beautiful in the world. When you comprehend and present all of these important reservations, even though they may appear miniscule, I acknowledge that the climate of Upper Louisiana is better than that of Lower Louisiana, than of most of the United States of America, even than many of the climates in Europe, Asia, and Africa that you might experience during the course of a long life. I acknowledge that with effort its products will multiply and become rewarding, that the country is picturesque, that it is generally fertile, and that in several areas it is even blessed with some traits which demonstrate that nature has from time to time cast benevolent eyes on it. But while acknowledging these virtues, I must persist in calling attention to the [200] problems that so often arise from nature's neglect or wrath, and to the difficulties that appear at every step. My objective was not to eulogize Upper Louisiana. I merely wished to present a description that would be true to the land and that would be appreciated by persons who could not see it for themselves. In such cases, one is in a good position to tell the truth. You can freely and dispassionately criticize things that are neither good nor beautiful, and also assign merit with the precise amount of praise that truth demands.[289]

289. Finiels' negativism in this paragraph contrasts with his previous comments that were more favorable about the Illinois Country. His tone here may suggest that he was fed up with the rigors of the New World and homesick for "la douce France." Another possibility is that he wanted to temper the exaggerated claims of Georges-Victor Collot, whom he had met in Philadelphia and who had some influence in France. Collot later wrote (*Journey in North America,* 1:286), "The province of the Illinois is perhaps the only spot respecting which travelers have given no exaggerated account; it is superior to any description which has been made, for local beauty, fertility, climate, and the means of every kind which nature has lavished upon it for facility of commerce."

WORKS CITED

BOOKS

Abel, Annie Heloise, ed. *Tabeau's Narrative of Loisel's Expedition to the Upper Missouri.* Norman: University of Oklahoma Press, 1939.

Adney, Edwin Tappan, and Howard I. Chapelle. *The Bark Canoe and Skin Boats of North America.* Washington, D.C.: Smithsonian Institution, 1964.

Alvord, Clarence W., ed. *Cahokia Records, 1778–1790.* Vol. 2,Collections of Illinois State Historical Library. Springfield: Illinois State, 1907.

———. *The Illinois Country, 1673–1818.* Springfield: Illinois Centennial Commission, 1920.

Alvord, Clarence W., and Clarence E. Carter, eds. *The New Regime, 1765–1767.* Vol. 11, Collections of Illinois State Historical Library. Springfield: Illinois State, 1916.

Ammon, Harry. *The Genêt Mission.* New York: Norton, 1973.

Axtell, James. *The Invasion Within: The Contest of Cultures in Colonial North America.* New York: Oxford University Press, 1985.

Beck, Lewis C. *A Gazetteer of the States of Illinois and Missouri.* Albany, N.Y.: C. R. and G. Webster, 1823.

Belting, Natalia M. *Kaskaskia Under the French Regime.* Urbana: University of Illinois Press, 1948.

Bemis, Samuel F. *Pinckney's Treaty: America's Advantage from Europe's Distress, 1783–1800.* Rev. ed. New Haven: Yale University Press, 1960.

Benson, Adolph B., ed. *Peter Kalm's Travels in North America.* 2 vols. New York: Wilson-Erickson, 1937.

Berkhofer, Robert F. *The White Man's Indian: Images of the American Indian from Columbus to the Present.* New York: Alfred A. Knopf, 1978.

Billon, Frederic L. *Annals of St. Louis in Its Early Days Under the French and Spanish Dominations, 1764–1804.* St. Louis: 1886.

Bowers, Alfred W. *Mandan Social and Ceremonial Organization.* Chicago: University of Chicago Press, 1950.

Brackenridge, Henry M. *Recollections of Persons and Places in the West.* Philadelphia: J. Kay, Jr., and Brother, 1834.

———. *Views of Louisiana, Together with a Journal of a Voyage up the Missouri River in 1811.* Pittsburgh: Cramer, Spear, and Eichbaum, 1814.

Bradley, A. G. *The Fight with France for North America.* London: Archibald Constable and Co., 1900.

Carter, Clarence E. *Great Britain and the Illinois Country, 1763–1774.* Washington, D.C.: American Historical Association, 1910.

Chateaubriand, François-August-René de. *Voyage en Amérique.* Edited by Richard Switzer. 2 vols. Paris: Didier, 1964.

Childs, Francis Sargeant. *French Refugee Life in the United States, 1790–1800*. Baltimore: Johns Hopkins University Press, 1940.

Chittenden, Hiram M. *The American Fur Trade of the Far West*. 3 vols. New York: F. P. Harper, 1902.

Collot, Georges-Victor. *A Journey in North America*. 2 vols. Paris: Arthur Bertrand, 1826.

Daniels, Jonathan. *The Devil's Backbone: The Story of the Natchez Trace*. New York: McGraw-Hill, 1962.

DeConde, Alexander. *This Affair of Louisiana*. New York: Scribner, 1976.

Dickason, Olive. *The Myth of the Savage*. Edmonton: University of Alberta Press, 1984.

Din, Gilbert C., and Abraham P. Nasatir. *The Imperial Osages: Spanish-Indian Diplomacy in the Mississippi Valley*. Norman: University of Oklahoma Press, 1983.

Eccles, W. J. *The Canadian Frontier*. Rev. ed. Albuquerque: University of New Mexico Press, 1983.

Ekberg, Carl J. *Colonial Ste. Genevieve: An Adventure on the Mississippi Frontier*. Gerald, Mo.: Patrice Press, 1985.

Favrot Papers, 1796–1790. Prepared by Historical Records Survey, Division of Professional and Service Projects, Works Projects Administration. 7 vols. New Orleans, 1940–1942.

Foley, William E. *A History of Missouri, Volume I: 1673–1820*. Columbia: University of Missouri Press, 1971.

Foley, William E., and C. David Rice. *The First Chouteaus: River Barons of Early St. Louis*. Urbana: University of Illinois Press, 1983.

Galloway, Patricia K., ed. *LaSalle and His Legacy: Frenchmen and Indians in the Lower Mississippi Valley*. Jackson: University Press of Mississippi, 1982.

Gayarré, Charles. *History of Louisiana*. 4 vols. New York: Redfield, 1854.

Geggus, David P. *Slavery, War, and Revolution: The British Occupation of Saint Domingue, 1793–1798*. New York: Oxford University Press, 1982.

Gesner, Konrad von. *Descriptio Montes fracti sive Montis Pilati*. Zurich, 1555.

Gilman, Carolyn, and Mary Jane Schneider. *The Way to Independence: Memories of a Hidatsa Indian Family, 1840–1920*. St. Paul: Minnesota Historical Press, 1987.

Gracy, David B. *Moses Austin: His Life*. San Antonio: Trinity University Press, 1987.

Haas, Edward F., and Robert R. Macdonald, eds. *Louisiana's Legal Heritage*. Pensacola, Fla.: The Perdido Bay Press for the Louisiana State Museum, 1983.

Hafen, Leroy. *The Mountain Men and the Fur Trade of the Far West*. 10 vols. Glendale, Ca.: Arthur H. Clark, 1965–1972.

Hamilton, Milton W. *Sir William Johnson, Colonial American, 1715–1763*. Port Washington, N.Y.: Kennikat Press, 1976.

Hammond, George P., ed. *New Spain and the Anglo-American West*. Lancaster, Pa.: Lancaster Press, 1932.

Holmes, Jack D. L., ed. *Documentos Inéditos para la Historia de la Luisiana, 1792–1810*. Madrid: J. Porrúa Turanzas, 1963.

———. *Honor and Fidelity: The Louisiana Infantry Regiment and the Louisiana Militia Companies, 1766–1821*. Birmingham, Ala.: privately printed, 1965.

———. *Gayoso: The Life of a Spanish Governor in the Mississippi Valley, 1789–1799*. Baton Rouge: Louisiana State University Press for the Louisiana Historical Association, 1965.

Houck, Louis. *History of Missouri*. 3 vols. Chicago: R. R. Donnelley, 1908.

———. *Memorial Sketches of Pioneers and Early Residents of Southeast Missouri*. Cape Girardeau: Naeter Bros., 1915.

———. *The Spanish Regime in Missouri*. 2 vols. Chicago: R. R. Donnelley, 1909.

Howard, James H. *The Plains-Ojibwa or Bungi, Hunters and Warriors of the Northern Prairies*. Vermillion: Anthropological Papers of the South Dakota Museum, no. 1, 1965.

Hutchins, Thomas. *A Historical and Topographical Description of Louisiana and West Florida*. 1784. Facsimilie ed. Edited by Joseph G. Tregle, Jr. Gainesville: University of Florida Press, 1968.

———. *A Topographical Description of Virginia, Pennsylvania, Maryland and North Carolina*. London, 1778. Rpt., edited by Frederick Charles Hicks. Cleveland: Burrow Brothers Co., 1904.

Innis, Harold A. *The Fur Trade in Canada*. New Haven: Yale University Press, 1930.

Jackson, Donald, ed. *The Journals of Zebulon Montgomery Pike*. 2 vols. Norman: University of Oklahoma Press, 1966.

———, ed. *Letters of the Lewis and Clark Expedition with Related Documents, 1783–1854*. 2 vols. 2d ed. Urbana: University of Illinois Press, 1978.

Jaenen, Cornelius. *Friend and Foe: Aspects of French-American Cultural Contacts in the 16th and 17th Centuries*. New York: Columbia University Press, 1976.

James, James Alton. *The Life of George Rogers Clark*. Chicago: University of Chicago Press, 1928.

Kinnaird, Lawrence. *Spain in the Mississippi Valley, 1765–1794*. 3 vols. Washington, D.C.: American Historical Association, 1946–1949.

Laussat, Pierre-Clément de. *Memoirs of My Life*. Translated by Agnes-Josephine Pastwa; edited by Robert D. Brush. Baton Rouge: Louisiana State University Press, 1978.

Leblond, Guillaume. *Eléments de fortification*. Paris: 1768.

Long, John. *Voyages and Travels*. Edited by Milo Quaife. Chicago: R. R. Donnelley and Sons, 1922.

Long, S. H. *Account of an Expedition from Pittsburgh to the Rocky Mountains*. Vol. 14 in *Early Western Travels*, edited by Reuben Gold Thwaites. Cleveland: Arthur H. Clark, 1905.

Lyon, E. Wilson. *Louisiana in French Diplomacy, 1759–1804*. Norman: University of Oklahoma Press, 1934.

McDermott, John Francis, ed. *The Early Histories of St. Louis*. St. Louis: St. Louis Historical Documents Foundation, 1952.

———. *Glossary of Mississippi Valley French, 1673–1850*. St. Louis: Washington University Studies, 1941.

———, ed. *The French in the Mississippi Valley*. Urbana: University of Illinois Press, 1965.

———, ed. *The Spanish in the Mississippi Valley, 1762–1804*. Urbana: University of Illinois Press, 1974.

Mackenzie, Alexander. *Voyages from Montreal through the Continent of North America*. London: T. Cadell, Jr., and W. Davies, 1801.

Mandrou, Robert. *De la culture populaire en France aux XVIIe et XVIIIe siècles*. Paris: Stock, 1964.

Meyer, Roy W. *The Village Indians of the Upper Missouri: The Mandans, Hidatsas, and Arikaras*. Lincoln: University of Nebraska Press, 1977.

Montalambert, Marc-René de. *La fortification perpendiculaire*. 11 vols. Paris, 1776–1786.

Moreau de Saint-Méry. *Voyage aux Etats-Unis de l'Amérique, 1693–1798*. Edited by Stuart L. Mims. New Haven: Yale University Press, 1913.

Morse, Eric W. *Fur Trade Routes of Canada, Then and Now*. 2d ed. Toronto: University of Toronto Press, 1979.

Moulton, Gary E., ed. *Atlas of the Lewis and Clark Expedition*. Lincoln: University of Nebraska Press, 1983.

———, ed. *The Journals of the Lewis and Clark Expedition*. Lincoln: University of Nebraska Press, 1986–.

Murdock, George Peter, and Timothy J. O'Leary. *Ethnographic Bibliography of North America*. 5 vols. New Haven: Human Relations Area Files Press, 1975.

Musick, James B. *St. Louis as a Fortified Town*. St. Louis: R. F. Miller, 1941.

Nasatir, Abraham P., ed. *Before Lewis and Clark: Documents Illustrating the History of Missouri, 1785–1804*. 2 vols. St. Louis: St. Louis Historical Documents Foundation, 1952.

———. *Borderland in Retreat*. Albuquerque: University of New Mexico Press, 1976.

———. *Spanish War Vessels on the Mississippi, 1792–1796*. New Haven: Yale University Press, 1968.

Nash, Gary B. *Red, White, and Black: The Peoples of Early America*. Englewood Cliffs: Prentice-Hall, 1974.

Nicolson, Marjorie Hope. *Mountain Gloom and Mountain Glory*. Ithaca: Cornell University Press, 1959.

Ott, Thomas O. *The Haitian Revolution, 1789–1804*. Knoxville: University of Tennessee Press, 1973.

Palm, Mary Borgia. *Jesuit Missions in the Illinois Country, 1673–1763*. Cleveland: Sisters of Notre Dame, 1933.

Perrin du Lac. *Voyage dans les deux Louisianes*. Lyons: Chez Bruyset ainé et Buynand, 1805.

Phillips, Paul C. *The Fur Trade*. 2 vols. Norman: University of Oklahoma Press, 1962.

Pittman, Philip. *The Present State of European Settlements on the Mississippi*. 1770. Facsimilie ed., edited by Robert Rea. Gainesville: University of Florida Press, 1973.

Primm, James Neal. *Lion of the Valley: St. Louis, Missouri*. Boulder: Pruett, 1981.

Provo, Daniel J. *Fort Esperance in 1793–1795: A North West Provisioning Post*. Lincoln, Neb.: J and L Reprints, 1984.

Quaife, Milo M., ed. *The Journals of Captain Meriwether Lewis and Sergeant John Ordway*. Madison: State Historical Society of Wisconsin, 1916.

Read, William E. *Louisiana French*. Rev. ed. Baton Rouge: Louisiana State University Press, 1963.

Rousseau, Jean Jacques. *Oeuvres complètes*. Edited by Barnard Gagnebin and Marcel Raymond. 3 vols. Paris: Bibliothèque de la Pléiade (Gallimard), 1959–1964.

Rowland, Dunbar, ed. *Official Letter Books of W. C. C. Claiborne*. 6 vols. Jackson, Miss.: State Department of Archives and History, 1917.

Saum, Lewis O. *The Fur Trader and the Indian*. Seattle: University of Washington Press, 1965.

Savelle, Max. *George Morgan: Colony Builder*. New York: Columbia University Press, 1932.

Scanlan, Peter. *Prairie du Chien: French, British, American*. Menasha, Wis.: George Banta, 1937.

Smith, G. Hubert, and W. Raymond Wood. *The Explorations of the La Vérendryes in the Northern Plains*. Lincoln: University of Nebraska Press, 1980.

Stiles, Henry Reed, ed. *Joutel's Journal of La Salle's Last Voyage, 1684–1687*. Albany, N.Y.: Joseph McDonough, 1906.

Stoddard, Amos. *Sketches, Historical and Descriptive of Upper Louisiana*. Philadelphia: Matthew Carey, 1812.

Stoddard, T. Lothrop. *The French Revolution in San Domingo*. New York: Houghton Mifflin Co., 1914.

Sturtevant, William C., gen. ed. *Handbook of North American Indians*. Vol. 15. Edited by Bruce G. Trigger. *Northeast*. Washington, D.C.: Smithsonian Institution, 1978.

Surrey, Nancy M. *The Commerce of Louisiana During the French Regime, 1699–1763*. New York: Columbia University Press, 1916.

Swanton, John R. *The Indian Tribes of North America*. Washington, D.C.: Smithsonian Institution, 1969.

Tanguay, Cyprien. *Dictionnaire généalogigue des familles canadiennes*. 7 vols. Montreal: Eusèbe Sénécal, 1871–1890.

Temple, Wayne C. *Indian Villages of the Illinois Country*. Springfield: Illinois State Museum Scientific Papers. Vol. 2, pt. 2, 1958.

Thomas, Rosemary Hyde. *It's Good to Tell You: French Folk Tales from Missouri*. Columbia: University of Missouri Press, 1981.

Thwaites, Reuben Gold, ed. *British Regime in Wisconsin, 1760–1800*. Vol. 18 of *Wisconsin Historical Collections*. Madison: State Historical Society of Wisconsin, 1908.

——, ed. *The Jesuit Relations and Allied Documents*. 73 vols. Cleveland: Burrows Brothers, 1896–1901.

——, ed. *Original Journals of the Lewis and Clark Expedition, 1804–1806*. 7 vols. New York: Dodd Mead and Co., 1904–1905.

Twain, Mark. *Life on the Mississippi*. New York: Harper and Bros., 1917.

Unrau, William. *The Kansas Indians: A History of the Wind People, 1763–1873*. Norman: University of Oklahoma Press, 1971.

Villiers du Terrage, Baron Marc de. *Les dernières années de la Louisiane française*. Paris, 1903.

Volney, Comte de, Constantin-François Chasseboeuf. *A View of the Soil and Climate of the United States of America*. London and Philadelphia: J. Conrad and Co., 1804.

Whitaker, Arthur P. *The Mississippi Question, 1795–1803*. New York: D. Appleton-Century Co., 1934.

Williams, Gwyn A. *Madoc: The Making of a Myth*. London: Eyre Methuen, 1979.

Wilson, E. Lyon. *Louisiana in French Diplomacy, 1759–1804*. Norman: University of Oklahoma Press, 1934.

Wilson, Samuel, Jr., and Leonard V. Huber. *The Cabildo on Jackson Square*. New Orleans: Friends of the Cabildo, 1970.

Winzerling, Oscar W. *Acadian Odyssey*. Baton Rouge: Louisiana State University Press, 1955.

Wood, W. Raymond, and Thomas D. Thiessen, eds. *Early Fur Trade on the Northern Plains*. Norman: University of Oklahoma Press, 1985.

ARTICLES

Baade, Hans W. "The Law of Slavery in Spanish Louisiana, 1769–1803." In *Louisiana's Legal Heritage,* edited by Edward F. Haas and Robert R. Macdonald, 43–56. Pensacola, Fla.: Perdido Bay Press for the Louisiana State Museum, 1983.

Baker, Vaughn, Amos Simpson, and Mathé Allain. "*Le Mari Est Seigneur:* Marital Laws Governing Women in French Louisiana." In *Louisiana's Legal Heritage,* edited by Edward F. Haas and Robert R. Macdonald, 7–18. Pensacola, Fla.: Perdido Bay Press for the Louisiana State Museum, 1983.

Barbeau, Marius. "Voyageur Songs of the Missouri." *Missouri Historical Society Bulletin* 10 (April 1954): 336–50.

Boyle, Susan C. "Did She Generally Decide? Women in Ste. Genevieve, 1750–1805." *William and Mary Quarterly* 44 (October 1987): 775–89.

Chapman, Carl H. "The Indomitable Osage in Spanish Illinois (Upper Louisiana), 1763–1804." In *The Spanish in the Mississippi Valley,* ed. John Francis McDermott, 287–312. Urbana: University of Illinois Press, 1974.

Chardon, Roland. "The Linear League in North America." *Annals of the Association of American Geographers* 70 (June 1980): 129–53.

Cronon, William, and Richard White. "Indians in the Land." *American Heritage* 37 (August/September 1986): 19–25.

Denman, David. "History of 'La Saline': Salt Manufacturing Site, 1675–1825." *Missouri Historical Review* 73 (April 1979): 307–20.

Din, Gilbert. "The Immigration Policy of Governor Esteban Miro." *Southwestern Historical Quarterly* 73 (October 1969): 155–64.

———. "Spain's Immigration Policy in Louisiana and the American Penetration, 1792–1803." *Southwestern Historical Quarterly* 76 (January 1973): 255–76.

Douglas, Walter B. "Jean-Gabriel Cerré—A Sketch." In *Transactions of the Illinois State Historical Society* 9 (1904).

Echeverria, Durand. "General Collot's Plan for a Reconnaissance of the Ohio and Mississippi Valleys, 1796." *William and Mary Quarterly* 9 (October 1952): 512–20.

Ekberg, Carl J. "The English Bend: Forgotten Gateway to New Orleans." In *La Salle and His Legacy: Frenchmen and Indians in the Lower Mississippi Valley,* edited by Patricia K. Galloway, 211–89. Jackson: University Press of Mississippi, 1982.

Emmons, Ben L. "The Founding of St. Charles and Blanchette Its Founder." *Missouri Historical Review* 18 (July 1924): 507–20.

Hall, F. R. "Genêt's Western Intrigue, 1793–1794." *Journal of the Illinois Historical Society* 21 (October 1928): 359–81.

Holmes, Jack D. L. "The Marques de Casa-Calvo, Nicolas de Finiels, and the 1805 Spanish Expedition through East Texas and Oklahoma." *Southwestern Historical Quarterly* 69 (1966): 325–39.

———. "Some French Engineers in Spanish Louisiana." In *The French in the Mississippi Valley,* edited by John Francis McDermott, 123–42. Urbana: University of Illinois Press, 1965.

Kyte, George W. "A Spy on the Western Waters: The Military Intelligence Mission of General Collot in 1796." *Mississippi Valley Historical Review* 34 (December 1947): 427–42.

Liljegren, Ernest R. "Frontier Education in Spanish Louisiana." *Missouri Historical Review* 35 (April 1941): 345–73.

———. "Jacobinism in Spanish Louisiana, 1792–1797." *Louisiana Historical Quarterly* 22 (January 1939): 47–97.

McDermott, John Francis. "The Battle of St. Louis, 26 May 1780." *Missouri Historical Society Bulletin* 36 (April 1980): 131–51.

———. "The Exclusive Trade Privileges of Maxent, Laclede and Company." *Missouri Historical Review* 29 (July 1935): 272–78.

———. "Myths and Realities Concerning the Founding of St. Louis." In his *The French in the Mississippi Valley,* 1–15. Urbana: University of Illinois Press, 1965.

———. "Paincourt and Poverty." *Mid-America* 5 (April 1934): 210–12.

———. "Travelers on the Western Waters." In *Proceedings of the American Antiquarian Society* 77 (1968): 255–80.

Morrow, Lynn. "New Madrid and Its Hinterland, 1783–1826." *Missouri Historical Society Bulletin* 36 (July 1980): 241–50.

Muench, Julius T. "Jean Gabriel Cerré." In *Missouri Historical Society Collections* 2 (April 1903): 58–76.

Nasatir, Abraham P. "Anglo-Spanish Rivalry in the Iowa Country, 1797–1798." *Iowa Journal of History and Politics* 29 (April 1929): 155–232.

———. "Anglo-Spanish Rivalry on the Upper Missouri." *Mississippi Valley Historical Review* 16 (June 1929 and March 1930): 359–82, 420–39.

———. "The Formation of the Missouri Company." *Missouri Historical Review* 25 (October 1930): 10–22.

———. "James Mackay." In *The Mountain Men and the Fur Trade of the Far West,* edited by Leroy Hafen, 4:185–206. Glendale, Calif.: Arthur H. Clark, 1966.

———. "Jean Baptiste Truteau." In *The Mountain Men and the Fur Trade of the Far West,* edited by Leroy Hafen, 4:381–97. Glendale, Calif.: Arthur H. Clark, 1966.

———. "John Evans." In *The Mountain Men and the Fur Trade of the Far West,* edited by Leroy Hafen, 3:99–117. Glendale, Calif.: Arthur H. Clark, 1966.

Parks, Douglas R. "The Northern Caddoan Languages: Their Subgroupings and Time Depths." *Nebraska History* 60 (Summer 1979): 197–213.

Price, Anna. "The Three Lives of Fort de Chartres: French Outpost on the Mississippi." *Historic Illinois* 3 (June 1980): 1–4.

Shoemaker, Floyd C. "Cape Girardeau, Most American of Missouri's Original Five Counties." *Missouri Historical Review* 50 (October 1955): 49–61.

Stewart, Frank H. "Mandan and Hidatsa Villages in the Eighteenth and Nineteenth Centuries." *Plains Anthropologist* 19 (November 1974): 287–302.

Thurman, Melburn D. "Cartography of the Illinois Country: An Analysis of Middle Mississippi Maps Drawn during the British Regime." *Journal of the Illinois State Historical Society* 75 (Winter 1982): 277–88.

———. "The Little Missouri River: A Source of Confusion for Plains Ethnohistory." *Plains Anthropologist* 33 (1988): 429–47.

Turner, Frederick Jackson. "The Policy of France Toward the Mississippi Valley in the Period of Washington and Adams." *American Historical Review* 10 (January 1905): 249–79.

Viles, Jonas. "Population and Extent of Settlement in Missouri Before 1804." *Missouri Historical Review* 5 (July 1911): 189–213.

Webre, Stephen. "The Problem of Indian Slavery in Spanish Louisiana, 1769–1803." *Louisiana History* 25 (Spring 1984): 117–35.

Wood, W. Raymond. "Nicolas de Finiels: Mapping the Mississippi and Missouri Rivers, 1797–1798." *Missouri Historical Review* 81 (July 1987): 387–402.

———. "Origins and Settlements of the Hidatsas." In *The Way to Independence: Memories of a Hidatsa Indian Family, 1840–1920*, 322–24. Edited by Carolyn Gilman and Mary Jane Schneider. St. Paul: Minnesota Historical Press, 1987.

COLLECTIONS AND PAPERS

Acts and Deliberations of the Cabildo, 1769–1803. New Orleans Public Library.

Archives Nationales, section d'Outre Mer, Aix-en-Provence, France.

Archives of the Archdiocese of New Orleans.

Archivo General de Indias, Papeles de Cuba, Seville.

Chouteau, Auguste. Narrative of the Settlement of St. Louis. St. Louis Mercantile Library, St. Louis, Mo.

Chouteau Collections. Missouri Historical Society, St. Louis.

Clark Family Papers. Missouri Historical Society.

Finiels, Nicolas de. Letters. Estados Unidos, 1808. In Archivo Histórico Nacional, Madrid. Microfilm copies in Library of Congress.

———. Maps. Servicio Histórico Militar, Madrid.

Laussat Papers. Historic New Orleans Collection, New Orleans.

Louisiana Notarial Records. Civil Courts Building, New Orleans.

Missouri State Archives, Jefferson City. Testimony before Theodore Hunt, Recorder of Land Titles, St. Louis, 1825 (commonly called Hunt's Minutes).

Ste. Genevieve County Probate Records, Estate Inventories. Courthouse, Ste. Genevieve, Mo. Microfilm copies in Western Historical Manuscripts Collection, State Historical Society of Missouri, Columbia.

Vallé Papers. Missouri Historical Society, St. Louis.

UNITED STATES GOVERNMENT DOCUMENTS

American State Papers: Public Lands. Washington, D.C., 1832–1861.

Fletcher, Alice C., and Francis La Flesche. *The Omaha Tribe*. Washington, D.C.: Smithsonian Institution, Bureau of Ethnology Annual Report, 1911.

Howard, James H. *The Ponca Tribe*. Bureau of Ethnology Bulletin, vol. 195. Washington, D.C.: GPO, 1965.

U.S. Congress. House. *Executive Documents of the House of Representatives, 1887–1988*. Washington, D.C., 1889.

THESES, DISSERTATIONS, REPORTS, AND UNPUBLISHED PAPERS

Jacobson, Jerome. "The Riddle of the Piasa." Illinois Department of Transportation. 1986.

Kinnaird, Lawrence. "American Penetration into Spanish Territory, 1776–1802." Ph.D. diss., University of California–Berkeley, 1929.

Lessard, Renald, Jacques Mathieu, and Lina Gouger. "Peuplement colonisateur au pays des Illinois." Paper presented at the twelfth annual meeting of the French Colonial Historical Society, Ste. Genevieve, Mo., May 1986.

Liljegren, Ernest R. "The Commission of Carlos Howard." Master's thesis, University of Southern California, 1936.

Nasatir, Abraham P. "Trade and Diplomacy in Spanish Illinois, 1763–1792." Ph.D. diss., University of California–Berkeley, 1926.

Quattrocchi, Anne Margaret. "Thomas Hutchins, 1730–1789." Ph.D. diss., University of Pittsburgh, 1944.

Rollings, Willard H. "Prairie Hegemony: An Ethnohistorical Study of the Osage from Early Times to 1840." Ph.D. diss., Texas Tech University, 1983.

Thurman, Melburn D. "The Delaware Indians: A Study in Ethnohistory." Ph.D. diss., University of California–Santa Barbara, 1973.

Usner, Daniel. "Frontier Exchange in the Lower Mississippi Valley: Race Relations and Economic Life in Colonial Louisiana, 1699–1783." Ph.D. diss., Duke University, 1981. [A revised version of this dissertation is in press at the Institute of Early American History and Culture.]

Africa, 126, 135, 136
Ahnahaway Indians. *See* Watasoon Indians
Albion River, 39
Allegheny River, 27
American Revolution, 2, 10, 34, 82
Americans, 108, 109, 110, 111, 114, 130, 131; as a threat to Spanish Illinois, 124; at Cape Girardeau, 119; energy of, 37, 52, 65
Amiens, Peace of, 8
Angry Creek, 89
Anse à Coco Coco (Coco Bend), 41, 42
Anse à Philippe (Philip's Bend), 86, 87; location of, 71
Anse du Bois Brulé (Bois Brule Bend), 41, 80
Antilles, 8, 25, 125, 127. *See also* St. Domingue
Arkansas River, 33, 90
Arks, meaning of, 31
Asia, 126, 135, 136
Assiniboine River, 101
Attakapas, 31
Aubry, Marin, 113
Austin, Moses, 48, 49
Avoyelles, 31

Bateaux, 4, 30, 52, 108
Baton Rouge, 6
Bayou de Pierre, 57
Belize, 29
Bellechasse, Mr., 64
Belle Fountaine, early American settlement at, 54
Belle Rivière, 27. *See also* Ohio River
Belle Source, 54
Big Field of Ste. Geneviève. *See* Pointe Basse
Bison (*boeufs sauvage*), 98
Blacks. *See* Slaves
Boatmen, on Mississippi, 109
Bois Blanc Creek, 89
Bonaparte, Napoleon, 107
Bon Homme Creek, 32, 71, 72, 87
Braddock, Gen. George, 66
Brush Creek, 89
Buenos Aires, 126
Bungis Indians, 100, 101

Cahokia, 54, 56, 81
Cahokia Indians, 80
Canada, 3, 35, 99, 100, 104, 108, 127
Canadians, 101, 118; in Illinois Country, 66, 108, 116

Canes River, 39
Caninawis (Conoy) Indians, 96
Cannon Ball River, 94
Canoes, birchbark, 100
Cap à la Cruche, 32, 33, 38, 39; three farmsteads at, 34
Cap à la Cruche River, 39
Cap au Grès, 84
Cap d'Ail, 41
Cap Pointe de Rocher (or Cape Rocky Point), 33
Cap St. Antoine, 40, 41
Cap St. Cosme, 41, 42
Cap St. Croix, 40
Cape Girardeau, 37, 38, 39, 41, 90, 119, 128, 129; diseases in, 130; forests of, 39; Indian villages at, 36; Kentuckians at, 36-37; location of, 28; Louis Lorimier commandant of, 34; overland route to Ste. Geneviève from, 40; population of, 36, 37, 43, 118; soil of, 37
Carlos IV, King of Spain, 6
Carondelet, or Vide Poche (Empty Pocket), 55, 56; agriculture of, 55-56, 119; cattle and horses at, 55; climate at, 130; location of, 32; maize produced at, 56; population of, 55, 120; tobacco produced at, 56; wheat produced at, 55-56
Carondelet, Baron Francisco Luis Hector de, 3, 4, 36, 51, 53, 60, 68, 103; appoints Lorimier commandant of Cape Girardeau, 34; dispatches Vandenbemden to St. Louis, 61; Finiels writes to, 61; sends troops to St. Louis, 3, 60
Casa Calvo, Marques Sebastian de, 6
Catepoi River, 101-2
Cattle, 47, 49, 132
Cedar, price of, 88n
Cerré, Gabriel, 66
Charbonnière, 71, 73
Chartres, village of, 54; abandoned by French, 81. *See also* Fort de Chartres
Chateaubriand, François-René de, 12, 14
Cheyenne Indians, 96
Cheyenne River, 94
Chicago portage, 84
Chippewa Indians, 15. *See also* Ojibway Indians
Choret Creek, 87
Chouteau, Auguste, 56, 58, 59, 105; influence with Osage Indians, 89, 90
Cincinnati, 38
Clamorgan, Jacques, 93
Clamorgan, Loisel, and Company, 93, 103

Climate: in North America, 125–29, 130–31; in Upper Louisiana, 117, 125–29, 130–35

Clothing, of French creoles, 112, 113, 115

Cold Water Creek, 70

Cold Water Rocks, 71, 73

Collot, Georges-Victor: account of upper Louisiana, 25, 136n; acquaintance with Finiels, 3; arrested by Spanish, 3; description of St. Charles, 74; moved to Philadelphia, 3

Company of the Upper Missouri, 93, 102, 103, 104, 107

Convoy Indians. See Caninawi Indians

Cordillière Mountains, 95

Corne-à-Cerf, early American settlement at, 54

Creoles, French, 12, 55, 111, 116, 124, 125; clothing of, 115; customs of, 120; health of, 130, 131, 132; in Illinois Country, 108, 117, 118; morality of, 13, 109, 115

Creve Coeur, cattle and horses at, 72; location of, 12, 71; maize produced at, 72; population at, 72; tobacco produced at, 72; wheat produced at, 72; wildlife at, 71

Crow Indians, 96

Cuivre Creek, 76

Currency, 121–23; peltries and produce used as, 122–23

Dardenne Creek, 71; colony on, 76, 77; location of, 76; significance of, 77

Delassus, Carlos, 4

Delaware Indians, 1, 14. See also Loup Indians

Des Moines River, 107

Des Peres Creek, 55; location of, 53, 72; settlements on, 69

Detroit, 66

Diet in Illinois Country, 131

Diseases in Illinois Country, 68, 130–32

Doe Islands, 71, 73

Dubois Creek, 87

Ecores à Margot (Memphis), 64

Education, lack of among French creoles, 115, 116, 118

Engagés, 52, 66, 85, 100, 119

Englishmen, 86, 97, 99, 100, 101, 105; engaged in fur trade, 28, 93, 98, 102

Europe, 108, 110, 114, 122, 126, 127, 129, 135, 136

Evans, John, 95–99, 103; contacts Mandan Indians, 87, 102; returns to St. Louis, 103

Falls of St. Anthony, 85

Farming in Illinois Country, 63–64, 133–34

Femme Osage River, 11

Fencing of common fields, 64

Finiels, Nicolas de, 1, 11–15, 95–102, 113–16, 121–36 passim; account of Upper Louisiana, 7, 10, 15;

arrival in North America, 2; arrival in St. Louis with family, 4; contact with Georges-Victor Collot, 3–4, 10; critic of French Revolution, 2, 3, 8, 25, 108; east Texas mapped by, 6; economic ideas of, 122–23; education of, 93; employed by U.S. government, 2; family of, 4, 6; interest in the Sublime, 12–13; living in Philadelphia, 3; opinions on French foreign policy, 109; purchase of two town lots, 5; romantic sensibilities of, 12–15; supporter of Carlos IV, King of Spain, 6; Upper Louisiana mapped by, 1; used Thomas Hutchins as a source, 10; worked for Spanish Crown, 1; wounded at Pensacola, 6

Finiels, Pedro Arturo, son of Nicolas, 6

Fire Creek Prairie, 130

Flora in Upper Louisiana, 69, 133, 134

Florida, 105

Florissant. See St. Ferdinand

Flourmills. See Mills

Forests, wasteful use of, 124

Fort Carondelet, 89

Fort Clarksville, 31, 38

Fort de Chartres, 81; ruins of, 46

Fort Duquesne: English defeated at, 66; location of, 27; visited by Cerré in 1755, 66

Fort Espérance, 101

Fort Kaskaskia, 81

Fort Massiac (or Massac), 39

Fort Niagara, 113

Fort St. Charles, 59

Fort Washington, 38–39

Fortifications, at St. Louis, 3, 4, 60, 61

France, 2, 15, 26, 27, 37, 105, 120, 125, 136; emissaries sent to Louisiana, 9; revived interest in Louisiana, 7, 8; revolution in, 6–8; secret acquisition of Louisiana, 6–7; sells Louisiana to U.S., 10; war with Spain, 25

French and Indian War, 7, 8

French Revolution, 2, 7, 25, 108, 116

Fur trade: British domination of, 99–102; in Missouri River valley, 90, 91, 92, 93–107; profits of, 78, 107

Gabouri Creek, 47, 51, 53; location of, 44, 51; mouth of, 43

Gasconade River, 87; importance of, 88; mouth of, 88; navigation on, 87

Gayoso de Lemos, Manuel: as governor of Spanish Louisiana, 6, 36, 73; impressed with Finiels, 5

Genêt, Edmond C., 25

Georgia, 26, 31

Gesner, Konrad von, 26

Grand Champ of Ste. Genevieve. See Pointe Basse

Grand Detour (Dogtooth Bend), 15, 33

Grand Detour (on the Missouri River), 96

Grand Glaize Creek, 89

Grand Pawnee Indians, 92
Grand Platin, 52
Grand Portage, 99, 100, 101
Grand Tower, 40
Grande Isle, 63, 73
Gravois Creek, 88
Great Britain, 2, 7, 8, 104. *See also* Englishmen
Gros Ventres Indians, 96
Guadeloupe, 8
Gulf of Mexico, 128

Habitants, 64, 86, 109, 114, 116, 118, 119, 134;
   characteristics of, 107-20; daily life of, 118-20
Havana, 6
Hay River (Big Muddy), 96
Health, of Americans and Creoles, 130-32
Hocat Indians, 96
Holmes, Jack D. L., 2
Hudson Bay, 127
Huron Indians, 2
Hutchins, Thomas, 10, 49

Illinois (American), 58, 80-85
Illinois Country, 1, 10, 12, 30, 45, 46, 51, 73, 79, 80,
   81, 84, 88; agriculture in, 69, 113; American families in, 53, 72, 81; Americans as a threat to, 38,
   39; Canadians in, 66; climate of, 64, 67, 126, 127,
   129, 130, 135; communications in, 28, 32; currency in, 121-23; customs in, 81; goods scarce in,
   62; Indian trade in, 85, 86; Indians in, 89, 90;
   inhabitants of, 81, 111, 116; introduction of
   sheep in, 64; lead production in, 78; livestock in,
   62, 132, 133; maize produced in, 78; maple sugar
   production in, 78; merchants in, 30, 66, 108;
   morality in, 111, 115, 120; mulattos in, 109; persons able to bear arms in, 79; population of, 27,
   66, 79, 82, 114; prices in, 79, 122; products of,
   78, 107, 132-34; religion in, 114; routes to, 4; salt
   production in, 78; settlements in, 31, 37, 50, 94,
   120, 131, 133, 135; smallpox in, 131, 132; tobacco
   produced in, 78; value of goods produced in, 78;
   wheat produced in, 78. *See also* Spanish Illinois
Illinois River, 84, 119; mouth of, 1, 13, 27, 32, 74,
   83; navigation on, 76; traders on, 86
Illnesses. *See* Diseases in Illinois Country
Indiana Territory, 82
Indians, 97, 112, 114; alcoholism of, 49; as bankers,
   121; as hunters, 12, 41, 89-98; as traders, 28, 85,
   105, 113, 121; customs of, 35; Finiels' advice on
   treatment of, 105, 106; Finiels' attitude toward,
   12, 14, 113, 116; opinions of whites, 105, 106;
   poisoning among, 93; settled at Cape Girardeau,
   34, 35; trade with, 28, 85, 105, 113. *See also specific tribal names*
Iroquois Indians, 36
Irujo, Carlos Martínez de: contact with Nicolas de

Finiels, 2; employer of Finiels, 4; Spanish minis-
   ter to the U.S., 2
Isle à Cabaret, 63, 73
Isle à Duclos, 51
Isle à la Course, 40, 80
Isle à Roinsa, 80
Isle au Bois, 52
Isle de la Glaise, 41
Isle du Platin, 52
Isle la Pensée, 87
Isles aux Biches (Doe Islands), 71, 73
Isles aux Perches, 41, 42
Isles de St. Charles (St. Charles Islands), 71

Jackson, Andrew, 6
Jesuit missionaries, in Illinois Country, 80, 81, 111,
   114

Kansa Indians, 91
Kansas River, 90-91
Kaskaskia, 11, 31, 38, 42, 46, 49, 50, 80, 131; as
   first French town in area, 80; governed by Jesuit
   missionaries, 80, 81, 114
Kaskaskia Indians, 80; drunkenness of, 49; settled
   in Ste. Genevieve, 49
Kaskaskia River, 38, 39, 41, 42, 46, 53
Kentucky, 28, 31, 36, 37, 38, 45, 119

La Fourche Creek, 89
La Rochelle, France, 8
Lac la Pluie (Rainy Lake), 100
Laclède Liguest, Pierre de, 56
Lake Erie, 127, 128
Lake Huron, 127, 128
Lake Michigan, 84, 127, 128
Lake Ontario, 127, 128
Lake Pontchartrain, 31
Lake Superior, 99, 128; traders on, 72
Lake Winnipeg, 72, 100, 101
Lamine River, 90
Laussat, Pierre-Clément de, 9, 10, 15; employer of
   Finiels, 9; prefect-appointee of Louisiana, 5, 8,
   10
Lead production: New Bourbon, 47; Ste. Gen-
   evieve, 50; Upper Louisiana, 78
Leblond, Guillaume, 61
Leclerc, Gen. Charles-Victor, 8
Leida, 92
Levana, settlement of, 36
Licking River, 38
Little Gravois Creek, 89
Little Miami, 38
Little Osage Indians. *See* Osage Indians
Little Osage River, 89
Little Saline Creek, 89
Little Turkey Creek, 89

London meridian, 86
Lorimier, Louis, 119; accompanied by Shawnees
    and Loups, 34–35; appointed commandant of
    old Cape Girardeau, 34; concession of, 39, 119;
    harried by General Wayne, 34; parents of, 35
Louisiana, 3, 6, 8, 10, 15, 26, 27, 62, 74, 105, 109,
    110, 112, 116, 121, 125, 126; climate of, 66, 127,
    129; diseases in, 130, 131; French desire to
    regain, 27; trade of, 85, 86, 107, 134
Louisiana, Lower, 39, 42, 66, 110, 111, 116, 117,
    124, 128; climate in, 129, 136; disease in, 131;
    rivers of, 33
Louisiana, Upper, 1, 3, 4, 9, 10, 12, 15, 32, 36, 40,
    43, 85, 108, 111, 112, 119, 123, 125, 128, 132, 133,
    134; agriculture in, 77–78, 134; boundaries of, 9,
    27, 28; Canadians in, 66, 101, 108, 116; climate
    of, 129, 132, 135, 136; communications of, 27;
    communications with New Orleans, 28; contacts
    with Lower Louisiana, 122; contacts with the
    U.S., 28; contacts with Upper Canada, 28; dis-
    eases in, 130, 132; flora of, 133; fur trade of, 28,
    78, 106, 107; harvests in, 70, 78, 134; lead pro-
    duction in, 78; livestock in, 47, 49, 132; maize
    produced in, 78; maple sugar production in, 78;
    population of, 79, 108, 109; products of, 70, 78,
    135; revenues of, 73, 78; salt production in, 78;
    settlements of, 32; tobacco produced in, 78;
    trade in, 104
Louisville, 31, 38
Loup (Delaware) Indians, 36, 118; follow Lorimier
    to Cape Girardeau, 34
L'Ouverture, Toussaint, 8, 25
Luzières, Pierre-Charles de Lassus de, 124, 131;
    commandant of New Bourbon, 44; house of, 46

McDermott, John Francis, 15
Mackay, James, 5, 95, 96, 97, 98, 99, 101, 103; com-
    mandant of Bon Homme Creek and Creve
    Coeur, 72; employed by trading company, 72;
    Finiels maps Missouri River for, 72; leads expe-
    dition to Mandans, 72, 87; returns to St. Louis,
    103
Maha Indians, 14, 93, 103, 107; population of, 92;
    trade of, 92; tyranny of chief, 92, 93
Mahomet, 92
Maize, 47, 49, 56, 69, 70, 71, 72, 77, 78, 97, 123;
    Carondelet, 56; Creve Coeur, 72; Illinois Coun-
    try, 78; Marais des Liards, 71; Meramec, 69; St.
    Charles, 77; St. Ferdinand, 70; St. Louis, 69; Ste.
    Genevieve, 49
Mandan Indians, 86, 87, 93, 94, 95, 96, 97, 98, 99,
    102, 103; contact with English traders, 72, 101,
    104; friendliness of, 97; fur trade with, 72, 102,
    103, 104; pottery of, 97; villages of, 95; visited
    by Spanish, 102
Manigua Creek, 89

Manitaris. See Gros Ventre Indians
Maple sugar, production of in Illinois Country,
    77–78
Marais de Crève Coeur, or Creve Coeur Marsh, 71
Marais des Liards (Cottonwood Swamp), 51, 71;
    cattle and horses at, 71; climate of, 70, 130;
    founded by Americans, 70; maize produced at,
    71; population of, 70, 71, 120; tobacco pro-
    duced at, 71; wheat of little importance at, 71
Maringouin (Indian name meaning "mosquito"),
    54
Marmaton River, 89
Martinique, 8
Meramec River, 48, 52; American settlement on, 69
Mexico, 133; mines in, 86
Michegamea Indians, 49, 80
Michilimackinac, 55, 56, 84, 86, 104, 112, 120
Mills, 37, 39, 49; Chouteau's, 56, 59, 60; horse, 56;
    saw, 65, 73; shortage of in Illinois Country, 3;
    wind, 75
Mines: iron, 37; lead, 48, 49
Mingrelia, 26
Misery (as nickname for Ste. Genevieve), 58
Mississippi River, 42, 43, 44, 76, 84, 88, 95, 96,
    101, 104, 107, 111, 124, 127, 128; banks of, 13,
    43, 82, 86, 130, 131; boatmen on, 119; current of,
    29, 83, 128; drinking of, 65; ferries across, 53–54;
    flooding of, 42, 58; length of from Natchez to
    New Orleans, 29; length of from St. Louis to
    New Orleans, 4; mouth of, 129; navigation on,
    38, 76, 80; once called Michacépé, 28; routes on,
    30–31, 54, 65
Missouri Company. See Company of the Upper
    Missouri
Missouri River, 37, 53, 55, 56, 58, 59, 71, 72, 74, 76,
    79, 84, 85–98, 101, 102, 104, 113, 119, 120; banks
    of, 32, 69, 86, 95, 96, 97, 98, 130; fur trade of, 98;
    Indian tribes of, 28, 88–99; mouth of, 13, 43, 53,
    59, 82, 94, 111; navigation on, 75, 87, 98; source
    of, 13, 95, 99; trade on, 28, 93, 107; width of, 97,
    98
Monongahela River, 27
Montalambert, Marc-René de, 61
Montreal, 99, 100, 129
Morals and mores of Creoles, 107–20
Moustier, Elénore François, 7
Mulattos: in Spanish Illinois, 107; in Illinois Coun-
    try, 108–9; morality of, 109

Nashville, 31
Natchez, 29, 30, 31, 51
Natchitoches, 31
New Bourbon, 40, 44, 45, 46, 47, 49, 50, 119; agri-
    cultural production of, 42; cattle and horses at,
    47; diseases in, 131; founding of, 44; house of
    Monsieur de Luzières at, 46; lead produced at,

47; location of, 32; maize produced at, 47; population of, 47; wheat produced at, 47

New Madrid, 1, 3, 4, 28, 31, 33, 35, 37, 45, 54, 60, 90, 125, 129; Peyroux commandant at, 45

New Mexico, 125, 129; boundaries with Upper Louisiana unknown, 28

New Orleans, 3, 4, 6, 7, 9, 10, 28, 29, 30, 31, 32, 44, 45, 55, 60, 84, 90, 99, 103, 104, 107, 113, 114, 122, 123, 125, 129; climate at, 126, 127; sugar refinery in, 78

Niagara Falls, 95, 128

Niangua Creek, 89

Norris, F. Terry, 11n

North America, 119

Northwest Territory, 28, 31

Ogle, American settlement, 54

Ohio River, 39, 45, 113, 119; mouth of, 27, 28, 38, 54, 80; navigation on, 31, 55

Ojibway Indians, 15, 101n

Omaha Indians. *See* Maha Indians

Opelousas, 31

Osage Indians: Chouteau's influence with, 89, 90; Finiels' attitudes toward, 90; fur production of, 90; population of, 89; trade of, 89, 107; warlike behavior of, 89

Osage Post, 45

Osage River, 86, 88, 89, 98

Ottoctata Indians, 92

Ouachita River, 31, 33

Paillissa Rocks, 76, 83

Paincourt (nickname for St. Louis), 32, 58

Palmyra, 92

Panimaha Indians, 92

Panis Indians. *See* Grand Pawnee Indians

Pelopennesus, 126

Pennsylvania, 28

Penobscot Bay, 127

Pensacola, 6

Peoria Indians, 49, 80

Peru, 133; mines in, 86, 122

Petit Platin, 52

Petit Rocher (Little Rock), 52

Petites Côtes (Little Hills), 73

Peyroux, Henri de la Coudrenière, 45

Piasa Bird painting, 76n

Philadelphia, 2, 4, 10, 60

Pinckney's Treaty, 31

Pittsburgh, 4, 28, 55

Plaine Basse of Ste. Genevieve, 49

Platte River, 86, 91, 92, 97, 98, 102

Pogniat, Bonnevie de, 11n

Pointe Basse, 44, 48; agriculture on, 46; fertile soil of, 42; flooding of, 42–43; location of, 43, 47. *See also* Plaine Basse

Ponca Indians, 94, 102; village of, 93

Population: Carondelet, 55; Creve Coeur, 72; Illinois Country, 79; Marais des Liards, 70–71; New Bourbon, 47; St. Charles, 77; St. Ferdinand, 70; St. Louis, 69; Ste. Genevieve, 49

Portage des Sioux, 58, 73

Prairie du Chien, 104n

Prairie du Pont, 81

Prairie du Rocher, 51; early settlement in Illinois Country, 81; ethnic French of, 82; Finiels spends night in, 67; stone houses of, 51; stagnation of, 81

Prairie Fire Creek, 90

Quebec, 99

Rainy Creek, 89

Remont à Baguette, 75

Ricara Indians, 102, 103; settled on banks of Missouri, 94

Rivière à la Mine (Lamine River), 90

Rivière à la Outre, 87

Rivière à la Pomme, 41

Rivière à la Table, 41

Rivière à Marie, 41, 89

Rivière aux Vases, 40, 42–44

Rivière Chératon (Chariton River), 90

Rivière d'Ardennes (Dardenne Creek), 32

Rivière de Chartres, 51

Rivière de la Glaise, 41

Rivière des Loup (Wolf River), 92

Rivière des Pères (Des Peres Creek), 53, 55, 69, 72

Rivière du Champ des Marmitons, 89

Rivière du Foin (Big Muddy), 96, 97

Roche Deboullée, 52

Roche de Bout (Standing Rock), 89

Rochers de l'Eau Froide (Cold Water Rocks), 71

Roches Brutales, 41

Rocky Mountains, 15, 86, 95, 97, 98, 101; Indians of, 96; sources of Missouri River in, 13, 87

Rousseau, Jean-Jacques, 12, 13, 14, 111, 112

St. Charles, or Petites Côtes (Little Hills), 71, 72, 73; cattle and horses at, 77; diseases in, 130; founded by hunters, 74; harvests at, 77; hunters at, 74, 119; livestock at, 75; lead produced at, 77; location of, 32, 74; maize produced at, 77; maple sugar production in, 78; mounds of, 76; obstacles on journey to, 75; origins of its nickname, 73; population of, 74, 77; residents of, 73, 75, 76, 77, 120; salt produced at, 77; stone tower at, 75; streets in, 74; "Three Breasts" of, 75–76; tobacco produced at, 77; water route to, 72; wheat produced at, 77; windmill at, 75

St. Charles Islands, 64, 71

St. Clair, Gen. Arthur, 39

St. Domingue, 4, 8, 25, 126

St. Ferdinand (later named Florissant): agriculture in, 70; cattle and horses at, 70; climate of, 130; founding of, 70; harvests at, 70; location of, 32, 70; origins of the name Florissant, 70; population of, 70; residents of, 70, 120; tobacco produced at, 70

St. Ferdinand River: confluence with Missouri, 73; location of, 70; Long family on, 73; sawmill on, 73

St. Francis River, 33, 37, 53, 90

St. Joachim Creek, 52

St. Laurent River, 41, 42, 44; American farmsteads at, 42

St. Lawrence River, 99, 127, 128

St. Louis, 7, 10, 14, 31, 35, 51, 54, 56, 57, 59, 60, 71, 73, 77, 86, 94, 99, 104, 109, 115, 117, 118, 121, 124, 125, 129, 130, 131, 133; American industry in, 65; American settlers in, 3, 62, 66; arrival of sheep in, 64; Canadians in, 66; capital of Spanish Illinois, 4, 56, 62; cattle and horses at, 69; Chouteau's mill at, 45, 60; climate of, 4, 62, 66, 67, 126, 127, 130; Creoles in, 12, 66; customs in, 62, 67, 68; defense of, 3, 61; fishing at, 63; flooding in, 64; food supply at, 63, 69; fortifications of, 59, 60, 61; French at, 66; garrison of, 59; harvests at, 69; houses in, 62, 74; hunting at, 63; Indian attacks at, 56, 60; iron production at, 65; livestock at, 62; location of, 69, 127; maize produced at, 69; merchants of, 1; morality in, 67, 120; overland routes to and from, 64, 65; population of, 11, 55, 62, 69, 119; Portage des Sioux near, 73; sawmills in, 65; size of, 119; smallpox in, 68, 131; tobacco produced at, 69; town lots in, 62; wheat produced at, 69

Saint-Maur, Comte du Pré de, 15

St. Philippe, 81

Ste. Genevieve (Misery), 4, 11, 32, 35, 40, 43, 50, 51, 77, 78, 109, 112, 113, 116, 118, 119, 129, 133; agriculture of, 42, 53; Americans of, 45; cattle and horses at, 49; customs of, 67, 68; diseases in, 131–32; Finiels' tribute to, 50; flooding of, 47; founding of, 111; hospitality of, 120; lead mines inland from, 48; lead produced at, 50, 78; location of, 11, 126; morality in, 67, 118; overland routes to and from, 43, 53; population of, 49, 50; residents of, 14, 42, 67, 115; salt produced at, 50; site of village moved, 2; tobacco produced at, 49; wheat produced at, 49

Salcedo, Manuel de, 6

Saline, 32, 40, 131; location of, 45, 199; settlement at, 44–45

Saline Creek, 34, 42, 44, 45

Salt production: Illinois Country, 78; Meramec, 69; St. Charles, 77; Ste. Genevieve, 50

Sandstone River, 88

Sauteur Indians, 101

Shawnee Indians, 36, 49; description of, 1, 14, 35; follow Lorimier to Cape Girardeau, 34; villages of, 35–36, 43, 118

Sheep, introduced to Illinois Country, 64

Shiwitoon Indians, 96

Sioux Indians, 96, 101, 102; attack on expeditions of Truteau and Evans, 103; ferociousness of, 97

Slaves, 69; in Illinois Country, 107, 124; morality of, 109; numbers of, 109

Smallpox, in Illinois Country, 68, 131, 132

Social customs of French creoles, 107–20

Spain, 2–8, 31

Spaniards, 3, 28, 97, 104, 105; visit the Mandans, 98, 102

Spanish Illinois, 85; capital at St. Louis, 51, 56; climate in, 4; diseases in, 131, 132; Frenchmen in, 82; government in, 82, 125; Stoddard describes, 28n. See also Illinois Country

Stoddard, Amos, 28, 77

Tennessee, 31

"Three Breasts" of St. Charles, 75, 76

Tobacco, 114; Carondelet, 56; Creve Coeur, 72; Illinois Country, 78; Marais des Liards, 71; Meramec, 69; St. Ferdinand, 70; St. Louis, 69; Ste. Genevieve, 49

Todd, Andrew, 103, 104

Treaty of Basle, 11

Treaty of San Ildefonso, 7, 8, 26

Tropic of Cancer, 135

Trudeau, Don Zenon, 5, 93, 94; as commandant of Spanish Illinois, 68, 69; popular with the people, 68, 69

Truteau, Jean-Baptiste, 95, 133; leads trade expedition to Mandan Indians, 102

Tuque Creek, 87

Turkey Creek, 89

Turtle Mountain, 101

United States, 31; as a threat to Spanish Illinois, 38; Congress of, 84; territory of, 82–85. See also American Revolution, Americans

U.S. Corps of Engineers, 11

Upper Canada, 28

Upper Louisiana. See Illinois Country

Vallé, François, 118, 122; as commandant of Ste. Genevieve, 50; owner of flour mill at Ste. Genevieve, 49

Vandenbemden, Louis: Finiels' opinion of, 4, 61; sent to St. Louis, 3, 60–61

Vermillon Creek, 89

Vide Poche (nickname for Carondelet), 55

Vincennes, 31, 39, 130

Virginia, 28

Wabash River, 31, 39, 130
Watasoon (Ahnahaway) Indians, 96
Wayne, Anthony, 34
Weather. *See* Climate
Wheat, 49, 55–56, 69, 70, 72, 77, 78, 123; Caron-
    delet, 55–56; Creve Coeur, 72; Illinois Country,

78; New Bourbon, 44; St. Charles, 77; St. Ferdi-
    nand, 70; St. Louis, 69; Ste. Genevieve, 49
White River, 94, 96, 102
Women, Creole, 115–17

Yellowstone River, 97; mouth of, 95